Learning to Play, Playing to Learn

Learning to Play, Playing to Learn

CURRICULUM AND ACTIVITIES FOR CLASSROOM AND PLAYGROUND MANAGEMENT

Reduce Bullying, Build Character
and Support Learning

....

by Charlie Steffens *and* Spencer Gorin

illustrations by Spencer Gorin
with a foreword by Rick Miller,
Founder of Kids at Hope

Creative Spirit™

Revised Third Edition
1-800-742-0708
Website: www.joyinlearning.com

We encourage participants to use their own good judgment when monitoring their well-being and activity levels. Creative Spirit assumes no liability for injuries.

Learning to Play, Playing to Learn
by Charlie Steffens and Spencer Gorin
First Edition 1997, Second Edition 2004, Third Edition 2007

Library of Congress Cataloging-in-Publication Data

Steffens, Charlie.
    Learning to play, playing to learn / by Charlie Steffens and Spencer
Gorin; illustrations by Spencer Gorin; with a foreword by Rick Miller.
      p. cm.
    Includes bibliographical references and index.
    ISBN 13:978-0-9747533-2-4
    ISBN 10:0-9747533-2-7
    1. Play. 2. Games. 3. Creative activities and seat work. 4. Socialization.
    5. Play therapy. I. Gorin, Spencer. II. Title.
    LB1137.S76 1997
    155.4′18—dc21   97-38131

Requests for such permissions should be addressed to:
Creative Spirit
2545 West Rapallo Way
Tucson, AZ 85741
1-800-742-0708

Publishing Consultant: Linda F. Radke, Five Star Publications, Inc.
Chandler, Arizona, www.FiveStarPublications.com
Design: Kate Mueller, Electric Dragon Productions & Rich Foster, Rich Designs
Cover Photo: SuperStock Inc.

Printed in Canada
10 9   8   7   6   5   4   3   2

Contents

Acknowledgments

We at Creative Spirit would like to acknowledge all the playful and creative spirit-masters who have been inspiration for our endeavors. Special thanks are directed toward the wizards at the New Games and Playfair foundations, Rick Miller and the staff at Kids at Hope, Ann Herbert, and Terry Orlick. This book is intended to promote healthy socialization through play and humor. Our Healthy Play Is a Solution/Learning to Play program is designed to educate people so everyone may achieve all the meaningful benefits associated with play.

The authors gratefully acknowledge the following sources for their contribution to this book:

Giants, elves, and wizards; blob; and the five Cs are adapted from *New Games & More New Games* © 1981 by Andrew Fluegelman. Reproduced for Creative Spirit by permission of Bantam Doubleday Dell Publishing Group, Inc. (1540 Broadway, New York, New York 10036). Further reproduction is prohibited.

Rolling logs, cooperative musical chairs, double simon says, and dragons dodgeball are adapted from the first and second *Co-*

Foreword

I confess, I Love To Play!

I cannot imagine a world where play does not serve as a cornerstone to that part of us that wishes to become self-actualized. I cannot imagine a world where play does not define our evolution as a civilized society. I cannot imagine a world where play is not valued as an integral element in each and every part of our existence. Therefore, I stand by my confession, reinforced by over 40 professional years in the youth development and education sectors, that as a concept, play defines our humanness.

So why even address this issue? We address it because we have lost our way as a society and play is a subject that has been pushed and trapped into a corner. Play must now prove that any time spent on it has a specific and immediate return on investment. How tragic this shortsighted debate has become. Although the concept of play can be overly studied and researched, it is a whole experience that enriches and adds value to our lives. Every emotionally and physically healthy person today can attest to the powerful and remarkable benefits play has had and continues to have in his or her life. Conversely, we can see something missing in the lives of children and adults who have not fully experienced the power of play as a part of their development and maturity.

When Charlie Steffens and Spencer Gorin asked me to write the foreword to *Learning to Play, Playing to Learn*, an emotional and soulful chord was struck deep within me for a number of reasons. First, I personally and professionally know Charlie and Spencer and have enjoyed many hours with them exploring the world of children and play. Second, we are practitioners who have effectively bridged research and practice and created strategies that offer unique insight and practical application in support of the success of all children, without exception. Third, I am a "graduate" of the *Learning to Play, Playing to Learn* workshop, or should I say "playshop." This personal and intimate experience complimented not only my understanding of Charlie and Spencer's methods but allowed me to observe adults of all ages and abilities rediscover their playful side. I witnessed them recognizing the wide application that games and activities offer to the healthy development of our children.

I was so taken by that experience that I could not wait to see the magic of Charlie and Spencer's approach as they worked directly with children. I wasn't surprised when I watched students in an elementary school truly learning to play and playing to learn. In just a short time, these young people modeled positive characteristics, skills, and traits through healthy play. These attributes will serve them well in school, careers, at home, and in support of their overall love of life. And they were having fun doing it.

I find it interesting that most corporations use the concepts of play taught in Charlie and Spencer's interactive sessions. These businesses have come to discover the interrelationship, interconnectedness, and interdependence that play, work and achievement represent. I sense these leaders recognized that too many of their colleagues lack, lost, or have forgotten the value of play in their business and personal lives. That may be the result of a rapidly changing society which is driven by electronics rather than relationships, by individual testing rather than group cooperation, and the belief that work shouldn't be confused with play and play shouldn't be confused with work. Whatever the reason, we have unintentionally or intentionally ignored the magnificent benefits of play as the first and greatest ongoing learning tool in our lives.

Play seems to strike at the heart of what we are and what we should be as a civilization. The process of play mirrors our most simple and complicated needs and values. It is the most natural form of expression and learning, yet we have relegated the importance of play to the category of leisure activity. As important as it is to use play as a part of our recreation, it should not be relegated to that dimension alone.

I am reminded of a common tongue-in-cheek memo that would find its way around offices. The memo states, "The whippings will continue until staff morale improves." With today's obsession regarding high stakes academic testing for students we are consumed with the industry of learning skills, but we are losing what truly drives our intelligence: spontaneity, creativity and the love of learning. We want our children to do well in academics, but we punish them by abandoning the basic principles of child development and human pedagogy that support their ability to become empathetic, creative, cooperative, responsible, optimistic, and holistically successful human beings.

So why is it important to read this book? This book reminds us about who we are and how we got to where we are. It provides a simple but compelling series of ideas and applications to restore and maximize our capacity to have fun and achieve. It is important to read this book because we need tools to help our children succeed academically by establishing a playful, safe, and effective learning environment. I am sure that after you read this book, and, more importantly, put its philosophies and practices to play, you will join me by unabashedly stating: I not only love to play, but I need to play and I have fun doing it!

Rick Miller
Founder, Kids at Hope

Introduction

About Play

Welcome! The Healthy Play Is a Solution Curriculum will be your most valuable tool for classroom and playground management. This curriculum is intended to be learned within a school semester. However, the ease of the lessons may make it easier to be completed even faster, almost immediately. Discover your natural rhythm and the readiness of your group of students when moving through the course. After completing the introduction, the Healthy Play (HP) curriculum will be covered in eight lessons. The first four lessons must be completed before playing with your students. The following four lessons will offer you practical ideas, activities and skills to meet all the objectives of this program. The final chapter in this book will give the reader additional ideas and methods to fine-tune the HP program with your students at your own setting. Once you and your students have learned the Healthy Play

Curriculum you will find ongoing reasons and joyous desire to utilize our effective methods for the remainder of your school career.

The basic premise of our Healthy Play Is a Solution course is that purposeful and therapeutic play can provide a solution to classroom and playground socialization and management problems. This program has a school-related focus with a target audience of teachers, school counselors, principals, after-school staff, teacher aides, park and recreation staff, community leaders and youth servicing professionals who are responsible for children in grades kindergarten through six. Other groups such as Campfire, Boy and Girl Scout leaders will find this course relevant. Additionally, parents may be able to utilize Healthy Play ideals and activities with their and other neighborhood families in a group format setting.

All the materials in this course are presented in a practical and logical order. This logical progression of activities guarantees greater success upon implementation. We encourage you to understand and use the game types (Creative, Trust/Compassionate and Soft Aggression Play) in succession as they are presented. But, you do not have to follow each game in the order that it is presented. We want you, as a reader, to feel free to move at your most comfortable pace. Discover your own readiness. Come to know the readiness of your own group of students or clients. To implement the program and to achieve the desired behaviors, you must first assess your group's needs.

When you reach the chapters that include games and activities, you will discover each game is described and followed by a "Gift of the Game." The Gift of the Game may be a vignette based on what we have witnessed or a touching story told by a teacher, counselor or parent. They may also indicate which behaviors can be nurtured by playing that particular activity and/or other benefits that might not be immediately apparent. At the end of the book you will find more helpful tips and ideas to fine tune and maximize the benefits of play. Occasionally, the reader will come upon a "Discussion Gift." The Discussion Gift is an extra that can enhance the idea presented, tell a related story or offer an additional technique. Each lesson has a suggested assignment. It is highly recommended that you complete this assignment to facilitate understanding, flow and skill building to receive the optimal benefit of reading this book.

Finally, please note that this course has two authors. We want to celebrate both our partnership and individuality which went into creating our program. Our writing styles may reflect this. Sometimes one or the other of us will be addressing the reader directly with personal experiences or feelings. For the most part, however, we will be addressing you jointly. We want you to be able to celebrate your own group as well as the individuals within your group that you will be playing with. As a reader, it might be helpful to imagine that we, both Charlie and Spencer, are there with you as you encounter successes, concerns and questions that arrive from implementing the Healthy Play program with your students.

Description of the Healthy Play program:

The Healthy Play (HP) curriculum is a character education, classroom management, violence prevention and conflict resolution program. HP has been primarily developed for use in the kindergarten through sixth grade classroom environment. Application of the curriculum is intended for both regular classes and for numerous special education class settings including mainstreaming of special needs students.

HP is an educational curriculum that promotes empathy and compassion for others. It allows students to achieve feelings of success and well-being as well as to manage or prevent the intimidating, aggressive, bullying or violent behaviors often seen in schools. HP provides practical opportunities for children to learn more effective social or behavioral management skills which they have not yet mastered. Simultaneously, it is a daily curriculum which allows students to practice optimal healthy behaviors throughout the total school day.

The educational focus of the HP game activities is based solely on the social interactions which the game experience provides. Game outcome and psychomotor skill development are less consequential in assessing the value of HP as a character education and violence prevention model.

HP in the K-6 educational setting has been designed to be a simple and uncomplicated process for both the teachers and students who use it. It is based on the knowledge that,

1. Children like and want to play.
2. Play is the most natural form of learning.
3. Play incorporates all eight of the multiple intelligence styles of learning.
4. When play is practiced correctly, it is a positive emotional experience for all the participants.
5. Of all the learning concepts involved in HP the most important one is the emphasis placed on the actual DOING of social skills/behaviors desired repetitively.

History of Healthy Play program development

The original underlying therapeutic play concepts now used in HP were developed by the authors in the in-patient psychiatric setting for children and adolescents with severe psychiatric illnesses and/or very difficult life experiences. These techniques were developed over a ten year period. Under the direction of psychiatrists and psychologists, a milieu of specific non-threatening experiences was developed. From these basic play experiences, children could better learn the skills of how to relate effectively with others.

All of the children's pathologies which the nurses and associated therapeutic staff were equipped to deal with surfaced during "here and now" play experiences. The focus during play could center on simple things like talking aloud, demonstrating a kindness to another, making a decision or just joining in. Sometimes it was as simple as having children move around vigorously to improve their attention span. The accompanying changes in serotonin and endorphin levels in their biochemistry made the children calmer and more content. Higher blood oxygen levels made them more alert which allowed them to view their life experiences in a positive way. A willingness to receive feedback on how others perceived their actions developed, and the children were given opportunities to make positive changes.

Play was not about exploring the depth of children's pathologies caused by trauma or organic disorders. It was not designed to resolve eating disorders, suicidal tendencies or psychosis; however, it did allow children to practice improved behaviors repeatedly. In our modern society, with a need for instant gratification, it has become standard to drop something if it doesn't work after the first try. In real-life situations, it was gleaned that for a behavior to become a new positive and normative habit, it had to be repeated at least 13 to 15 times. Learning clearly involves repetition and reinforcement. Essential for success utilizing HP is an understanding that the outcome (score) of the game is inconsequential. The play activity is merely an effective tool. The methodology of utilizing play is about processing aspects of the child's behavior during a game or activity.

With successful reintegration of in-patients back into their former schools, the authors received numerous requests from schools to model our techniques and procedures for their classrooms. School administrators and teachers realized that traditional character education techniques were failing students because they tended to be too abstract or intellectual and did not meet children at their developmental and emotional levels. They recognized that the key to our success was that we respected the importance of a motivating and experiential program that celebrated children as children and not as little adults. It was during this initial period that we solidified the HP philosophy and rules into the successful program we now share with teachers and faculty to use in their schools nationwide.

A brief historical and current perspective of play

In the beginning - well, soon after - there was play. Every culture has developed and used play as a means to teach children the necessary skills of living. Playing is not a way for children to waste time until they finally grow up and get a job. It is the natural way that children learn. Through play, children can practice over and over the behaviors and tasks necessary to become adults. This process of play repetition is essential in all grade levels of education.

Until about seventy-five years ago, it was easy to correlate the usefulness of play activities with becoming a successful adult. Play activities centered around food gathering, hunting, animal husbandry, clothes making and mock parenting. But, as our culture became much more urbanized, the focus of play has been redirected to two areas: entertainment and competition. While these two concepts of play are somewhat useful in helping humanity cope with living in compact cities, far too frequently, entertainment and competition are overused extremes that no longer represent the true meaning of play and/or its educational potential.

Millions of dollars have been spent on play research and volumes of reports have been written documenting the values of play. It is not our goal to add any more academic rhetoric that intellectualizes, rationalizes, or analyzes play dynamics. These excesses have overcomplicated play issues and created a perception that only those with Ph.D.'s can use the play process beneficially. Creative Spirit believes it's time to empower everyone to just start playing in a healthy manner.

Why the Healthy Play Course Utilizes Play

Play IS the most natural way that children learn. Play reaches

ALL children because it is the only medium that incorporates all eight ways of learning known as the multiple intelligences. It incorporates logical, verbal, intrapersonal, interpersonal, visual, kinesthetic, rhythmic and naturalistic intelligence.

Play is the essence of life. It is universal, collaborative, and expressive. Play supports intrinsic internal motivation and development of self-esteem and competency. Play contributes to cognitive development and problem-solving skills, supports children's language and literacy, promotes positive social skills, and constructs longer attention spans, which facilitates exploration into all subjects.

Play is the most joyous learning method. It becomes easy to see that play contributes to social, cognitive, physical, and emotional learning. Play enables children to test out ideas, theirs and others, consciously and unconsciously, internally integrating them as they put into service information gleaned from their play experiences. (Sponseller, 1974)

Positive play is an incredible motivator, especially for children, even though it has been our experience that it is quite true for adults as well. When something feels good to do and success results from it, people want to do it again. The power of play as an effective medium for learning is irrefutable.

Research and Studies

Confucius said, "What I hear, I forget. What I see, I remember. What I do, I know." In fact, the more senses involved in the learning process, the greater the impression it makes and the longer it stays with us.

Many people are put off by the word "Play." It often invokes images of frivolous and childish actions. In truth, play is a highly effective tool for assisting children to learn social skills. Play is the arena where children practice all the values that any character education program views necessary. Issues of compassion, conflict resolution, diversity, fairness, honesty and communication are acted upon in play settings. Once these behaviors are learned and practiced in play settings it is very easy, using simple dynamics, to transfer them throughout school and neighborhood community settings.

Play is something that children are drawn towards and will enable them to modify their behaviors effectively. If we offer children a program that they are drawn to we have greater success that they will actually do it. And, if we offer mindful adults, educators, counselors and community liaisons a program that is elegant, cost effective, and easy to implement they also have a greater chance to follow through on their responsibilities. Play is actually the most effective classroom and playground management tool.

Since 1992, we have had the opportunity to utilize Healthy Play with over 250,000 children, teachers, parents and youth service professionals with great success. Common sense and practical experiences have shown us over and over again the importance of play upon healthy socialization and learning. Our experiences as mothers and fathers, brothers and sisters and as adults who were once children ourselves reinforce the power of play. Additionally, there is a multitude of research that supports why play absolutely belongs at school. Traditionally, this research is often ignored by teachers due to fears of being perceived as not correctly doing their jobs or by caving into the national trend in high-stakes testing hysteria. We encourage teachers to do what is right and to reach children in the most effective manner in which they learn: Play.

Important research and study findings on play:

A Florida State University study of 334 K-2 children reported an average number of 212 aggressive incidents per 20-min period. Virtually every child assigned to the playground engaged in some form of inappropriate behavior when given nothing better to do. When structured activities were introduced the incidents were halved to a mean of 91 (Murphy, Hutchison, and Bailey, 1983).

Positive attitudes toward the play of children can be traced to the longstanding belief that play behaviors assist in the development of pro-social aptitudes and the formation of moral character, while at the same time nourishing the intellectual and language development of the child (Klugman, 1990).

Games played at recess are implicated in children's social competence and adjustment to first grade. Children's social competence develops in the context of interacting with their peers is especially important as children are rapidly losing opportunities to interact with peers. There are signs that children of primary school age have fewer opportunities out of school for interacting freely with peers and thus developing social skills and thus competence...Recess may be one of the few times during the day when children have the opportunity to interact with peers and develop social skills (Pellegrini, Kato, Blatchford, & Baines, 2002).

Brain-based research shows that physical movement plays a vital role in the formation of neural circuitry which promotes academic learning (Sprenger, 2002).

What children play, they become as adults. Two simple 20-minute observations of children's behavior during recess at the 5th grade are part of highly predictive formula for juvenile delinquency five years later. During play, children learn how to increase certain skills that help them in life, and they learn how to inhibit other actions (Walker, Colvin & Ramsey, 1995).

How big is the aggression problem on a playground? One study shows the rates are about 700 acts per hour. Very high risk schools or groups may be higher and much more serious rates of aggression (e.g., White & Bailey, 1990).

Cooperative games can reduce racism on the playground (Rogers, 1981).

Cooperative games also reduce negative behavior toward developmentally delayed children (Acton & Zarbatany, 1988).

From *The Owner's Manual for the Brain, Everyday Applications from Mind-Brain Research* by Pierce J. Howard, Ph.D. (2006) comes the following important research about play:

- Peer feedback is more influential than teacher feedback in obtaining lasting performance results. Approval or disapproval of one's peers is the best reinforcer.

- Generating epinephrine and norepinephrine will help fix memory. Suggested ways to generate such chemical change occurs by being active; i.e., walk about, exercise, do isometrics, climbing stairs, walking and through play.
- Memory is learning that sticks! Practice clarifies and strengthens (information and neural connections) that are formed while learning.

According to B. Fauth, author of Linking the Visual Arts with Drama, Movement, and Dance for the Young Child, (1990), we retain:

- 10% of what we read;
- 20% of what we hear;
- 30% of what we see;
- 50% of what we hear and see at the same time;
- 70% of what we hear, see and say; and
- 90% of what we hear, see, say, and do (acting out, dramatizing, dancing, drawing, constructing, playing).

Specific research and studies on Creative Spirit's Healthy Play IS a Solution program:

Healthy Play methods of delivery are based on Gardner's theory of multiple intelligences. HP content and instruction are presented in many different ways and formats, including lecture (linguistic), planned and spontaneous role-play (bodily-kinesthetic), experiential activities (spatial, interpersonal, bodily-kinesthetic), group discussion (linguistic, intrapersonal, interpersonal), facilitated strategy sessions (logical-mathematical, naturalistic), and in-classroom teacher feedback sessions (linguistic, spatial, interpersonal, intrapersonal). Thus, participants (a) become actively engaged in problem solving through play, (b) understand the eight learning styles in the context of play, and (c) learn through participation in the game activities ways to support academic and behavioral learning in the classroom.

Teachers see the results. "After five years of Goals 2000 study at 29 schools evaluating Creative Spirit's Healthy Play program, 85.5% of the teachers who used it in their curriculum 3, 4 or 5 times each week reported a behavioral problem reduction of 50% to 100% in acts of aggression, bullying, threats, non-cooperation and teasing."

The 1996-97 principal cross-reference study revealed a 52% reduction of children seen in the principal's office for behavior problems.

"After three years of utilizing the Healthy Play program our school went from 654 to 275 behavioral referrals a year. Of significance is that we went up from 992 to 1089 students. We also saw a 35% increase in SAT9 Reading scores." Deborah Bailey, Principal, William C. Jack School

Independent Suspension Studies:

In a study of two schools in Moreno Valley Unified School District, each reported a reduction of suspensions by 80% after implementing Creative Spirit's Healthy Play Is a Solution program. Jan Thaxton, MVUSD Project Coordinator

The most exciting recent research on the Healthy Play program is the three year study done at Lincoln Elementary School. The entire teaching staff participated in a full HP training and was given a two hour follow-up training for the second year. Additionally, the full faculty used a reading discussion process to explore all the concepts in the Learning to Play, Playing to Learn book. They implemented the program daily during PE, after lunch and during recesses. The results were a three year reduction of 62.4% in the number of students suspended, a 70.5% decrease in the total number of suspensions and a 72.0% reduction in the number of days students were suspended. What is so impressive about this research is that the gains indicated nearly equal progress in all of the categories and more importantly were sustained over a three year period. Additionally, at the conclusion of this research project Lincoln reported in 2004-2005 that it had now achieved an API total of 761, a score that approaches the statewide goal of 800. The three year gain of 120 points on the California API is very substantial. Although the research design does not allow for speculations of any specific academic gains by using Healthy Play, we can conversely state that the daily curriculum time that it took to implement this program did not have a negative effect on student achievement. We can only speculate that the increase in school safety, daily physical activity, improved social skills, and time saved by students and faculty in not having to deal with problematic situations contributed to a healthier learning environment.

Healthy Play Objectives:

Promote Healthy Social Skills

We named our program Healthy Play Is A Solution because play is one of the solutions to behavioral problems that arise at schools. There is no one methodology or program that will remove all behavior problems from occurring. But, as the studies on our program show, teachers experience an average 70% reduction in behavior problems. A 70% reduction is pretty impressive and significant! Would you like to deal with 70% fewer problems with your group of students? This course is designed to allow children to learn and develop healthy, positive social skills while playing. This is the real goal: healthy social skills. When purposeful play is facilitated and monitored by caring elders of your school community, wonderful social enhancing gifts will be discovered.

Manage Aggressive Behaviors

You can use Healthy Play to reduce and manage aggressive behaviors in your class and on the playground. When teachers utilize the philosophy, rules and activities of the HP program, healthy-play behaviors of their students transfer to free-play settings and throughout the entire school community. As mentioned above, teachers report a decrease in anti-social behaviors by an average of 70% when they utilize the HP program. A safe school environment becomes the foundation where learning can occur.

Increase Self Esteem

Every child can be nurtured to develop a positive self-concept. You can't just talk or read about having good self-esteem, children are far too concrete in their thinking to learn that way. Self esteem is something that develops from things you do. Healthy Play ideals are inclusive of everyone, therefore reducing feelings of alienation and promoting a beneficial sense of belonging. Humiliation and ridicule, bullying and intimidation are not tolerated, reduced and hopefully eliminated. Every student can succeed in either playing a HP activity or enacting HP rules. This gifts students with a sense of mastery over skills that promote a stronger sense of self.

Develop Social Relatedness

Play is where you really practice how to get along with others and to make friends. The inability to relate to others was the unifying condition that linked all children that Charlie and I served in the in-patient psychiatric setting, no matter the age or diagnosis. How well your students can relate to themselves, their peers, their teachers and other adult staff can make all the difference in a successful academic career and emotional connection with others. The ability to make friendships is paramount in the emotional development of school aged children. We all intuitively feel a deep sense of loneliness without friends; friendship may be the best antidote for our feelings of alienation. When students connect meaningfully with others, they develop a sense of belonging and comfort that will promote a readiness to learn and live productively as individuals and groups.

Maximize Participation

The Healthy Play approach gets every person involved. Once you broaden your play focus beyond "who is best," all students will be willing to try to be their own individual bests. All kids really want to play, but only when it is safe and when they know they can't be physically or emotionally hurt. Feelings of isolation dampen learning and healthy socialization. All children want to feel included among their peer group. No matter of abilities or disabilities, everyone has a bountiful capacity for joy.

Promote Positive Life Values

Healthy Play promotes positive life values. Children will practice caring, sharing, being compassionate and honest. Importantly, HP activities become the place where children take personal responsibility for their actions. A key to this program is holding every student accountable for the things he or she does. What you really want to do is to reinforce the things they are doing well. You'll find that the things Healthy Play teaches encourages such comments as, "Gee, that's a great job," or "Thanks for taking care of me." Peers and elders alike will learn to praise each person's accomplishments during a game. Likewise, it is everyone's caring responsibility to critique areas where a child's behavior needs improvement and where additional learning needs to occur. These issues can be safely addressed during Healthy Play activities.

Increase Emotional and Physical Health

Playing daily is good for students' physical and emotional health. Kids don't have six-hour attention spans. They really don't. Really! A study on Stanford University students indicated that those students only had a 15 minute attention span for lecture.

Brain research studies, and our own experiences show, that we learn best in short learning blocks of lecture followed by brief physical movement to cement that learning.

When students just can't stay in their seats any longer, get them out of their seats. They have already stopped learning. Your students have a natural need to get out of their chairs frequently. When this occurs, no matter how good an educator you are, you've stopped effectively teaching. Oh, you may think that you are still teaching because you are verbalizing the lesson, but you might as well save your breath. Your students' fidgety behaviors are telling you that, for right now, they've stopped learning. Don't let this situation become an endless battle of control between you and the students. When play becomes a time for teaching social values, games become part of valuable curriculum. You're not just wasting time; brief exercise and laughter will release natural body chemicals that will relax and stimulate more productive student behaviors. Additionally, we are seeing increased amounts of obesity and juvenile diabetes in our children. As educators, we have an obligation to improve the physical health of our students. Developing a healthy heart, lungs and muscles are not bad secondary benefits of play. Once you get past the limited concept that play is just entertainment, you can start to use play as a healthy solution to all sorts of daily classroom problems.

Develop A Positive Peer Culture

The last, but certainly not one of the least of our key components is to develop a positive peer culture. We're going to use peer pressure as a tool for teaching desirable social behavior. We tend to think of the negative aspects of peer pressure so often that we overlook positive aspects; we get lost in the fact that peer pressure is often why kids do drugs or join gangs. However, peer pressure is also why we all brush our teeth, fix our hair, take a shower, stop at red lights, go at green lights and create laws. As you will see, Healthy Play concepts reinforce and empower those students who demonstrate or are mastering positive values. Those children will receive a lot of validating attention and will ultimately be in control of the class and able to mentor other students needing support as indicated by their dysfunctional actions. The message that you and the positive peer culture will say is, "If you want to play in our class, this positive way of playing is how it will have to be done." Because the class will want to play, they will practice how to do it right. All students are motivated by play, even those whose behaviors initially tell you otherwise. They too will modify behaviors so that they can rejoin an activity. What the students learn and the positive culture they create will then transfer to every aspect of the entire school day becoming the normative model for your class and school.

Summary

There must be a joy in learning. This course is about rediscovering ourselves and others through the most basic and fun way possible: Healthy Play IS a Solution!

We learn many hurtful and helpful behaviors as children through our play experiences. We learn about relatedness and socialization through our play. The reason so few adults and many children are no longer playful is that we've had the play beaten out of us. Play is no longer seen or experienced as being fun, and as a culture, we see little value in play or fun.

Many adult and children's sports and game activities do not protect our sense of self-esteem or self worth. Too few people play fair anymore and the majority of us end up feeling like losers. That is why we've stopped playing, and that is why as a culture we have stopped winning in the arenas of relationships, marriage, industry and education. How can we love our spouses when we haven't learned to share, care or problem-solve? How can we work together when we can't cooperate with our co-workers? And, how can we learn in our schools when we fear for our self concept, safety or even our lives? We can't. Or rather, we can't if we continue on this fearful and hurtful path.

The good news is that we can meet all our needs when we choose to change our attitudes and values about how we play and work with each other. As we change our ways of thinking, we change our behaviors, and our interactions with others become more successful and intimate. Our process awakens our sense of joy and pleasure. At school, we can get on with learning because we are not distracted by ridicule and threats.

This course is about discovering the freedom to be creative, innovative and humorous. It is about giving permission to take risks and return an atmosphere of joy back into learning so we may succeed at school, and ultimately, in life. It is about recapturing the attributes that make us all good neighbors, effective learners, good workers, good mentors, parents, partners, teachers and friends. And, it is about passing those wonderfully infectious values to those who surround us.

Throughout this course, you will find more than 80 unique activities aimed at enhancing socialization skills. While participating in this course, you will be given the knowledge and the tools to create a safe and nurturing activity experience. If you focus on the needs of your students or clients first and foremost, the magic of individual and collective experiences will open up harmonious, socially satisfying and productive forces. We would like to invite you to join with us in discovering how many ways Healthy Play Is a Solution to contemporary challenges confronting our youth. We invite you to open your heart, mind and body as you discover the joys of Learning to Play and Playing to Learn.

The following lessons will explore how to start setting up the Healthy Play program in your classroom or setting. Never stop playing! Never stop learning!

If you have any questions or want more information regarding this course or Healthy Play resources you can contact the authors toll-free, at 1-800-742-0708, email us at info@joyinlearning.com or write to us care of Creative Spirit 6062 E. Beverly, Tucson AZ, 85711.

Lesson One:

Healthy Play Philosophy: Why Do We Play?

Setting up the Healthy Play Program for your Setting

Introduction

Let's start at the beginning. First, we must unload the common assumption that children are the experts on play simply because they are children. If this were true, our playgrounds, schools and neighborhoods would not be battlefields and you wouldn't need this book. Children are not the experts on play. They seem to have "unlearned" the ability to play enjoyably with each other. They have unfortunately forgotten or haven't been taught how to explore, imagine and create. Children now find themselves engulfed in the world of entertainment which is not the same thing as play. Entertainment is something that you receive passively, that is done for you, and often to turn you into a consumer of that entertainment.

Play occurs actively. It is something that a child or children create. Though you can be in a movie theater with a hundred people or in a stadium among thousands of others, your experience is still a non-interactive one with the action going on up on the screen or out in the field. Certainly, sitting with a joystick in hand in front of a computer game is incredibly isolating. Additionally, if it is a violent video game, research now supports that violent behaviors of the viewer are increased.

Play is something that one creates with others. It is inclusive and experiential. It brings children joy and allows for creative exploration of their world and how they can find a healthy place in it. As responsible elders of our school communities, we must recreate an environment where children can rediscover the value of being fully actualized human beings.

The reader is highly encouraged to read and complete all the information and suggested assignments in this and the following three lessons before attempting to play activities with their students.

Why the Philosophy Is Important

To utilize play as a classroom and playground management system, you need to focus on two essential philosophical principles and two valuable rules of the HP program. The games and activities, utilized alone, without the philosophy and rules, are not enough to make any significant behavioral change. There is a clear need to put attention into the intention of why you are using games as a tool to meet character education goals. Students can successfully integrate abstract behavioral ideals internally and then express them externally only when the philosophical framework and rules are implemented. The biggest mistake teachers make when starting the HP program with their students is going directly to playing the games. Without providing a concrete framework to identify the reasons why you would play at all in a school setting and giving a mechanism to make play purposeful, you only reinforce the same problematic behaviors you are trying to eliminate.

The first PHILOSOPHICAL PRINCIPLE of Healthy Play is the following:

We play to have FUN.

For the remainder of this lesson we will focus on this first philosophical point of play. The following lesson will cover the second essential point. As we mentioned earlier, it is essential that the reader cover the material in the first four chapters before playing any activities with their students.

Creating Poster # 1

The Healthy Play program starts with the creation of two posters on paper that will reflect students' values. The effective use of HP in the classroom must begin with the identification of your students' desired outcomes involving play at school. Each group of children must create their own classroom's play commandments. This concrete exercise will provide both a visual lesson and lay the groundwork for creating an awareness of what can be gained emotionally and behaviorally from play. The posters become concrete tools based on two very important questions. You and your students will return to these posters as needed or desired to validate successes and/or to fine tune any problems. Keep them up all year. Throughout the year you might want to create art and writing assignments that reflect the values on the posters. Whatever you do, don't laminate this year's completed poster and use it with next year's students. Though their answers will most likely be almost exactly the same it is important that each year's crop of kiddos "own" the answers that they give. As the children discover that each year they give the same values/answers it will reinforce and validate those behaviors. As the children advance in grade level they will most likely give more age appropriate responses.

Based on your assessment of your students' attention you will have the children come to a collective setting in front of the class or remain in their seats. The teacher leads a simple exercise to create a visual poster of the children's values. It centers on answering the question, "Why do we play?" All grade levels give approximately the same responses. They play to make friends, get energy, take a break, go outside, exercise, win, exercise, learn and have FUN. Additionally, the teacher asks the students, "How do you want to feel when you play?" They always respond that they want to feel, "happy, good, nice, safe, and accepted." The typical poster usually has ten or more responses, but the critical answer for the teacher and students is that they play to have FUN. Students are now part of the process of establishing their own criteria and values for play. The teacher now holds them accountable to these expectations when they play. From this point forward, only students playing by their identified positive class values will be allowed to continue playing.

Let us imagine that we are setting up the program in your classroom or with any group of children. (From hereon any reference to a classroom can be interpreted to mean any group of children or teenagers in any setting.) We must help children identify their own set of values and feelings that playing evokes. When children identify these values on their own, they are more likely to buy into the program. They are more likely to accept their own and their peers' ideas rather than being spoon-fed an adult's suggestions, especially as they get older. However, once they identify their values and feelings, we as teachers and elders, must be responsible for holding them accountable to those values.

POSTER # 1: WHY DO WE PLAY?

Using a big piece of butcher block paper, at the top write the question: Why do we play? In the middle of the paper draw a big, empty circle with a #1 in one corner of the circle.

The following script is a suggested way to present the creation of the posters to your class. It will foster a sense of playfulness and set the tone for behavioral expectations right from the beginning:

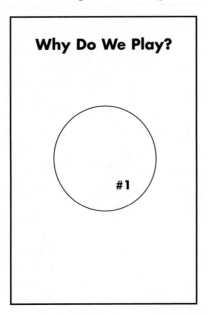

Why Do We Play?

#1

TEACHER: "We are going to create two posters from the answers to two very important questions that I'm going to ask. Now, the first question I'm going to ask is, 'Why do we play?' But, I need to let everybody here know that we are going to answer this question as if we were on a TV game show. On our TV game show there is a number one answer. I want to see it right here. *(Point to the circle with the #1 in it).*

You will be happy to know that additionally to the number one answer there's going to be 101 other really great answers. All really important and great answers will be placed on our poster. And, I'm going to only choose people that are being good listeners with their hands raised to answer this question." *(This last sentence helps set the tone for expected behavior responses.*

Sometimes just mentioning the word play can automatically stimulate hyper student behaviors. It is essential to maintain classroom management. Children that are jumping out of their seats or yell out are gently reminded that they won't be called on. Expectations are something that children can live up to. Positive reinforcement of successful behaviors will help bond children with their teacher and also give them a sense of contentment for living up to expectations.)

"The first question I have is, "Why do we play? If you think you know the answer raise your hand. All right, Kay Anne, why do you play?"

KAY ANNE: "It's fun!" *(It is essential that FUN is the only answer that gets to be the number one answer for this question. The framework for the program will be seriously sabotaged if you allow another answer to be number one. Just imagine if you let the number answer be, "To win prizes." You will be setting yourself up for a token economy system that will defeat the purpose of play, squash any hopes of classroom management and end up costing you to surrender your paycheck in order to buy candy bars, pizza and toys. You get to be the benevolent dictator of your classroom. FUN IS the only number one answer to this question.)*

TEACHER: "It is fun. Kay Anne got the number one answer. I need to let Kay Anne know that if this were an actual game show she would have won the trip to Disneyland, the red convertible car and the washer/dryer combination set. But, since she's here at our elementary school, let's give her a big, loud round of applause." *(Being the playful and quasi-creative guys we are we like to give interesting and enjoyable applause or cheers. Instead of a round of applause we often go directly to the dancing snake applause. For the "dancing snake" kids are instructed to take either arm and create an undulating snake-like silent cheer toward the child who gave the number one answer. We can't encourage you enough to be playful with your students and to inject smiles and humor into every possible appropriate situation.)*

"That IS the number one answer. We play to have fun! Raise your hand if you also play to have fun. *(The kids raise their hands. This visually and very publicly validates that this is the uniform answer that the majority of students agree upon as the number one reason why they will play from here on.)* It looks like almost everybody here plays to have fun! Who has another reason why we play? Why else would you play? Saul?"

SAUL: "Exercise."

TEACHER: "Exercise. Great answer. Exercise builds strong muscles and good cardiovascular systems. Why else would we play?"

KIM: "To learn."

TEACHER: "Exactly. Play becomes a fantastic place to learn new things. And, today we're going to learn new things. Shillana, why do you play?"

SHILLANA: "To make friends."

TEACHER: "To make friends. That's a very important answer."

(All kids want to make friends but many do not have the skills to do that. Just go out on your playground sometime and watch. Some are just absolutely horrible with each other. They call each other rotten names and treat each other with bullying and aggressiveness. And, they will not get friend-making skills by watching television or playing violent video games. But, they can when they learn how to play purposefully.

When kids give that answer, "to make friends," what we generally do is stop the questioning for a moment and ask the children to raise their hands if they like to make friends. Universally, everybody wants to make friends, and almost all, if not all, students will raise their hands. Then, we verbally and visually reinforce this to the students, saying, "If you want to make friends in this class, probably a great way to do it is to play with your friends. And, seeing all the hands raised, many friendships can be found in our class. Will you make friends if you are hurting others? Not likely. You will probably lose a friend. Will you make friends if you tease or bully? Once again, not very likely. You will probably lose a friend if you did that. Do we want to have people play with us who hurt and tease us?" The majority of the students will answer, "No!" You might continue to intervene this way, "Let's put this to a vote and see if we want this to be a classroom rule. Since being bullied, teased or purposefully hurt is not fun, who votes that those people who tease, bully or purposefully hurt others don't get to play until they can stop doing those hurtful things, but the rest of us do?" Every classroom we have gone into all voted on that rule for their class. This is great way to start practicing democracy and also begin to establish a positive peer culture for your classroom where children who do well are rewarded and children who need support by limit-setting are given motivation to want to change destructive behaviors. These concepts of how to make or lose friends may seem so simple and simply a matter of common sense, but many children have not yet to master them.

We, as adults, abstractly know that the easiest cure for a sense of alienation is friendship. Children don't begin to experience the world abstractly until they are teenagers, so we must reinforce basic knowledge concretely and linearly).

TEACHER: "Why else do we play? Amber?"

AMBER: "Relieve stress."

TEACHER: "You're right. Play is a great way to relieve stress. Why else do we play?"

JESSE: "To create. To use our imaginations and pretend."

TEACHER: "Oh, another wonderful answer. Who else has an answer?"

MALIA: "To share."

TEACHER: "Excellent answer!"

ERNESTO: "I play so I won't be bored."

TEACHER: "Fantastic answer, Ernesto. I think being bored is totally boring. Who here also plays so that they won't be bored? Raise your hand." *(Boredom is a big issue for children and teenagers. Kids have a hard time finding things to do with themselves and with each other. Much of their entertainment is pre-packaged for them. They need to learn how to entertain themselves).*

It is essential that while working on the same poster, to ask the children about their feelings regarding play. This acknowledgment of feelings will allow children to identify their own personal desires in how they want to feel and provide a gateway into discovery of empathy for other people's feelings which they too share.

TEACHER: "How do we like to feel when we are playing? Roxanne, how do you like to feel?"

ROXANNE: "I like to feel happy."

TEACHER: "Great answer. How else do we like to feel, Rick?"

RICK: "Like a winner."

TEACHER: "We all like to feel like we're winners. Raise your hand if you like to feel like you're a winner. Most of our sports and games are designed for one person to feel like that winner. But, at school, we are going to play activities where everyone can feel like a winner because that's how we all want to feel, like winners. How else do we like to feel?"

FORREST: "We want to be relaxed."

TEACHER: "Ah, we want to be relaxed. There's a nice kind of exhaustion that sometimes comes from playing, from having a good time with ourselves and each other."

EDGAR: "I want to feel included."

TEACHER: "Me too, Edgar. No one likes to feel left out." (*Feelings of belonging are important to elementary aged students. Let's face it; they are important for everyone regardless of age. However, if a child feels alienated and/or excluded from their peer group they, most likely, will have issues of poor self-esteem. Being invisible or being left out leads to various forms of compensating behaviors. At the best end of those behaviors, a child might overcompensate and become involved in an isolating skill that might be helpful academically, but prove to also be ineffective socially. At the negative end of the spectrum, a child might act out in self harmful behaviors or behaviors harmful to others*).

Discussion Gift: We came up with a playful technique to help children better focus on some of their feelings and would like to share it with you. And, if this technique appeals to you, after you have elicited some feelings from the students write the word

"GREX" on the poster. Charlie invented the word, GREX years ago. Then tell your students that when you play you like to feel, G-R-E-X. By now you will be able to look around to see the collective puzzled looks on their faces as they ponder what GREX could mean. Explain that the GR stands for the word, "great", and the EX stands for the word, "excellent." When you play you like to feel both great and excellent, therefore you like to feel, GREX. Ask them to raise their right hands if they too want to feel GREX. They will respond quickly to your enthusiasm. Tell them to raise their left hands if they want to feel excellent. Their other hands will briskly go up. Their next instructions are to raise and wave both hands in the air if they want to feel GREX. It's at this point that I tell everyone that we are now applauding in American Sign Language. (Gee, we're learning something new already.) You now have the power of this playful technique at your disposal. It has facilitated laughter, smiles and easy buy-in with children everywhere. Feel free to have your students come up with one of their own words that highlight two concurrent feelings. That would probably be even more memorable and meaningful to them. Pretty GREX, eh!?

The number of answers, for your posters, that you elicit from class to class may vary but most primary classes can come up with about eight, while intermediates can call out up to 15. For teachers and school counselors working with kindergarten aged students you will have to be realistic with answers that they can give you. Kinders tend to get the number one answer that we play to have fun. Some kinder students have the skills to answer the poster questions like their older schoolmates. However, don't be surprised when you ask for additional answers that they might sound like the following responses: "We play to have lots of fun. I play to have a lot, a lot of fun. We play to have really, really lots of fun, etc." Oh it's cute but it doesn't go anywhere fast in terms of making this exercise useful for kindergarten. You might have to help them fill in answers after the fun answer has been given. "Who here plays to get exercise? Great, let's put that on our poster. Who here plays to make friends? Wonderful! It looks like we all want to. Making friends goes on our poster. Who wants to feel happy when we play?" Continue the poster exercise until you have the answers listed that you deem important for healthy character expression of your students. You might even want to have the children spell out the letters as you list them to make this an academic lesson as well as creating an exercise for social skills enhancement.

After literally visiting thousands of classrooms and seeing thousands of posters, the above-mentioned values are pretty much the same answers that we universally hear and see mentioned on the posters. Once you have the answers listed it is now time to review the answers.

TEACHER: "I think we've got enough great answers here. In this class, these are the reasons that we've identified as to why we play. We play to get exercise, to feel relaxed, so we won't be bored. We're going to learn when we play. We're going to play to create and pretend, feel included, feel happy and GREX, to relieve our stress, share, feel like winners and to be with our friends.

But, the number one reason we play is to have what?"

KIDS: "FUN!"

TEACHER: "All right, you got the number one answer. OK, so once again, we play to have what?"

KIDS: "FUN!"

Problem solving possible poster problems

We've seen tens of thousands of posters created in as many classrooms. We rarely see any big problems with the creation of the posters. Occasionally, there will be a child who gives a silly or inappropriate attention-seeking answer. The following are potential problems you might encounter and suggestions on how to deal with them.

Incongruent answers

Every so often in a kindergarten or first grade class we encounter a child who, when asked how they want to feel will reply with this big happy grin on their face that they like to feel, "sad." Some say "sad" just because they recognize it as a feeling and want it listed on the poster with other feelings. Others may say, "Sad" because they genuinely feel isolated or unhappy with their peers or at home. Without discounting that answer we acknowledge that being sad is a feeling. When our pet died we felt "sad." But, ask your class, is "sad" how we want to feel when we play?" They, and often the child that gave that particular answer, will congruently identify that they would rather feel happy while playing.

Interesting answers

Children will sometimes say that they like to play to feel "hyper" or "silly." These two answers provide a wonderfully quick lesson on where to put those feelings into action. Put those answers on your poster as they are truly valid responses. Validate that children and adults often like to feel and act silly and hyper but there is a place and time for that at school. I ask students the following questions: "Can we act hyper or silly when our teacher is teaching us math?" They, of course, will say, "No." Can we be hyper and disrespectful if our teacher is trying to teach us science?" "No." Can we act silly or hyper when I am explaining the rules to a game?" "No" However, can we be silly and hyper as long as it is safe during a game?" "Yes!" This removes potential anxiety for healthy fidgety children when they know they will have an opportunity to be what they are, wiggly and squirmy bodies that do need to get out of their seats throughout the day. It will also help them to develop self control and learn how and when to channel these child appropriate feelings and actions.

Sarcastic and inappropriate answers

Charlie and I have conducted thousands of poster exercises in thousands of classrooms and have had extremely few children (less than five) who said that we should play to hurt or tease others and want to put those answers on their class poster. But, this scenario could come up in your classroom with your lil' sarcastic Skippy. (Skippy is the generic name that we have affectionately given to represent all children who might, or do, act out. I am sure you have seen a few Skippys in your class from time to time). Try to use the positive peer culture within your classroom to temper and rechannel negative responses. If your challenging student says that we play to "hurt others" ask the other students, "Do we want students to play with us if we think they might hurt us?" Of course, the other students will say, "No." Reflect to the challenging student that his or her peers just made a rule that students who will intentionally hurt others won't get to play. Ask if they would like to change their answer so that their peers will feel safe with them and let them join in. I imagine they will quickly change their original answer.

Sarcastic answers are usually verbalized to get attention and to possibly indicate dominance. Your appropriate response will enable the other children to create a safe culture within their classroom. If, by chance, one goofy inappropriate answer to the question, "Why do we play" ends up with a cascade of additional goofy answers, you might want to just end the discussion on play at this point and try again at another time. You are the benevolent dictator of your classroom and are absolutely the person in charge. Your role is to make sure that the dominating and bullying children do not prevail or sabotage the creation of a safe learning and play environment during the poster creation.

Once again, we have worked with over 250,000 students and we have had extremely few incidences with such inappropriate answers given. We just want to offer some suggestions if this were to happen in your classroom. We think you will be surprised at how similar the answers that children give are the same ones that adults give. When we conduct our trainings at schools with the teachers and staff and perform the poster exercise with them it is validating to see such similar responses.

Summary

When reflecting back to your students the answers listed, point out that they wisely didn't give negative answers like playing to tease, humiliate or hurt each other to be placed on their poster. Reiterate that they didn't state things that would prevent play from being fun, to be placed on their poster. Compliment them on the positive values that they chose. This program has a lot of opportunity for positive reinforcement of good answers and actions. We can not stress enough how important genuine praise is for establishing a bond with students. Students will utilize praise as a way to internalize a desire to do well and to feel good about helpful actions.

We recommend that you never or rarely use "token economies" as a way to motivate children. Some teachers, parents and counselors liberally hand out stars, pluses, candy, or pizza as gifts for desired student responses. When used very minimally, token systems of rewards can cause no harm and be motivational. However, when misused, as they often are, they can sabotage behavioral change and set up a system where children will come to expect some kind of financial or gifting reward for an action which should have no bartering or consumer trigger. Children should begin to associate positive internal feelings and the praise of peers and people they respect in response for their moral actions as appropriate rewards for doing or saying the "right" thing. Your role as an effective teacher can facilitate this important developmental step.

TEACHER: "These all are excellent reasons why we play. This is important because we are all going to be responsible for upholding and following through with these values. I don't see being sad, putting down, hurting or humiliating anybody here on our poster. We were smart to leave them off. That is really important because those of us who can't follow through with these values will be asked not to participate until they decide to play with our values in mind and action. They can watch the game until they are ready to play. "So, would you rather watch the game or play?"

KIDS: "Play!"

TEACHER: "Would you rather tease someone or have fun?"

KIDS: "Have fun!"

TEACHER: "Do you want to hurt others or have fun?"

KIDS: "Have fun!"

TEACHER: "Smart Answers."

Congratulations, you are one-quarter of the way there because this is the first philosophical tool and underlying principle for using play therapeutically for classroom and playground management. We play to have FUN. Remind your children frequently that at their school the number one reason they play is to have fun. This becomes the goal they must achieve when they play. In fact, make this answer, "We play to have FUN," your school's mantra. If we can keep this simple underlying philosophy in mind, then all the other identified values gleaned from children regarding play and listed on their poster become available to us. Through play we learn rules, cooperation, responsibility and much more. And, through the Healthy Play principles, children will learn healthy socialization and develop a greater chance of success in their lives.

The next lesson continues with the second philosophical component of play and completes the poster creation exercise. Discussing only the first philosophical component of the Healthy Play program with your students is not enough to illicit effective behavioral change. It is highly recommended that you do both poster questions as discussed in chapters two and three at the same time with your students to provide a logical continuity.

Suggested Assignment:

It is time to initiate the Healthy Play program with your students. Create a poster for your group of students which will answer the question, "Why do we play?" To save space in your classroom, you can combine this question with the next one in the following lesson on one 36 by 24 inch sheet of paper. For separate posters for each question, we recommend 24 by 18 inch posters. Be colorful. Use colored sheets of paper. Charlie likes those yellow ones. Use colorful markers as well. Write all positive suggestions on the poster. Upon receiving the number one answer, "Fun," and a few other answers, don't forget to ask the following question, "How do you want to feel when you play?" during this part of the poster creation. Compliment your students for all their positive answers. Acknowledge and praise that you didn't receive negative answers. End this part of the exercise with the question, "Why do we play?"

Have children cheer out, "Fun!" before going on to the next poster question, "What is the most important part of every game?" It is HIGHLY recommended that you do the assignments for this lesson and the following three lessons sequentially and at the same opportunity for optimum results.

Lesson Two:

Healthy Play Philosophy: What IS The Most Important Part of Every Game?

Introduction

In order to utilize play in school you must have a philosophy that is both educational and curriculum friendly. In this lesson we will continue to explore some of the preconceived belief systems about play and then demonstrate why the Healthy Play philosophical model can meet your needs. Let's start with a question. What could possibly make play at school part of your daily curriculum? Developing an understanding of how play can be an incredibly useful educational tool takes some thinking. In many instances, it may take some unthinking.

Educators must initially deal with many myths and biases that we all have about play. There are two major categories for most of these issues. The first group is composed of adults who view play as a frivolous activity. It's something to say to children to make them disappear for a while. "Go out and play." When the children return several hours later and do not bring back any money or food this seems to validate that it was just wasted time. Such a limited bias mostly views play as something which fills the vacuum of time until children grow up and get a master's degree and go off to work.

The second major group of adults has constructed a rewards/work ethic approach to the use of play. The focus of this model determines that the value of play activities can only be measured in ribbons, medals, trophies and wins. It starts by identifying a specific set of gross motor tasks for a particular sport, i.e. baseball, soccer, basketball, etc. Next, countless hours are dedicated to perfecting these skills. The value of this model only occurs if you become better than anyone else. However, the vast majority of these experiences will not be used by participating children during most of their adult lives.

Neither of the two myths or biases are meaningful rationales for the use of play as part of the educational curriculum. We're all smart enough to see that. They fail as school oriented models because they don't teach very much of anything. Play is so much more than that. Just look at all the values and feelings your students identified when they answered the first philosophical question of "Why do we play?" They play to make friends, exercise, learn, reduce stress, share, win, not be bored, pretend, and feel included, happy and good. Ask yourself the question, "Do I want my students to learn how to do, to be, all those things and feelings?" If so, then a successful philosophy about play to support daily curriculum must be comprehensive enough to allow for all these learning experiences.

Why the philosophy is important

The second essential philosophical tenant in Healthy Play curriculum is the answer to the question, "What is the most important part of every game?" It doesn't matter if the game is jump rope, basketball or hockey. It doesn't matter if it's Chess, Monopoly or Duck-duck-goose. No matter what the game is, what is the single most important part of the game? The answer to this question is the heart of the Healthy Play Is a Solution program. Our focus is that the PEOPLE are the most important part of the game.

Unlike the question, "Why do we play?" where FUN was the obvious response, this second philosophical point of PEOPLE has proven much more elusive for both adults and children to identify. The negative modeling in our culture has so permeated our beliefs about play that all too often we have lost sight of the big picture. Most of your kindergarten through sixth grade students will not quickly recognize the PEOPLE concept until it is brought to their attention.

Once the understanding that people are the most important part of the game becomes your reality, a whole set of possibilities springs to life. You can't pay lip service to this concept. If you do, you'll give the same mixed message that is so often given to play. You've heard well meaning adults say, "It doesn't matter if you win or lose it is how you play the game." In theory, the right words were just uttered, but in practice, how many parents have you seen run up to their child on the winning team and say that? They don't! As a kid, you know you're a loser when you hear that speech. Our children have learned when our actions are not in harmony with our words.

At school, unequivocally, the focus must be the PEOPLE. Not just sometimes, but all the time. This is a logical perspective for you and your students. Are there any games without people? Is there ever score without the PEOPLE? Let's broaden this even more. What's the most important part of reading? Who writes the books? Who reads them? What's the most important part of math? What is the most important part of your whole school? It's the PEOPLE.

This philosophy now makes it practical to view every aspect of the game activity as a potential for student learning. Your curriculum can be totally based on the experiential moments of the activity, not the outcome. Simply stated, it's all about what happens with the interpersonal interactions of your children during the game. That's where the ongoing real learning is always occurring.

POSTER # 2: What is the most important part of every game?

Depending on whether you have chosen to have two separate pieces of paper or just one, divided in half, you are now ready to ask the second question to your class. Plan to spend about five minutes of class time doing this activity.

Write the question, "What is the most important part of every game?" at the top of the paper. Just like the first poster, have a big circle with a #1 placed inside it, so the key response will be highlighted once it has been given. Now begin to solicit answers from your class.

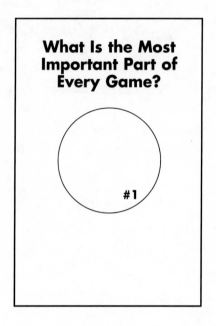

In general, your students will give the following answers: The most important part of the game is: "Winning, taking turns, teamwork, safety, being a good sport, cooperating, rules, equipment, playing fair or no cheating." Again, when you receive vital responses like playing fair, taking turns or safety, be sure to take time to process these concepts with the class. You know what the issues your particular group of children are having difficulty mastering. You've probably been dealing with the aftermath of these factors on a regular basis after lunch recess everyday. It's time to take advantage of a classroom management opportunity. This is where you will begin to expand your students' limited concrete knowledge of certain values. This part of setting up the HP program will begin the process of developing your class's concepts (not just the teacher's) of what the right way to play at school will be.

TEACHER: "Who in this class likes it when we play fair during games?" *(The vast, healthy majority of students will raise their hands.)*

Teacher: "Who likes it when someone cheats or is dishonest?"

(You may have some hands go up.)

TEACHER: "Is it FUN when we don't play fair?"

CLASS: "No!" will be the majority class answer.

TEACHER: "With whom are you more likely to make friends; students who play fair or those who cheat?" *(Here's a key place to develop the community ethic for playing fair.)* Re-state, "Raise your hand if you like playing fair." The raised hands are always a majority, but this is now a visual indicator for everyone in the class to see.

TEACHER: Your summary on this point will be, "Our class has just voted that only students who play fair will be allowed to play the games. We will now give brief time-outs *(usually no more than 30 seconds)* to students who need to learn how to play fairly. By watching, they can see how to have more success making friends."

You have just put all the children with positive values in charge of the games. The educational issue is that you are concretely helping your students identify a social skill they need to practice: honesty. Feel free to emphasize one or two more by having students vote for safety or taking turns.

Back to our question:

TEACHER: "What is the most important part of every game? You still have yet to discover the number one answer. I do agree that it is important to have fun, show respect, feel challenged, get better, participate, be responsible, and take care of the equipment." *(Also include other responses the students have given. The poster exercise is a wonderful opportunity to emphasize critical character skills which your school has identified as important to learn. Giving positive verbal acknowledgement to the students who state them is the type of reinforcement we endorse.)*

In many classes, and especially in kindergarten, students will readily supply something we refer to affectionately as the "No list." "No fighting, no kicking, no pushing, no hitting, no bad words." We like to list these responses because the children are used to hearing and listing values expressed this way. They just need the elders to help them correctly follow through correctly when they are playing.

TEACHER: "By now you must be wondering just what is the most important part of every game? Here's a hint: It starts with the letter 'P'." (*It might be necessary and give a second hint.*) "You can't play any games without this part." (*Ahhh! The light goes on.*) "PEOPLE are the most important part of every game." (*Make a big deal of this. Switch the lights on and off several times, whistle, cheer, clap and boldly write PEOPLE in your #1 circle on your poster.*)

Now make the same points with your students that we emphasized with you earlier in this chapter. Ask your students the following questions:

"Are there any games without PEOPLE?"

"Do jump ropes jump by themselves?"

"Do basketballs roll out of the classroom by themselves?"

"Do the puzzles glide off the shelves and put themselves together?"

"Is there any score in a game without PEOPLE? *(Through this series of questions, your students will quickly begin to understand why PEOPLE is the rational number one answer for this poster. Then to reinforce the number one answer you will ask the following question):*

"So which is more important, the PEOPLE or the score?" *(To accentuate this point with older students, ask them to remember two years ago on this same date, "Do you remember the scores of the games you played that day?" They won't have a clue. Then ask, "Do you remember who your friends were on that day?" Clearly the kids will see that PEOPLE are more important. Use the expanded questions about the most important part of reading, math and the whole school. By doing this, their understanding of why PEOPLE are the most important past of their school becomes transferable throughout their whole school experience).*

To reinforce learning through various senses you might have primary students do the following exercise, which will add visual and kinetic components:

TEACHER: "Everybody point to a girl and say to her, 'You're the most important part of the game." *(If some of the students don't want to acknowledge a girl, go back and do it over. Let the students know that there will be no tolerance for even the subtlest lack of acceptance at school. Say something like, "I didn't see everyone point to a girl to tell her she was the most important part of the game." Have them try it again, and then have the students point to a boy and say, "You're the most important part of the game.")*

Another valuable answer to the question, "What is the most important part of every game?" is listening. If the students don't suggest it then bring it up by asking:

TEACHER: "Do you think it's important to listen when we're outside playing?"

CLASS: "Yes."

TEACHER: "As one of the PEOPLE, do you think I'm having FUN when others don't listen?"

CLASS: "No."

Teacher: "If I'm not having FUN, do you think we'll take time to go out and play?"

CLASS: "No."

TEACHER: "Is this a class that likes to play?"

CLASS: "Yes."

TEACHER: "Then listening will be one of our guidelines. If someone forgets to listen we'll ask then to briefly watch the game as a way to help them learn." *(This game listening protocol will help a lot with classroom management. When students get busy talking to others instead of paying attention you will ask them to go to the side boundary. Instruct the student to count to twenty after the games starts. At that point they can join the game).*

Here again you have established that the play arena will provide you and your students with practice opportunities to learn valuable social and academic skills. The poster demonstration begins to make the transitions of the social skills from the games to every part of the school day. The carry-over will start immediately. To end the lesson, have your kids verbally answer the question, "What's the most important part of every game?" Students will response, "PEOPLE!"

Processing the classroom discussion

We have made thousands of posters in all grades. The above dialogue and specific techniques we suggest almost always generate the correct responses from children. However, there are students who just have to create some attention for themselves by giving undesirable answers. The key factor in replying to the majority of these inappropriate comments is to remember to say, "This is how we are going to play at school."

Over the years we have seen some powerful social cliques try to show off that they like "cheating." You can acknowledge that if they wish to do so elsewhere it's up to them, but it's not a very good idea. Even if they were just clowning around we encourage you to respond with a non-punitive but serious response. Additionally, to keep building your student community of support, restate, "But, playing fair is how we will play at school."

Again, most often in the older grades, there may be a student(s) who believes winning is the most important part of the game. Give this student emotional space to have this personal belief. A good non-judgmental response might be to say, "In your sports league, your parents and coaches may teach other priorities. Here in class, people will be the most important part of our games. It may be different from other places where you play, but 'people' will be the number one focus when we all play at school." Students can differentiate what actions are permissible in different settings. They will quickly accept that people are the most important part of the game at school because that will be how everyone is playing.

Occasionally, we've seen students create a power struggle and actually win a class vote on an issue you know is inappropriate. Your best option is to terminate the lecture. You might say, "As your teacher, I can only use school time if we agree to play the right way. It doesn't seem like were able do that today so let's move onto something else. Maybe we'll try again tomorrow or later in the week." Once you've made a decision to stop, make it firm and truly stop. Do not negotiate to the pleas the students will make. Be pleasant, but stop, for this is a wonderful classroom management learning moment. Use this, and other, opportunities effectively and everyone will benefit. If, when you talk again, 90% of the class is willing to be serious, go forward and finish the process with them. When it comes time to play, remove the two or three students who have persisted in being uncooperative from the game. In the Healthy Play curriculum you will notice there is room for flexibility. Use your discretion on when an issue needs a logical group consequence or when it's time to have an individual consequence.

Normal growth and development issues exist when creating the posters with kindergarten children. First and foremost is that they have a very short attention span. Second, they always like to raise their hand to be called on. However, this does not mean they wish to say something about the topic at hand. Third, even if they do have a proper response, the frequent twenty second pauses before they start talking can rapidly exhaust the previously mentioned short attention spans of their peers. Fourth, and always a danger, is that the response to your question of what's most important could be something like, "To wash our hands after we go to the bathroom." This response will trigger the next kid to say, "To close the door when we go outside." An equally excited third child will steer this train of thought even further of the track by adding, "We should always say please." Since this is a possible reality we recommend a much quicker paced process when doing the poster with kinders.

We encourage you to have five to seven values in mind before you start the process. Basic kindergarten values might be to; be safe, play fair, listen, follow rules, share, take turns and be kind. Read the question and say, "How many of you think it's important to play safe? If you do, please raise your hand." The class will look like you just started "The Wave." Continue this hand waving process with the remaining ideas as you write them on the poster. This should take about thirty seconds. Now, in your own style, add a little extra trumpet flair and tell your students that the number one answer is PEOPLE. About a minute of embellishment will cover the topic of why people are most important. Complete the process by pointing to each other and saying, "You're the most important part of the game." When asking kindergarten students to chant the answer to, "What's the most important part of the game?" there will probably be some confusion when some say

FUN. After a few days, and some practice, they will be able to differentiate the two questions with the proper responses.

Summary

Our goal in Lesson two was to identify a play philosophy that would be both educational and curriculum friendly. To achieve this we have offered that the most important part of every game, are the PEOPLE. With this understanding, we can be open to the learning potential of the student's experiences which are always present during a game.

The creation of the second poster allowed for everyone to participate in the discovery that the PEOPLE are the most important part of our games at school. Additionally, it's the full balance of the students' 20 or more answers on both posters that makes this program rich and meaningful. All we have to do as the teachers (elders) is to hold the children accountable to the values they have given. These are their answers. They just need countless opportunities to practice how to turn their words and beliefs into actions.

During the dialogue we took several opportunities to model and highlight how every aspect of this program can be utilized for its learning potential. You will find many chances to build community, practice voting, empower a positive peer culture and have a useful mechanism to support your classroom management. That's the philosophy. Play to have FUN. PEOPLE are the most important part of the game. It makes your role as the teacher simple. If all the students are playing, having FUN and taking care of the PEOPLE, then keep playing. Everything is fine.

Suggested Assignment:

It's now your turn to complete the development of the second philosophical poster with your class. Be sure to have some fun while you're doing this. It's a chance to share other aspects of your own personality. Be silly or dramatic. Laugh with your students. Tell your kids you are reading a book on how they can use a little school time to play, but only if they play the right way! When you are done with the poster be sure to find a place in the room where you can keep it visible ALL YEAR. (The poster stays on the wall so you can always refer back to it). As mentioned in Lesson one, you should do both philosophical posters at the same time. Plan for about ten to fifteen minutes. It's how long we usually take to do it. In kindergarten, you may want to do each 3-5 minute lesson separately which is more age appropriate for lectures.

Lesson Three:
Rule # 1, the Empathy Rule

Introduction

Knowing the two philosophical principles – "We play to have fun" and "People are the most important part of the game" – you now find yourself half-way to being able to use play therapeutically. Your students have identified the values we all want to foster with the creation of your posters. Now, to set up a safe learning community, from your classroom to the playground, throughout the whole school and enable students to learn, practice and solidify these values, we must focus on two essential HP rules that you and your group must adhere to.

Why do children perpetrate violence upon each other?

It is because they lack empathy. Surely, if they had a sense of empathy they would not be so over-abundantly cruel to each other in acts of bullying and violence. How do you teach empathy? Oh, you could talk about it. Some people learn that way. If we go back to the research, we do learn 20 % of what we say. We could have our children read about it. We've seen anti-violence posters mass-marketed in almost every school up there on the walls of school cafeterias higher than the eyesight lines of most children. They all have wonderful words on those posters that we do want our children to embody such as; responsibility, respect, compassion, etc. Once again, we do learn 30 % of what we see. Talk about it? Hey, we've added another few percentage points. The point that we must always remember is we must give our children real-life opportunities to learn and practice empathy and compassion repetitively. The addition of experiential practice is where retaining 90 % of what we learn comes in, through the art of doing something. Rule # 1, our rule to learn and practice responsibility, nurturing, compassion and empathy is practical and easily implemented.

Rule # 1 Defined

RULE # 1: IF ANYONE IS HURT, EITHER PHYSICALLY OR EMOTIONALLY, THE CLOSEST PERSON MUST STOP PLAYING, TAKE CARE OF AND STAY WITH THAT PERSON.

Regarding rule # 1, it is very significant that no blame is attached to who causes an injury or problem. The focus of the HP learning opportunity is now centered on caring for the injured person vs. catching the culprit. However, in reality, this process always catches the perpetrator. Of course, they were closest when the injury occurred. It is not relevant whether the act was intentional, an accident or just being out of control. It is now simply an issue of proximity and the closest person must stop and help. Additionally, even if a student trips and no one caused the injury, the closest person must stop and render immediate assistance. For children this makes perfect linear sense and fits developmentally, enabling them to easily see this form of simple logic. The HP emphasis is on the students, not the teacher, taking the responsibility to DO the caring. This is how students learn personal responsibility for their actions. If a student tags another aggressively and hurts that child, they are the one who must stay with the injured child until that student is ready to return to the activity. A hard, hurtful tag means that the aggressive child will not be playing for the time of their responsible Rule # 1 intervention. That child will gain a practical opportunity to learn about the consequences of their actions while developing empathy and nurturing skills. The injured child will feel nurtured and also see the aggressive child as potentially able to also be fair and responsible. But, it is essential that empathy and compassion now becomes the responsibility of the students and not just the teachers.

With this gentle system of logical consequences - play without hurting others and you continue to play, but if you hurt others you are removed from the fun to take care of the person you injured - kids start to learn (a little bit at a time) how to play with others more successfully. They will eventually learn, usually after only a few short episodes being out from the action, that they can actually play the game without hurting anybody. They will learn to find greater satisfaction in making friends then hurting others. And, the wonderful thing about this program and this rule is that the kids who need to practice playing without hurting others get all the practice they need. Usually, they will practice over and over again until they get it.

Now, for the child who knows how to be responsible after accidentally hurting a peer, this rule provides a wonderful opportunity to foster and hone nurturance. As educators, mental-health professionals or as parents, we know that wonderful feeling and power that comes when you walk over to a crying child and they stop crying quickly because they feel better just being in our presence. As an adult, it is so wonderful having this effect over hurt children, rescuing them from their pain by our mere touch, our mere presence. As teachers we experience many such opportunities daily seeing children being hurt by other students. We swoop down out of the sky like Wonder Woman™ or Superman™ and take over the nurturing duties. Teachers are such caring individuals. Most go into this profession because they feel a sense of passion for teaching and a great concern for children. So, it is easy to see teachers immediately running across a playground when they see a child injured by another taking full responsibility for healing opportunities. And, as this happens, the child who caused the injury goes blissfully off to injure others, intentionally or unintentionally, without learning how to solve this problem.

If the teacher is the only Good Samaritan, without thinking, we rob the experience of nurturing from the children who can learn from having accidentally hurt another. Turning the responsibility over to the children gives them a chance to practice nurturing. We give them a chance to share in the responsibility of making that person feel better. They become part of the healing. They learn personal responsibility and responsibility towards others. Responsibility belongs in every aspect of all school curriculum.

Safety Issue:

Charlie and I are NOT advocating that you stand idly by watching all the playground injuries that can occur in a day. Be smart! If you see teeth, blood, guts or gore get your sweet nurturing butt over there immediately! Be a sharp responsible elder for your students. Use your good adult assessment and common sense skills. You really know when you need to be there. You know when you need to be right up close and with a child. But, for those kids that can take care of each other, give them a chance to practice. These kids will, in turn, feel a sense of empowerment and a sense of care-taking that is going to be a truly powerful tool in their success as a healthy, social being.

Explaining Rule # 1 to your students

Explaining Rule # 1 is done by teacher discussion and having students role model what they might say or do if they see someone hurt.

Upon completion of your classroom posters have your students go through the following chant:

TEACHER: "At our school we play to have what?"
STUDENTS: "FUN!"
TEACHER: "The most important part of every game are the who?"
STUDENTS: "The People!"

You will then tell your students, "To make sure that we, the people, can have fun we will have two important rules. Let's first talk about rule number one."

Clearly explain Rule # 1.

Rule # 1: "If anyone is hurt, either physically or emotionally, the closest person must stop playing, take care of and stay with that person."

Whenever somebody bumps a head, bonks an elbow, falls down or is emotionally hurt, the closest person stays with that person and is out of the game, care-taking the injured child until the injured party is ready to play again. There are no exceptions about implementing this rule. All students must commit by a show of hands to follow this rule if they wish to join any of the games at school.

So, have everyone in your class very publicly and visibly raise their hands if they can promise to follow this rule. Remember, this is how you continue to build your Positive Peer Culture. If you have a child who won't promise, and you most likely will, firmly uphold the group's positive expectations always acting non-punitively. Most often when you have a child refusing to promise to care for others it is because they are hoping for the cheap laugh and have found that their past negative actions gets them peer or teacher attention. Usually, when it is repeated that without a promise that child just won't get to play, faster than greased lightning, most children will promise and raise their hands in commitment. But, still make sure you accept that even when children raise their hands in a promise that does not mean they will be ready to keep that promise. The hand raising enables the teacher to have something concrete to go back to, to hold children accountable to if they break or simply forget to follow Rule # 1. However, any child who will not raise their hand, indicating their refusal to be a responsible caretaker is instructed that they will have to watch the activity from the sidelines. Do not allow that child to play until you feel comfortable that he/she can join in with a promise to caretake and not hurt others intentionally.

Tell this child that everyone must be mindful and take care of each other. Let the child know that you'd prefer having him/her safely play than watch the game. You might even verbalize that you want to help them learn the behaviors which will make them more friends. Your group of children is looking towards you for modeling and mentoring. You, as the local responsible elder, are going to hold your "Skippy," (once again, our affectionate generic name for all the acting-out children out there) and all people accountable for everybody's safety.

Role plays are powerful tools to help children learn the words and actions that are expected of them. When I am conducting this aspect of explaining rule # 1 in a classroom setting I go around and feign having a hurt nose or sore knee. I will ask the students to identify the child who is closest to me and my hurt nose. This is important because upon giving children an opportunity to receive positive attention for nurturing many elementary students will say they are, or will want to be, the closest to my hurt nose even though they are actually on the other side of the classroom. For the sake of teaching personal responsibility and not additionally creating an unsafe situation where the whole class might pounce unsafely upon an injured student with a desire to do good in their hearts, help students learn that ONLY the closest person needs to comply to Rule # 1. Help students learn to ask an injured person, "Are you okay?" Role model this with you being the injured person. Quickly expand the role play to the students. Pick a few students to role play what they would say and do if the child next to them became injured. We would suggest that you publicly do this role play with your "Skippy" who probably needs to learn this rule the most.

Be realistic regarding your most challenging students. Your "Skippy" student, who might be the class bully, is not going to learn nurturing skills right away, but they will be able to learn from logical consequences. The exciting game that Skippy wants to play is going to be a powerful motivator. To get to play, he, or she, will have to modify their behaviors. Once they put it together that it is their hard tag that results in having to comply with Rule # 1 which keeps them out of the exciting action of the game they will quickly learn to tag softer and not injure others. Play is such a motivating factor. All children want to play. They also want to be successful making friends and praised by peers and elders that they have bonded with. Rule # 1 gives them a real life opportunity to accomplish this.

With older students in the fourth through sixth grades, it may be useful to use a specific age appropriate game like soccer for the role play. Have one student be the goalie and another pretend to be a player on the opposing team. Have them lightly bump into each other and instruct the goalie to fall down safely. Ask the class the following questions, "Is the goalie one of the people in our game? Doesn't that make her the most important part of the game? Is she more important than the score or who wins the game? Is a hurt person having any fun? Of course she is the most important part of the game and that is why the closest person to her has to stop and care for what's most important! Both teams will need to know that if a player who is closet to the injured person does not stop to help and continues to play, even making a score, that score just will not count."

This demonstration allows you to connect your posters to a likely situation which will probably occur in your students' games, especially in the early implementation of the program.

While you are playing activities with your students, you, as the teacher, are to remain aware of when children need to implement Rule # 1. Some students will automatically implement it. Some will not even be aware that they have hurt another child as they may be distracted by the excitement of the game activity. There will be a need, especially at the beginning of implementing the HP program, that you will have to point out to students when an injury has occurred and who was the closest to the hurt child. All the front-loaded attention and intervention pays off as students soon

learn how to internalize empathy and caretaking.

Problems you may encounter:

Oh, the things we've learned over years!

Students who refuse to promise to take care of others

We have a story to share with you regarding some children making a "promise" to use Rule # 1. We've worked directly with over 250,000 students and the majority of them have promised very easily. Somewhere around 248,271 have. However, it has also been our experience that some children initially refuse to promise in an attempt for that class "clown" kind of attention they desire, but quickly change their minds when they realize that they will not get to play until they do promise. And, then there are those few rare compassionate children who uncharacteristically can't seem to "promise" to take care of their peers. We were initially puzzled why these particular children would not promise as they seemed so well behaved and compassionate. This is what they taught us. There wasn't a problem about their compassion, there was a problem with our use of the word "promise." It turns out that their religion believed that men and women should not make "promises" because it is humanly impossible to live up to every single promise made. To rectify this we said, "Raise your hand if you agree to take care of the injured person and are the closet." This they could easily live with.

Now back to those powerful class "clowns," negative peer leaders, their followers and what to do with them. Most students in the younger grades who go for the easy attention seeking negative response of not promising quickly change their tune when they discover in a non-punitive manner that by not promising they are not going to play. However, for those of you who teach intermediate grades where negative peer pressure makes some students not want to promise, you may want to try some of the following interventions:

I always let students know that there is a finite time for play activities as we have other tasks that we need to accomplish during our school day. Many students recognize that the opposition from the class clown is actually harmless and that he or she is just going for a laugh. However, when I point out that the time it takes for me, or the teacher, to address the class clown comes out of the class play time, the attitudes quickly shift. Instead of being entertained by the class clown they are now losing valuable playtime. Where there was once support for inappropriate behaviors there is now frustration and impatience because the whole class is affected by the inappropriate actions of an individual and they will want it quickly remedied. I often ask the class as a whole, "By me having to address this issue, because it is my responsibility to make sure our play can be fun and safe, we as a group have just lost play time. We now have had three minutes taken from us that we could have used playing. Do we like losing our play time?" The kids will respond with a resounding, "No!" Upon feeling such strong positive peer pressure from their classmates, the child who initially compromised the amount of playtime, generally promises to comply with Rule # 1 very quickly. This solves this problem about 85% of the time.

But, there may be a very powerful Skippy in your class. Once he or she refuses to promise, their cronies start to get in on it as well. You have a few options here. If a majority of students were to refuse to comply for reasons of just being oppositional, going for a laugh, or just not being willing to comply with caretaking, we recommend stopping the lesson at this point. Be verbal that you liked that people were honest about their unwillingness to take care of others but that we all previously agreed to make our activities "fun" and would take care of the "people." "Since that no longer seems to be the case, then our class just doesn't appear to be ready to play now." Perhaps you might return to this rule after some academic lessons or try again the following day. Some children develop a habit to "test" us adults. This can be a wonderful opportunity to demonstrate to our students that we will walk our talk. We will not conduct or allow unsafe activities. We will however, provide opportunities for learning compassion and how to play well and safely. We will help them live up to the expectations and values that they listed on their posters which will make them better students and friends.

Let's imagine that there are only a handful of students that are unwilling to promise to Rule # 1. The Alpha Skippy got a few of their buddies to go along with him. It might be that clique of girls or group of boys that often act like a little unruly mob in your classroom. We always praise kids for being honest with their response that they refuse to care take others. We then use some of the following techniques:

Take your class outside and play with all of the students that can promise to care take of others. Remember, this is a program for the success of all the students and not just the Skippys or "kids at risk." However, do not let the kids who couldn't promise sit together as a group. Divide and conquer! Have them either watch or do something else that is constructive like homework or academic lessons. This IS class time. Most of the students chose to play as class time, those who didn't, could perhaps do a written lesson on why they felt they wouldn't want to take care of others. Let them know, like any language arts lesson, you will be grading them on grammar and spelling. That alone gets most students quickly wanting back in the game with a solid promise.

Discussion Gift: A teacher and I were gifted with a valuable learning opportunity from a small group of her very articulate eighth grade students who refused to participate, promise or care for others. This opportunity was ultimately helpful at problem solving and facilitating positive change. In this classroom, there were four students who refused to help specific students. It turns out that the students they refused to care for were bullies. Feeling a need for retribution, they wanted to acknowledge that if their former tormentors got hurt they would be just fine to let them suffer for their past mean acts. Until this point, the teacher was not even aware of a bully problem among her students. Like many educators, this teacher had never played with her children, so was unaware of the "Lord of the Flies" scenario that was going on daily out on the playground. But, now the situation was made public. The teacher was able to facilitate needed dialog between the appropriate parties, additionally laying down rules for expected conduct. Within minutes everyone was able to participate without fear of purposeful harm and demonstrated expected compassion. This intervention changed cruel and non-empathetic children into mindful and friendly ones. When I returned to this school a few months later all the children reported a greater sense of compassion and fewer problems. This was evidenced by the teacher's ongoing observations when she played with her students which was at least "three times per week." Additionally, I saw the same positive dynamics when I played with them as well. Ah, the power of play!

Sometimes, an option of doing academic work during playtime will not work for every one of your most challenging students. As the students who promised to comply with Rule # 1 are playing, remove yourself from the game and go up individually to each student who refused to promise. The divide and conquer approach, tied in with individual one-on-ones, tends to break down that group machismo and opposition. We've rarely seen a child give up playing for longer than two rounds of a game. The whole class's attention has now shifted from the acting out child to their enjoyment of the game activity. Most kids who act out love being "timed-out" because it offers them such an opportunity to be powerful and the center of attention. But now it no longer works because their classmates are having too much fun to notice inappropriate behaviors. The time IN is now way more motivating than a time OUT. Most time-outs are conducted ineffectively. They are either too long where the child forgets why they have been timed out or they provide little opportunity for learning. Many time-outs are given just to give the teacher a break. The Healthy Play approach makes brief time-outs more effective tools for the teacher AND student to use.

There will be those rare children who just don't want to promise and be caretakers. It is extremely rare, but we have seen a handful of them. Some have problems that will need approaches that are definitively more therapy than our therapeutic approach to children. Our program is called Healthy Play Is A Solution. It is a powerful solution, but not the only solution. There will be students who you will discover, through this program, that need and deserve more intensive interventions.

As always, we encourage you to recognize that students may remove themselves from the Rule # 1 promise, or activities in general, to protect themselves or others. A refusal to promise to care take may just be a genuine way of keeping safety or their esteem protected. Tolerate students demonstrating personal readiness. Invite, but do not force children to make a commitment that they are not ready to make.

Too many helpers

Teachers working with kindergartners and first graders will often report that when one student gets hurt everyone wants to be their helper and do Rule # 1 "en mass." It might take a small amount of time for this young group of children to recognize that the rule only applies to the closest person. It is a learning experience. Too many Rule # 1 helpers might cause additional injuries if the whole class comes cascading to the rescue of one injured kiddo. But, if it is just a few, tolerate it until they learn about the concept of "closest." Remember, this is the age group that when you set boundaries for an activity will totally go out of bounds for a while until they master such simple concepts. It will not take too many rounds of an activity for them to "get" who is closest with your modeling that concept.

Kids who purposefully act injured

This problem occurs in the younger grades as some children discover that if they fake being injured by falling down while playing they will have a whole group of potential friends running to their rescue. This is easy to see among the most attention seeking children. While the game is going on you will remove a child who is manipulating this rule to the side of the game outside the boundary. We will further discuss taking children out of an activity using Rule # 2 in the next chapter. However, let the child know that it seems that she is getting hurt a lot, and remind her that we play to have fun and not to get hurt. State that you are responsible for taking care of all the people. Let the student know that you will have to remove her from the game for her own safety, unless she can keep herself from getting hurt. Once the younger children logically get that their manipulation keeps them from playing they start to change that behavior. This might take a few interventions for them to learn this. Older children that can be confronted with their manipulations directly will benefit by your promise to remove them from the activity to keep them safe and to help them learn that manipulation is not a healthy way to make friends.

Injuries happen

All the bicycle helmets in the world will not prevent some children that ride bicycles from getting hurt. All the banning of tag games at some campuses will not stop kids from getting hurt when they play other games. All our well intentioned best wishes will not keep our students free from injuries. Accidents happen. Getting hurt physically and emotionally is a part of being a child, teenager and adult. Being kinetic frees us; movement makes us physically healthy, emotionally happier, and even makes us better learners. However, it also makes us vulnerable. Charlie and I will never make a promise that you or your students will be free from injury. And, we won't accept responsibility if that were to happen. The truth is that people get hurt when they play or move about, and people can also get hurt if they don't play or move about. Children will experience a scraped knee, a bloodied nose, a tumble, a fall and we will have to be accepting of it when it happens by accident. What we are trying to do here is make a difference in purposeful acts of aggression, violence and bullying. This is something we can help our children with. Aggression, violence and bullying are things that we will not tolerate or allow. Students can be taught how to become good friends, fair players, soft taggers, and be compassionate and empathetic human beings.

Summary

We've had teachers say that Rule # 1 is a liberating concept because every time they would traditionally take care of two children that were hurt and had their back turned away from the other children, three more acts of aggression would happen. They saw themselves spending recess or PE time treating, limit-setting and mediating the entire playground. After being placed in this joyless position repeatedly many teachers just stopped playing or facilitating play for their children.

Now, we give the power and responsibility back to all the children who demonstrate or need to learn successful nurturing social skills. Help the children and the adults to focus, not just on scoring goals, but on demonstrating that in your school community, the people truly are the most important thing. By making this concept of "people and caring first" a foundation for all curriculum, in and out of the classroom, we optimize all forms of learning and education.

What you will find most effective about the use of the two HP rules are the logical consequences that occur for students. The students who cause the most injuries or argue the most will be the recipient of the most learning opportunities to practice correcting these problems. The two HP rules are meant to be a framework for teacher guidelines. They are not written in stone. The HP curriculum promotes that teachers use their good discretion. If the injury is of a greater magnitude, the teacher will absolutely become involved. Remember, seeing teeth, blood, guts and gore will be your clues that you should be there in a jiffy, directly intervening. In the younger grades, the teacher might initially, and always, when safety and assessment dictates, join the student who is providing compassion, and model and assist in the nurturing. However, the long term and desired goal is for students to act responsibly by themselves in these situations.

HP in the educational setting goes beyond classroom lectures and slogans on the bulletin board. These are some of the ways of how children learn and we have included them in our program. However, it's the actual concrete, hands-on life experiences which are the most critical learning factors for children ages 5-12. HP utilizes the playground environment where the vast majority of students' daily problems actually occur. The playground is where children accumulate the practical concrete experiences that will become the learning base for future abstract thinking and problem solving skills.

Like any other subject taught in school, the eventual goal for these learned behaviors and skills is to transfer them into the students' total life environment. The HP process is initiated through the use of daily play, but it is expected to carryover to encompass the entire school day. The HP rules are used by all, both students and adults, at the school throughout the day. If a student from another class falls on the way to the bus, the nearest student must immediately use Rule # 1. As the students constantly see these guidelines being modeled and expected by the teachers they soon learn that they too are empowered to initiate the appropriate rules with their peers. Week by week and month by month the simple concrete focus on DOING the correct social skills is transferred across all settings.

Compassion and empathy can be learned and nurtured by our students if we delegate personal responsibility and expect them to live up to values that will serve them individually and collectively. Rule # 1 will gift our children opportunities to practice empathy. Frequently, and every time you take your students out to play say the following: "When someone gets hurt, do you stay with them or run away?"

The only acceptable response will be a resounding, "Stay with them!"

Suggested Assignment

After completing the poster exercise, verbalize rule number one with your students. Role-play what are appropriate responses to say and do when a student is closest to an injured person. Have your group of students demonstrate who is willing to agree to Rule # 1 by a show of hands. During a game activity, remain focused on the players and point out and direct students to conduct Rule # 1 if they do not implement it on their own. Praise children when you see them utilizing Rule # 1 and nurturing others.

Lesson Four:

RULE # 2: THE DISAGREEMENT RULE

Introduction

It is natural to have disagreements and to argue about them. It's normal. Human beings can disagree about everything. What is critical is learning how to come up with a peaceful process and solution when arguing. It's a bad news, good news situation. The bad news is that games are loaded with the grist for potential arguments. You can hear them daily during every recess:

"I tagged you."

"No you missed."

"You're out."

"No I'm safe."

"It's my turn."

"You took cuts in line."

The good news is that playground squabbles provide a perfect situation in every school where teachers can help the students learn how to deal with these conflicts.

This is the strength of the Healthy Play curriculum. Play will provide your students with countless situations where they can practice over and over how to resolve their disagreements. It's the experiences during the game where the ongoing learning occurs. Discovering how to resolve disagreements makes playing games useful. It is not our intention to teach you any one particular method of conflict resolution or peer mediation. The goal of this lesson is for the teacher to identify that there is a controlled means which allows students to learn more successful communication skills.

Failure to successfully deal with arguments impacts upon academics in school. In the short term, dealing with constant arguments is disruptive, takes time, is often frustrating and can be stressful for everyone involved. In the long term, the impact is even more significant. Research has shown that over 90% of employees who are fired from a job aren't fired because they can't read, write or do the work. They are fired because they do not get along effectively with others. Using the Healthy Play curriculum will make a positive impact in helping your students learn to disagree effectively with their peers. It's a skill they need to master to become successful adults.

Rule # 2 and the role of the teacher defined

RULE # 2: IF TWO INDIVIDUALS HAVE AN ARGUMENT OR DISAGREEMENT DURING A GAME, THEY MUST LEAVE THE GAME UNTIL THEIR ARGUMENT IS PEACEFULLY SETTLED.

The great thing about the Healthy Play curriculum is its logical simplicity. It makes things easier for you and understandable for the kids. Arguing is not one of the reasons we play. Use your posters to point out that arguing is not listed there. It's not FUN. Therefore, since the arguers are not having FUN, they must leave the activity. They are out of the activity until they resolve their problem and can enjoy the game as much as everyone else. Using this rule, we've taken the power away from those kids who can stop an activity every time they want to have an argument. From now on, they're the ones who need to go process and figure out a solution. (This is a healthier way of thinking.)

This rule and concept works because it continues to empower the students who are doing well. They are having FUN, and with this system, the game immediately continues for them. The frequent negative attention that so often accompanies arguments is now given minimal acknowledgment by the teacher and class. The teacher, or any student, can simply say, "If you two have an argument, take it out of the game." Only the two students involved leave. No gang of friends can accompany them. If more than two students disagree with someone, each discussion must be done by just two students at a time until everyone has had their say. By reflecting the disagreement back to the children, you coerce them to do the learning.

Important when implementing this rule is your understanding that an argument is just a problem that the students can gain practice in solving. All day long your students solve math problems, spelling problems, reading problems and science problems. A disagreement is just a social problem that has occurred during a game; it's a game problem. You must clearly convey to your class that having a disagreement does not mean they are in trouble. Highlighting the difference between a problem and trouble is critical. A problem is something the students solve. Trouble means that the teacher, principal and parents will be getting involved. Our baseline behavior in resolving disagreements is, "No bad words and no fighting." We'll explore this concept more when it comes to role playing this rule with your students.

Defining the role of the teacher when using Rule # 2:

When implementing this concept you will need to accept some different priorities when playing games at school. This is not the NFL. A disagreement does not mean you'll stop the game and review the video tape for two minutes to guarantee that the correct call is made. There are no championships, trophies or millions of dollars involved. Remember, this is school. No one really needs to care about who wins today's fourth grade kickball game. Your primary role when implementing Rule # 2 is to become the validator. As the validator, you are the person who verbally praises the kids for resolving their argument peacefully.

Being a validator changes how you will interact with your students. The first factor to address is that the teacher has traditionally assumed the role of absolute authority in the game. You must abandon this long established role for adults during play. Now you can model that you should be treated as an equal by your students while they play. Too often the adults have enjoyed the authoritative role for the subtle power given to the person who makes the final judgment. It's based on the idea that the "students need my wisdom." But, it's a trap. If the teacher is always the person who resolves a difference of opinion, then the students will always need to seek you out for every problem that occurs. Not just during game time, but all day long! Being this authoritative actually reinforces "tattle-tale" behaviors. Children manipulate this situation because it usually means the teacher will pronounce a judgment of, "You're right" on one student, and, "You're wrong" on the other. Instead, a validator says, "I'm glad you two worked things out. Good job!" Much of the rationale for having the adult make all of the judgments comes from the fact that it is expedient. It kept the game going. But, we've fixed that. Rule # 2 sends the two disagreeing parties over to the side so the game can go on.

The next factor about not having the teacher resolve all the conflicts may be more difficult to accept at first. As a teacher working with children you probably have a very strong desire to make their world one that is filled with liberty, justice and fairness. As adults, we have far greater experiences in life. Therefore, our judgments are usually better. However, we are now going to ask you to do things differently so the students can begin to develop this same positive understanding. It will mean that even if you saw the play at second base and a player was clearly out or absolutely safe, you will not make the decision. When students say, "Teacher, tell him he's out." "No I'm safe." You will simply respond, "Sounds like a disagreement, use Rule # 2." Here's the tough part. Thirty seconds later they come back and the decision they made without bad words or fighting is the opposite of what you saw happen, you must accept their results. Simply say, "Do you both agree on this answer?" If yes, "Then get back in the game." A little later we will address what to do if a student manipulates the Rule # 2 process by always "winning" the disagreements even when he, or she, isn't being fair.

As always, the teacher can join in to facilitate a productive peaceful discussion. Use your good judgment. If you see one student who is the equivalent of gasoline and the other one is matches, get there before the explosion occurs. In these cases, your wisdom is initially needed to model how a non-violent argument is processed. They need you to prevent it from turning into a fight. Support your students so they can keep a disagreement as a problem and not let it escalate into trouble. Even when you leave, the game continues for everyone else. On the practical side, you finally have a couple of minutes to help some students one to one. You're doing this during game time without it interfering with your academic lessons.

Explaining Rule # 2 to your Students:

Spencer and I strongly encourage the use of role play for introducing Rule # 2. It makes the learning so much more effective. In this role play you will pick two students to have a disagreement. You get to play the teacher and commentator for this scene.

Ask for a volunteer's to help you do the role play. If the "Skippy" in your class, who argues with everyone, happens to raise his hand, this could be a perfect opportunity to pick him. If you can demonstrate to the class that there is a successful way to argue with this person then you'll be getting an extra benefit from this lesson. However, if this is too much to expect that he'll be helpful, then pick a less problematic Skippy or other student. Also pick someone who normally acts responsible and has good verbal skills. We'll call her Susie in this dialogue.

The following is a suggested dialogue for how this scene usually goes. Feel free to copy this Rule # 2 script for you and your students to act out.

Set the scene: Skippy and Susie are going to have a disagreement. Skippy is the pitcher in the kickball game and when Susie was coming into second base he ran over there with the ball and believes he tagged out. Susie disagrees and thinks she's safe. They're going to argue over if Susie is safe or out. Before you begin the role play, complete the scene setup by asking your class the following questions:

TEACHER: "Does our poster show that we play games to argue?
CLASS: "No."
TEACHER: "But let's be honest. How many of us have had arguments when we play games?"
CLASS: Everyone including the teacher raises their hand.
TEACHER: "Then it's normal to have disagreements. The important thing is that we learn at *(use the name of your)* school how to do it the right way."
TEACHER: "When we argue at *(your school)* school are we allowed to say bad words?"
CLASS: "No." *(If you get some 'yes' answers, firmly address the situation immediately. The reality is, you will only have FUN playing as a class when your students know the expectations are uncompromis-*

ingly clear. You are constantly role modeling for the good kids in your class).

TEACHER: "Since we can't say bad words I need both Skippy and Susie to shake hands and agree that they won't say bad words." *(Skippy and Susie must shake hands).*

TEACHER: "Since we can't say bad words are we allowed at *(name of school)* to punch, fight or hit each other?"

CLASS: "No." *(Have Skippy and Susie shake hands that they can't fight.)*

TEACHER: "Then here we go. Susie, pretend you're running into second base and Skippy pretend to tag her with the ball. Start your disagreement"

SKIPPY: "I tagged you. You're out."

SUSIE: "No you missed, I'm safe.

SKIPPY: "You're out."

SUSIE: "I'm safe."

SKIPPY: "I got you."

SUSIE: "No, you missed."

SKIPPY: "Out."

SUSIE: "Safe."

SKIPPY: "I got you."

SUSIE: "No you didn't."

SKIPPY: "Did too."

SUSIE: "No way!"

SKIPPY: "Your foot was in the air when I tagged you."

SUSIE: "No, it was already on the base."

SKIPPY: "Teacher, teacher, teacher! Tell Susie she's out."

SUSIE: "Teacher, tell Skippy I'm safe."

At this point you will explain the disagreement rule.

RULE # 2: IF TWO INDIVIDUALS HAVE AN ARGUMENT OR DISAGREEMENT DURING A GAME, THEY MUST LEAVE THE GAME UNTIL THEIR ARGUMENT IS PEACEFULLY SETTLED

TEACHER: "It sound like you two have a disagreement so go over to the side and solve the problem of who's safe or out. *(The role play continues.)*

TEACHER: "Skippy, you were the pitcher but since you now need to have an argument I'll pick Damon as the new pitcher. Batter up!"

Skippy and Susie now walk over to the side of the classroom demonstrating that they have left the game to have a private disagreement.

TEACHER: Ask your class, "Should we wreck our FUN in this game because they're having a disagreement?" *(This will achieve the positive peer culture buy-in you desire when the class says, "No!")*

Have Skippy and Susie continue the disagreement. The "Out/safe" debate is repeated a few more times.

TEACHER: "Skippy and Susie, I'm going to ask the class a question. Their answer may look like bad news for you. However, it's an important question and I need to ask it."

TEACHER: "Class, raise your hands if you think Skippy and Susie are in trouble because they are over there disagreeing?"

CLASS: *(The majority of hands will be up. There may be some students who correctly think they are not in trouble and that's great).*

TEACHER: "This looks pretty bad for you two. Most of the class thinks you're in trouble But, I don't think that at all."

TEACHER: Addressing Susie, "Did Skippy say any bad words to you during the disagreement?"

SUSIE: "No."

TEACHER: Addressing Skippy, "Did Susie any bad words."

SKIPPY: "No."

TEACHER: "Did Skippy punch or hit you?

SUSIE: "No."

TEACHER: "Did Susie try to fight or hurt you?"

SKIPPY: "No."

TEACHER: "Since you both had to leave the game and everyone else got to play, are you wrecking our game?"

BOTH: "No."

TEACHER: "Then you're not in trouble. *(Give some time for this dramatic point to sink in.)* You have a problem, but that's very different from trouble. The problem Skippy and Susie have is that he thinks she's out and she thinks she's safe."

TEACHER: Asking the whole class, "Do you solve math problems at school? Reading problems, spelling and science problems? Sure! At school we learn to solve problems. Skippy and Susie have a game problem, but not trouble. Do you know how you can tell the difference between a problem and trouble? All you have to ask, 'Is the teacher or the principal going to call my mom or dad to tell them about this?' Do you think I would call Susie's mom tonight and explain that during an argument she said the word, 'safe'? Oh yes! Susie said 'safe' eight or nine times. There's no way I'm calling a parent to tell them that. If Susie had said, 'bad word, bad word, bad word, I'm safe,' do you think she'd get a call home then? Of course I'd call her parents. But, in this case I wouldn't call because she didn't."

"Do you think a principal would call Skippy's mom or dad to tell then he had said, 'Susie, I tagged you and you're out?' Absolutely not! If he had punched her, that's when he'd be in trouble. That's when he would get suspended. But neither of them did any fighting. They're not in trouble. But, they still have the game problem to solve."

SUSIE: "Skippy, I want to get back in the game. If we agree on something the teacher will let us right back in."

At this point postulate several alternatives for the students. Susie could agree to be out. Skippy could agree she is safe. They could both agree to do a redo. You might even ask the class for some ideas. Have Skippy and Susie chose one of the options and have available and agree.

TEACHER: "I'm really proud of you two. Good job! Get back in the game." *(It makes sense that the teacher should reinforce the proper behaviors and peaceful resolutions when students have had a successful argument.)*

At the end of the role play have everyone give the "opera" applause (lightly tapping one palm into the other) to the two wonderful students who did such great acting. In your best British voice say, "Bravo, Susie! Nicely done, Sir Skippy."

Finish the role play with a class chant.

TEACHER: "According to Rule # 2, if you have a disagreement, do you do it in the middle of the game or out of the game?"

CLASS: "Out of the game!"

Some hints, issues of flexibility and concerns you may have

Spencer and I have highlighted ten of the issues pertaining to the use of Rule # 2. They are just beginning guidelines. You will regularly find the issues and behaviors of your students will not always fit the concepts we have described. Absolutely feel free to do what you know is best in these situations. Be flexible.

1. Be clear that there is a specific area where those with disagreements must go and stay until resolution occurs. Students may not go wandering off, get a drink of water or do something else, which would probably be more FUN. They need to stay with the class, just one step outside the boundary of the game. Let your kids know that they can use the disagreement rule during class. Have a specific spot where they should go; our preference, either inside or outside, is that they go to a place where you can still easily observe and intervene if necessary.

2. If one child doesn't want to talk, then both students still need

to wait, at least, for a little while. Silent stubbornness is often an effective tool for children who haven't mastered verbal communication and are poised against a stronger peer. The stronger peer may learn that intimidation no longer works in this class because the other student's silence keeps them both out of the game. The children experience logical consequences in action. Sometimes you'll need to demonstrate flexibility. If one child truly makes attempts to solve the problem, but the other child uses silence, manipulation or non-compliance, you may let the compliant child return to the game. At this point, you can support the other child to search for and learn more effective problem-solving techniques. This is that brief one-to-one time that's so hard to find when teaching academics. After you have helped the student get more comfortable, bring the other student back to finalize a resolution.

3. For some students, just practicing how to stand close or even ten feet from someone they disagree with, is an important skill. It's the best this child can do. Accept that this is where their learning will start. This is the kind of discretion we want you to use when implementing Rule # 2. As we mentioned, the Healthy Play curriculum does not advocate any one specific peer-mediation methodology. From our experiences, we feel many kids aren't always ready for a cookbook or step program approach to happy endings. We're content if they don't fight or say bad words. At least no one has gotten into trouble. On the long term, it's great if you can teach some of the basics

A   Look the person in the eyes.
B.   Speak in a calm voice.
C.   State your feeling about the issue by saying, "I feel... when you..."

However, in reality, many adults haven't mastered these conflict resolution skills. This is elementary school and learning is a bit by bit process. Maybe next month the child will talk a little. Maybe two years from now, with daily practice, he will make some effective assertive statements. Kids aren't psychiatrists, they're just kids. Let them reach their own conclusions. Then, when it's really necessary to advance someone's learning, you can step in. (See next hint.)

4. Remember earlier we said you would have to go along with the decision of the two people arguing even if you saw things differently. That's still true. But, there is also room for flexibility. Obviously, you are going to have students who must always get their way. First start the disagreement process on the peer to peer level regardless of the outcome. Once you have spotted a dominating, manipulative and reoccurring pattern, then you can use the same rule the kids are using to begin teaching some useful lessons to the dominator. Immediately, after the two kids are finished, approach the dominator and inform her that you want to argue with her. While you are "arguing," you can address the real issues of social relatedness and making friends with the child who is ineffectively dominating her peers. You can help the child learn effective behaviors that will result in successful friendships. Winning every argument is seldom a great quality to have in making friends. That's the real point you want to share with this student. It is not who is tagged or not tagged. Additionally, be sure to let the child with the dominating behaviors know that you will always be ready to help re-remind her by using Rule # 2 if you see her winning every disagreement unfairly with her peers.

5. Let a student stay out of the game in the designated watching area if they don't want to play or if they are too angry or upset to use the conflict resolution process. For even more special students we have seen teachers let them go twenty or thirty yards away and that seemed very correct. Personal readiness often means removing oneself from a situation one is

not ready for. The goal of these educational activities is not forced participation because everyone must be participating to be happy. You are not a bad teacher if kids are watching on the sidelines; you are just giving the students the time they need to compose their feelings safely. When they have settled down and are ready to resume having FUN, they will let you know. Be sure to reinforce what was good about their behavior. It may take looking at the overall progress this child needs to make. You might say, "Good job for walking away and keeping this as a problem we can still try to solve." "I liked how we talked this over quietly." "I'm proud of how you...."

6. With kindergarten children we usually wait to explain Rule # 2 until far later in the school year. For the most part, they really need to see some teacher modeling on how to solve their problems. Some kindergarten classes never advance to using the disagreement rule, while in other years, you may have the class from heaven and they are ready to try this by October. Just do what the students are ready to learn. There are no standardized tests requiring the learning be done by a certain grade with our concepts.

7. In the primary grades you may want to make the conflict in the role play argument involve a game of tag. "I got you." "No you missed." and, so on. Make it a situation your kids will relate to. Use you own style on how to cover the key concepts.

8. Kids are quick to find and exploit any and all possible flaws in our basic guidelines. Some will fake arguments just so they can go over to the side and talk. Others will want to keep the discussion going forever and still others will just make token agreements so they can hurry back into the game. Feel free to develop additional approaches or even consequences. Set a time limit of no more than two minutes. Make them write out their thoughts if they don't want to talk or can't agree. Have a

student go to someone else's class during the time you play. In more extreme cases, assign the problem as a homework assignment to be signed by a parent. Let the parents get involved.

9. One of the solutions being promoted by some other programs to help children solve disagreements is the use of, "Rock, Paper, Scissors." We actually tried using it for a short period of time. On some levels this system looks like it has some useful applications. No bad words, no fighting, it's quick, but we came to the realization that it wasn't teaching anything of greater value to the students. The resolution was completely arbitrary. It often completely minimized one person's legitimate feelings and the opportunity to share them. It turned problem solving into a game of chance. We feel the use of coin flips, odd or even numbers and rock, paper scissors is just using a gimmick. We believe the students can learn more responsible and respectful resolutions.

10. As much as possible, let your students address the issues that arise from the game. While playing, you may readily see dozens of infractions during the game, such as people going out of bounds, not staying frozen, not sharing, etc. Do not constantly stop the game or create an argument with every child. Sooner or later, usually sooner, one of your kids will identify the same issue, and then they get to practice dealing with it. You can always highlight an observation between the start of a new game. "Remember everyone, you can use Rule # 2 if you see someone going out of bounds." Then you get back to the more useful role of validating when they did a good job.

One of the higher critical thinking skills that develops over time is the ability to decide when it's best to ignore something. As adults, we are often saying, "Just ignore Skippy when he's doing...such and such," We, as adults, came to this useful insight after experiencing hundreds and hundreds of picky, petty, little squabbles and determining that most are certainly not worth wasting any time over. Now your students can start to figure this out for themselves. Do I want to leave the game over this issue or not?

You may be thinking, "This sounds too easy. It's never going to work with my students." For some it won't. Research projects conducted on the Healthy Play curriculum show it works an average of 70% of the time. That 70% can offer you quite a relief and we feel that this is also a very impressive percentage. We know that you will think so as well. However, you might still need to utilize other tools, trying your best, to help certain kids approximately 30% of the time. So, don't forget to utilize these other tools and school procedures that are also available to you. We caution you not to reject this HP concept because of unrealistic exceptions that it will solve 100% of your problems 100% of the time. Nothing works 100% of the time. Just as the students learn in their reading, science and math classes, they will become more effectively socialized each month that they practice this concept.

Summary

Having disagreements is absolutely normal. Practicing how to effectively resolve these problems where they occur most often, during games on the playground, just makes sense. Healthy Play provides structured curriculum opportunities which will help students learn how to deal with these conflicts.

The role of the teacher is to instruct the students to briefly remove themselves from the activity and use Rule # 2. It's the student's responsibility to come to a mutual understanding about their disagreement. The basic guideline is that there will be no bad words and/or fighting. The focus is about keeping issues at a problem level which are solvable by the students and not escalating them into trouble where parents, teachers or administrators have to intervene. Upon successful completion of the disagreement utilizing Rule # 2, the teacher validates the outcome and praises the students for solving their problem the right way.

As with all of our concepts, be flexible. Always intervene or be ready to take an active role in helping students who need more support. Because the game continues for the other students, you can take advantage of this opportunity to help your challenging children learn how to communicate more effectively. Eventually, the students will use this concept by themselves and solve most of their playground and classroom disagreements without needing to involve the teacher.

Suggested Assignment

Plan and lead a role play and discussion about the Disagreement Rule # 2. Approximate time is ten minutes.

Lesson Five
TIME TO PLAY

Introduction

Hooray! You finally get to go play while getting paid for doing it. In this section we want to help prepare you to lead your first activities with your students. Although the Healthy Play philosophy and the two rules are all you need to play any game, we have created and collected a number of games which really focus on the curriculum values you want the students to learn. Feel free to use all the games we suggest or choose just one to complete the assignment.

Additionally, there is one last essential element in our curriculum called, "Compliments" which we'll need to explore. It will be the process which cements the positive learning which occurs during the game. We will also cover some helpful hints which Spencer and I have picked-up over the years that make game leading easier. Plan to have some FUN!

Leading Games at School

The role for the teacher is to be actively involved with your students while they play the game. Get right into the middle of the action; teaching is not a spectator sport. The active role in the middle of the game conveys a message to children that play curriculum is important. You wouldn't lead a math or science lesson by standing just outside the door of your room. For some of your children, seeing you participate means they can try the game and you will be near them when they join in. Wherever the teacher is standing is usually a safe place to be.

Don't panic! Being in the middle of the action only indicates where you need to be physically located. It's the best place for observing what the students are doing. We didn't say you had to run, tag, pitch, bat, crawl, skip or do summersaults. If you don't want to play in the activity, that's perfectly okay.

Active involvement means you are in position to regularly give positive feedback to students. Let them know you like it when you see them play fair and stay frozen after they were tagged. Acknowledge when you see a tag that is gentle. From the middle of the game, you can remind a student if they were the closest to someone who might be injured. Point out to them that they need to see if someone is alright. At first, your students will likely need regular coaching to do Rule # 1. As time goes on, they will understand what they are responsible for. Additionally, from the center of the game, you are close enough to see if you are needed or not.

When you look like you're participating, it is easier to delegate the disagreement rule. As students approach to tell you about a game problem with another student you'll be able to say, "I'm having FUN in the game. You need to use Rule # 2 and go over to the boundary." Initially, the students might need you to say, "Skippy!

Susie Cue has a disagreement with you. Go with her to the side and solve the problem." Over time, students will recognize that's what they have to do. However, at first, they'll need your close support and direction.

When you stand outside the game you are subtly encouraging some children to come over and watch with you. You'll attract children that are shy, withdrawn, overweight, not very physically skilled, scared or the ones that just like having the teacher's attention. These are the very students who will benefit the most from having successful social play interactions with their peers. It's a mixed message to tell those children they need to go run around and be physical while you act like a spectator.

Join the game if you can. Do as much as you feel comfortable doing. Even slow running or just walking is fine with your students. At 56, I don't run or jump hardly at all in the games. There are a lot of times I get frozen and no one has even touched me. In some games, I'm hoping I won't get saved because I'm just fine being frozen. Yet, the students always remark how much they liked that I played with them. The comments are just like when I was 30 when I did a lot more running around.

Being in the game models many important messages. It's why schools ask teachers to model personal reading during free reading periods with the kids. Valuable modeling during any activity mostly shows that, regardless of your ability, if you're just having FUN, that's all you have to do. By being in the game you have more effective teaching options to help your students. When you see a student standing at the side you can go over and explore what the issue is. Again, a game can offer you brief one-to-one time with students that you don't normally get when teaching academics. However, when you reach the point where the student now needs to take a healthy risk by joining in, you have a reason to leave and a place to go. Usually the students will follow your lead. If not the first time, maybe they will by the second or third.

On the other hand, many teachers are in peak condition. You will want to run and do all the different aspects of the game with your students. The games are exciting and they will bring forth joyful emotions you remember from when you were a kid. Join in actively, but remember your participation is not to prove you're the best athlete. The teacher's goal is to facilitate learning. It is not being able to go home to family and friends and relate how much stronger and faster you are than first or sixth graders. If you are knocking kids over or twisting an ankle, and we've seen teachers accidentally do this, you need to reevaluate what you are doing. Slow down and return to giving feedback to your students on how you see them playing the activity.

You can pick any time of the day to do HP. In some elementary schools the teacher is responsible for doing some or all of the student's physical education. This fits perfectly. Some teachers (you "Golds" know who you are) like to set a specific time. That's fine. It is often best to try to identify a time in the day when you know the kids need to get moving around. A good time may be after a prolonged mandatory subject when you realize the students are long past their attention span. It could be to wake them up first thing or wait until the afternoon lull when fidgety behaviors occur. Any time is fine. Actually, Spencer and I are less formal about when to play. We encourage you to observe your students. Be flexible. A short break when the students need one can oxygenate their body, boost their natural body chemistry and make them better learners. Some days you might want go out a second spontaneous time just because it makes sense.

The single factor we do not encourage you to use is making play a reward. "If you are good, we'll go out later." Healthy Play is a curriculum where you plan to help students learn. There is very little transferable classroom management or education involved when you use play as just a reward. Doesn't it seem that some days the children are extra wound up? Why make everyone suffer for hours trying to be good when you can chose to quickly burn off that energy by doing something physical and educational. You'll find the time lost while playing will be recovered when the students regain control of their naturally age appropriate high energy levels.

Stopping a game

As the game leader, your single most effective learning tool is that you can STOP the game. If multiple students are not having FUN or if something is not safe, bring the whole game to an immediate halt, and let everyone grumble about having the game stopped. By taking away something the students want to continue doing, you have created a positive situation to motivate them to do better. Initially, it may feel like you've made things worse because some students are unhappy, but you haven't! This problem is likely to occur sometime, somewhere, every day you play. But, today you are going to take time and practice fixing it. Sure you're losing game time today, but your students didn't even have game time to lose before you started doing HP. Gather your students together and calmly reflect to them the problem you see happening. Then turn this problem over to them to resolve. Listen to their ideas and give positive praise where appropriate. In the end, have the students vote or commit to the class solution. Return to playing to see if things are better. Most of the time, you will find that your students will arrive at a successful resolution.

Game Set-up

The best place to start is to decide whether you want to play outside or inside. Offer the students a chance to vote on the location they prefer. (**Hint:** the students will always vote to go outside. In Phoenix, when it was 115 degrees; Parker, where the wind was blowing at 35 mph; Chicago, where it was 20 degrees with snow, they always voted to go outside.) We think it's important for adults to recognize how confined students often feel in their classrooms. Children have regularly answered the poster question of why they play with the response, "So we can get out of our chairs." Most of the activities we will share with you happen outside for this very reason. So, now that you have selected to go outside you need to pick a place. Most games are best played on grass. It's softer and safer. However, some schools have no grass or it may be too wet. In those cases, use a basketball court or other paved area.

In most of the games, we will give you an idea how of how big a space you will need. A general rule is that the younger the children, the more space they need. Younger students have not developed the coordination and/or the awareness of all the things happening around them. A game that fifth graders could play on half a basketball court may require two full basketball courts worth of space for K-2 students. By giving them more space you reduce the potential for any collisions.

Many of our games will use the basketball court. The courts are great because of all the boundary lines painted on the ground. This makes game set-up easy and the variety of lines are useful in many ways for different games. However, playing on pavement causes more abrasions when children fall. Be observant for behaviors that may require more limit setting while on pavement than on a grassy playing field.

The Healthy Play curriculum does not require expensive equipment. There are a few pieces of equipment that we use, but most of the time, you already have similar equipment at school or can find alternative objects for little or no additional cost. At some point you might want to get the following:

1. A laundry bag (cheap substitute is a pillow case) to put your equipment in.

2. Six bandannas (cut up a towel in six pieces if you don't want to buy bandannas).

3. Three TuffSkin™ or soft Palos Sports RuffSkin™ balls. These balls are very kid friendly because they're softer and cause fewer injuries. They can be purchased through Palos Sports, 1-800-233-5484. Softer balls are becoming increasingly rare at the usual department, toy or sports store.

4. 12 low cones (they are only a few inches high and do not have a point. You can spend about $10.00 for a dozen and buy them at the local sports store or Target, K-Mart etc.).

5. One small pointy cone (or substitute an empty plastic soft drink or dish detergent bottle).

6. One small plastic bottle the size of a salt shaker.

7. Sometimes paper and pencils.

8. For your own comfort, you might want to keep some tennis shoes at school to change into for game time. (This will also model that kids should be wearing such footwear instead of the latest fashion).

Although we find the few aforementioned items really useful, we will always offer you activities to choose from that use no equipment.

Before you actually get to play a game, we have one last important detail to share with you. Paradoxically, it's how to end a game. The most effective means we have discovered for ending the game is to get your students to chant a 5, 4, 3, 2, 1 countdown. This makes them actively involved in your classroom management. When the countdown is completed all students must remain frozen like statues and be totally quiet. Frozen in place means students are standing on two legs in a comfortable position. You will probably have to clarify this position or you will have numerous students in out of balance stances which sooner or later fall. Simply tell students when they hear you call out FIVE, that they need to verbally join in the countdown (loud but no screaming). Practice the countdown one or two times before you play your first game. Additionally, when the kids are so joyously playing, they lose track of what is going on around them. Sometimes you will have to do the count down twice. The first time got 50% of the class to join in, the repeat will make contact with the others. If the countdown does not successfully stop everyone, feel confident that you can practice the countdown over and over thus wasting game time.

Discussion Gift: Charlie and I had conducted many HP trainings at multiple schools in the McKinleyville/Eureka, CA area. The wonderful thing about doing so many schools there was there were full communities of teachers and students who knew all about HP and our techniques. One creative McKinleyville school teacher shared the following story with us regarding her creative usage of the 5, 4, 3, 2, 1 countdown. She was at the local burger shop trying to have a pleasant dinner. However, there were numerous screaming children there who were making her dining experience anything but pleasurable. She recognized that a few of the children were from her school and figured she had nothing to lose so she yelled out, "5!" Well, immediately all the kiddos yelled back, "4, 3, 2, 1!" Suddenly, the burger shop was pin-drop quiet and filled with tiny well behaved frozen statues. She said the parents were looking around at their immobile and now totally quiet children like they had entered a parent friendly episode of the Twilight Zone. She explained that this technique was part of her school's character education curriculum called Healthy Play. Parents verbalized that they liked the effect they saw and would start to use the countdown at home as well.

Three Games

Here are the first three games we suggest you choose from to start your Healthy Play experiences. These activities will quickly convey to students the concepts of why we are playing at school. Each game can be played as many times as your students want to play them. The games do not take long which allows teachers the freedom to decide how long to play.

"Like, totally it" tag

LIKE, TOTALLY IT TAG
(All grades, any number of players, large playing area, no equipment)

How It's Played
This is the ultimate freeze tag game and a perfect place to start focusing on playing fair. Set up a playing area (in the grass is best) and make sure everyone knows the boundaries (a single basketball court size for older kids and bigger space for younger). Form your students into a circle so everyone can hear you explain the game. If students have difficulty forming a circle because they are pulling on someone's arm, or squeezing a hand, you have your first opportunity to send two people to the side to use Rule # 2. Remember, as soon as they problem solve the issue they are immediately back in the game.

In this game, all the players are simultaneously "It." The rules are simple. Whoever tags another person first, freezes them. In younger grades you might want to model tagging with a student helper. After you tag your student helper make sure your class realizes that the person you tagged became frozen (and not you) because you tagged them first. Then continue modeling by pretending to be trying to tag someone while having a student come up from behind you, tagging you before you could tag someone else. Once again, make sure the students know that, this time, you would have ended up frozen. Be ready for the students to ask the question of, "What happens if we both tag at the same time?" Don't tell them the obvious answer. Let them make the suggestion. "They are both frozen." At this point, call for a vote, "How many agree that if you tag at the same time both people will be frozen. Looks like a majority. Then that is our rule."

(The constant involvement of the positive peer majority bonds them to the concept that everyone, not just the teacher, is responsible for the rules.)

Ask the question, "In our class are we going to tag hard or soft?" After the desired answer is given, have your students model a soft tag to the person next to them. (This demonstration may create another opportunity for using Rule # 2 if someone tags too aggressively. "Susie Cue, please take Skippy to the side and show him how to tag nicely.")

Once players are frozen they stay that way until the game ends. Many tag games have a way to get unfrozen, but this doesn't happen in Totally It Tag. Play continues until only a few players are left unfrozen (about six). At that point, have everybody who is frozen yell out a 5, 4, 3, 2, 1 countdown to indicate the game is coming to an end. To have like a "toad-a-lay awe-sum" time, this game should be humorously explained in your best Valley girl or boy accent.

After explaining the rules, state that you are going to pick a student who was listening (a value from the poster) to help you start the game. Ask this person, "What is you favorite food?" "Pizza!" Announce that the game will start when you say the secret word, "Pizza."

(At this point you may have some carry over from Rule # 1 when everyone was asked to promise to care for each other. Without fanfare, quietly ask those students who did not promise to go to the side to watch the first round of the game. After every round of the game give these students a chance to agree to follow Rule # 1 and get them into the game.)

Since everyone is it, before starting, allow the students a few seconds to spread out and get away from each other. (This will probably give you another chance to re-clarify the boundaries since some students will go past them.) "Everybody ready, OK, spaghetti!" By saying the wrong food you will find out quickly who was listening and comprehending. Stop the players who have started playing and have them affirm what the correct word is needed to start the game. Try a second false start. By the third time you will have perfect listening so truly start the game. This is a fast game and a good one to explore what effect different size boundaries have on a game. Play it many times before moving on to something else. Pick a new student each time and give them a different question like; favorite animal, color, book, subject at school etc. to find a word to start the next round of Totally It Tag. Eventually, have the student who has been picked, be the person who starts the game. Turn as many aspects of the game as you can over to the children.

THE GIFT OF THE GAME

Ah, traditional freeze tag had its moments, but they often were too short and enjoyed by too few. Remember being "It" with that impossible task of freezing all the players? You could try to tag your friends from now till next December and still never accomplish your task. And, remember standing around feeling wistful and uninvolved as the person who was "It" went after one solitary runner on the other side of the playground. Boring! You could only get into the action when, and if, you were noticed by the person who was "It." LIKE, TOTALLY IT TAG changes all that. Players shine even before the game begins as everybody is encouraged to call off the name of the game in their best Valley girl or boy accents (high-lighting all children's attributes of humor and acting).

This is the game we usually start with when playing with a new group of students. This game sets the tone for all the liberating game experiences that can and will occur. This is the ideal game to equalize all the players right from the get go. Everybody gets a chance to play. No waiting. No need to take a number. Immediately, participants experience and will easily buy into HP philosophy and rules with this activity. LIKE, TOTALLY IT TAG becomes one of your strongest "marketing" tools when initiating the Healthy Play curriculum with your class. All the socialization dynamics that hook a person into wanting to play in a healthy manner are introduced at once: acceptance, equality, total participation, fairness, excitement, safety, compassion, humor and fun. Like, oh, my Gawd! LIKE, TOTALLY IT TAG is so the one to start with! Totally! Fur shur!

TROLL TREASURE

(First grade and up, eight or more players, 30-x-30 foot outdoor or indoor space, a piece of "treasure" like an empty plastic bottle with 2 inches of dirt in the bottom to give it some weight or a field-marker cone 8 to 12 inches tall)

How It's Played

Telling a story will set the tone for this game of fantasy, strategy and sneakiness. There once was a huge Troll; a gnarly, grumpy type who liked to find treasures and keep them hidden away. The most valuable of all the treasures was the "Beautiful pearl-white dish-soap bottle," which the Troll stole from the school library. (When explaining the game have the children say, "Ooohhh!" every time you say, "Beautiful, pearl-white, dish-soap bottle.") Now, the "Beautiful pearl white dish-soap bottle" ("Ooohhh!") was kept in the middle of the Troll's den. (Place the bottle on some significant spot in the middle of your playing area. Half of a basketball court works really well since there are nice boundary lines on all four sides. You could also make the den out on the grass using cones to delineate boundaries.) The citizens from the school found the Troll's den and sent their bravest people to retrieve the "Beautiful pearl-white dish-soap bottle" ("Ooohhh!") from the Troll and return it to the library.

Now it's very important to know some facts about Trolls. First of all, if they touch you, you turn into stone and then you can't move anymore for the rest of the round (for safety reasons all stone statues must be standing up). A second fact is that Trolls can run around inside the boundary lines of their den, but they can't go past those boundary lines. Thirdly, they can't touch the treasure with their feet or hands and they must stay standing up unless they are tagging someone.

While telling the rules and background story for this game, students should be lined up on one side of the basketball court. Randomly pick one student to be the first Troll, and have the Troll stand guard over the treasure (Here's a great method for random picking. Ask one student to give you a number between 5 and 15. Now go to a different student in the line and ask them to give you a direction "right" or "left." Use the second person as your starting point and going the direction they chose, count the number the first person gave. Where you end up counting will be the person who becomes the Troll.) Return to the beginning of the line; count off five people to be the first challengers to attempt to retrieve the treasure from the Troll. Have them go half way down the sideline to their starting position.

The game begins by having the Troll give a ferocious warning roar to the first five treasure hunters. Upon hearing the roar, only those five enter inside the boundary area and move around the Troll from all angles, each trying to snatch the "Beautiful pearl-white soap-dish bottle" ("Ooohhh!") from the middle of the playing area. Every time the Troll touches one of the players they become immobilized (turned to stone, staying right where they were tagged) and a new player is sent in from the line. If someone takes the treasure but is tagged before they get past the boundary line, they also are turned to stone on that spot. The Troll returns the treasure to the middle of the playing area. For safety reasons the treasure hunters cannot kick or pass the treasure to anyone else. Only the troll can pick up a cone that has been knocked over and replace it to the correct position. Eventually, one of the good citizens grabs the treasure and races outside the boundary line on any side. This person becomes the next Troll. Any player who was on the court becomes unfrozen, will go to the end of the line and a new round of the game begins. Like our other games, which foster sharing, you can only be the Troll once. If you do swipe the treasure again, you get to choose someone who has done something nice that day to take your place.

THE GIFT OF THE GAME

This is a wonderful game to help children practice playing fair. They must acknowledge if they were frozen and learn to settle minor disagreements instantly or leave the game to use Rule # 2. When leading this activity prepare yourself for various scenarios to happen. Sometimes, in an attempt to get the Troll's Treasure a student might fall to the ground. At first, other students will be so excited to get the Troll's Treasure they might forget to ask, "Are you okay?" to the injured child and instead go after the treasure. When this happens, stop the game immediately so that the closest person can check out if anyone got hurt. Even if they look fine, have them go through the motions of asking. Keep the kids focused that the PEOPLE are most important part of the game.

The other likely occurrence is when someone falls and the troll does the right thing and checks the person out. However, while the Troll mindfully complied with Rule # 1, someone else took advantage and stole the treasure. Here again you have a perfect opportunity to stop the game. The class can discuss what seems fair when someone was caring for another person. Publicly, the class determines fairness and creates positive peer pressure in a non punitive manner for all individuals. With practice they will develop strategies of sacrificing themselves to get caught at critical positions. This will block the Troll from tagging someone else, thus assisting the successful retrieval of the treasure. The structure of the game also teaches children patience as they wait their turns in line. Even the beginning of the game, when the Troll roars, gives children the chance to practice being silly and taking healthy risks. They enjoy returning stolen treasures to their rightful owners.

Universally, this game is a playground and neighborhood favorite. Children and teens will play this one for a long time. We know monitors at many schools who start their recess with Troll Treasure for their First graders and continue the same game, in the same location, as each grade comes and leaves recess time. We have also seen multiple games going on simultaneously. Ooohhh!

BROKEN WHEEL

(Kindergarten and up, 8-36 players, large open area playing space about 2/3 of a basketball court, no equipment)

How It's Played

Here's a game where you get to invent the wheel and then fix it every time it gets broken. Players sit on the ground in one of four rows, one behind another. The number of students in a row will depend on the size of the group (rows can have different numbers of students). The sitting groups are arranged, so they resemble the spokes of a wheel. All of the players in the spokes will be facing the center of the wheel. You get to stand in the center of the wheel to direct the action. Now you're ready to start the game.

Select one person to be the leader. This person starts by walking around the outside of the wheel. (For kindergarten children make sure everyone sees what direction the person is walking. Bring in academics and call it clockwise. Ask the kids, "In what shape are they walking?" "Yes, that is right. It is a circle!") Eventually, the leader taps the shoulder of the last person, in line, of one of the spokes and says, "BROKEN WHEEL!" The person who was

Broken wheel

tapped and all the players in the chosen spoke now race along with the leader around the outside of the wheel. Only one spoke of the wheel races around per turn. Players are allowed to pass other runners including the leader. No cutting is allowed through the spokes. The race ends when players reach their original spoke's location and sit back down behind each other, facing towards center, to reassemble the spoke. (Again, in kindergarten, have the children do a walking demonstration to show the proper direction. Include in this demonstration that you cannot go through the wheel but must go around the outside.) The last player to make it back becomes the next leader and will walk around and "break" another part of the wheel. (Students who are use to playing Duck, Duck, Goose will need to be reminded that you are racing to get back. They are NOT trying to tag the person who started the game.)

Once everyone has the basic race down pat, the time for innovation begins. The wheel breaker can call "BROKEN WHEEL, hop on one leg," or "Skip," "Go the opposite way," "Slide steps," or

"Sing 'Row Row Your Boat,'" "Count by 5's" and so on. For those teachers in charge of PE, this game will allow you to check and see which students can do these various gross motor skills. Monitor the activity well, so the people in the race don't collide or run through the middle of the wheel. As always, refocus your students if someone falls down to immediately use Rule # 1.

We guarantee BROKEN WHEEL will give you several chances to model the use of Rule # 2. Quickly your students will figure out that if they are last, they get to be the next leader. Therefore, as the race nears completion you will actually see kids slowing down and even go backwards so they can be last and become the leader. Of course, they want to be the center of attention. They're kids. You can use the disagreement rule to remove the purposely slow student to talk about playing fair. If this happens, pick another student to carry on with the game so you can utilize Rule # 2 with the child who was manipulating and help them learn about fair play. Additionally, like most of our games, you can only be the leader once. If a student legitimately was the last one back to a spoke for a second round, they would have to pick someone else to take their place as leader. This is particularly important. Kids in wheel chairs or who are obese and very slow will not end up winning the race. We want them to try their best but we won't punish them over and over by making them the leader.

Don't hesitate to veto any unsafe running suggestions. Sometimes children will want to run or walk backwards. Our experience has shown that running backwards and even walking backwards results in children getting frequently injured. You don't want to set up an activity that will guarantee children toppling down, especially on a hard surface. You are the benevolent dictator of your classroom; become comfortable vetoing any idea that you suspect or know is unsafe.

THE GIFT OF THE GAME

BROKEN WHEEL has given us one of the funniest experiences we have ever had. Usually we teach this game to younger classes because it is the next creative step beyond Duck-Duck-Goose. However, one day we were dealing with a particularly aggressive fifth-grade class that was dominated by boys wanting to play Dodge Ball. Dodge Ball, for this group of students, was not going to be FUN for everyone, so we selected different games to allow everyone a safe time.

What a treat! The game had quickly progressed from the simple phase of racing around and sitting down to creatively allowing the leader to call out whatever running option he wanted. The five dominating "cool" guys were all in one spoke of the wheel when this girl, thoughtfully and with premeditation, tapped the last boy on the shoulder and said "Broken Wheel, CARTWHEELS." With the precision of a gymnast, she preformed a dozen rapid cartwheels around the outside of the wheel and sat down. The five boys floundered like fish out of water as they somersaulted, rolled and basically tumbled their way around the circle. It was hysterical, but it was clear to all that no one had made fun of them. During the compliments processing after the game, the girl received many kudos for a skill others now respected. The gift of play should allow everyone to shine.

COMPLIMENTS

A LITTLE PROCESSING GOES A LONG WAY. This is the last essential component of the Healthy Play curriculum. This activity nurtures and strengthens the values which the children first identified on their posters ("Why do we play?" and "What is the most important part of all games?") and later used in their playing. This is the culmination of why you used school time to play. Additionally, the processing time allows the students to physically and emotionally compose themselves and settle down before returning to the classroom.

Right after any activity session (whether the kids play one game or many) you must facilitate a short processing or dialog session. Find a quiet area as far away from distraction as possible and sit closely together on the ground. These sessions should last two minutes or longer if necessary or desired by the students, teacher or counselor.

During the processing time, ask the children to identify only the positive experiences they felt or observed while playing. When students make complaints like, "I saw Skippy cheat" or "You tagged me too hard," redirect them that they should have dealt with those complaints during the games. Remind them, as often as needed, that the processing session is a time to discuss positive behaviors only. Left to their own devices, kids can become the kings and queens of put-downs because that's what they've been taught. Lots of times they think these comments are funny, but they're not. It misdirects the children to find fault with themselves and others. They need your guidance to find the jewels within themselves and their peers. Processing provides the learning opportunity to say kind things. It allows the teacher to transform play into an effective tool for class management and school curriculum.

Praising only positive behaviors helps make those actions, ideas and values a reality in the children's lives. They experience that inner glow of personal joy and recognition. This is what helps children find their place within their own moral selves and positive peer culture. This positive peer culture tells kids how they must act if they want to be part of the fun and caring group. Active praise produces the best way for long term internal change to happen for children in the real world.

Teachers have often told us that these after-games processing sessions become the "favorite time" or "highlight of the school day" for both students and themselves. The processing also carries over easily to other academics. This means greater group cooperation and team work because of the success of the individual child. Praising positive behaviors while reducing the emphasis on negative behaviors make those positive behaviors the norm. It's a win-win situation for both the child and the class. These are the childhood experiences that help us succeed in our relationships, families and jobs as adults.

Nominations for Compliments

Our favorite form of processing uses the concept of nominations. Ask your kids if they know what a "nomination" is. Define the concept to make sure everyone understands. Simply stated, a nomination is when you pick someone and publicly announce their name and why you are choosing them. Explain to your students that from now on every time we play, we are going to watch each other and see who are playing well. We are going to watch and remember which of our classmates are playing fair, safe, or who's taking care of the people, using teamwork, sharing, listening and arguing the right way. We'll do this so at the end of our games we can nominate these people for a compliment.

As the teacher you can model one or two nominations, but do not dominate this process. This is where the students need to learn how to say good things to each other. As the teacher, you might look for students who do real well but seldom get the recognition they deserve. We recommend your first nominations center on the two rules. "I want to nominate Susie Cue and Skippy for settling their disagreement about holding hands. You solved your problem the right way! I also want to nominate Juan, because when Xavier fell down, he stopped playing and immediately took care of him. That was an excellent job doing Rule # 1." Now open the process to the class. Make sure lots of different people get chosen for compliments and not just the most popular kids. Help students get past the superficial compliments like, "I like Jenny's shoes." When students get stuck on one particular value ask that the next nominations be on different concepts. Nominations for scoring well are okay, but always expand the process to encompass the greater social values of the game. It is truly amazing to watch the growth children can make in just a few weeks practice of saying nice things to each other.

We recommend that immediately following each nomination you and the class reward the child chosen with a special applause or cheer. We make up all types of creative applause and encourage the children to also do so. Creative applause such as "twirling pinky, spider doing a pushup on a mirror, disco, train, sky rocket, sprinkler, butterfly, Addams Family, opera, and the seal of approval" cheers are just the beginning. Use your imagination to create additional applause to further reinforce the positive behaviors growing in the group.

For children in K through second grade, it's probably best if you just call the process "giving compliments." Make sure these youngsters know what a compliment is before going out to play. Sadly, we have discovered that many five, six, seven or eight year olds have gotten this far in life without knowing what a compliment is. No wonder it's easier for them to put themselves and other people down, rather than to praise each other.

Time to Play Summary

This section has been all about going out for the first time to use the Healthy Play curriculum with your students. You will always want to be aware that you have the power to make play valuable curriculum time. Before playing any games have your students chant the answers to "Why do we play? What is the most important part of the game? If someone is hurt do you stay with them or run away? Do you do your disagreement in the game or out of it?" before leaving the classroom. Practice the 5, 4, 3, 2, 1 countdown before playing any games as well. Stay actively involved in the middle of the game by intervening and directing students to utilize Rules # 1 and 2. Praise your children often for all the things that they do well. If your students have questions about rules don't always give them the obvious answers. Allow them to come up with creative ideas and vote on choices. Veto any unsafe ideas. Saving a short processing time will be one of your most useful tools to cement positive behaviors learned and practiced by the students during the games

Don't worry if you forget some of the rules. It's just a game. Spencer and I forget rules regularly. It becomes obvious soon enough when you start playing that you forgot something. You just stop the game and tell the kids what you forgot. Don't get too concerned that you personally have to enforce all the rules you observe being broken. Sometimes adults can be such perfectionists. If the students aren't upset about these game rule infractions, except caring for the people, then why should you? Pick critical times to intervene where your modeling will help empower the most children. Mostly, be patient and wait for the students to see the same problems. However, if the players aren't having fun and/or the game becomes unsafe and no student is properly intervening, then it is up to you to stop the game. As we have mentioned before, stopping an unsafe activity is both highly appropriate and motivating.

In kindergarten and first grade, all the children agree that they know what the boundaries are for the game. When the game starts, however, only gravity seems to keep kids on the planet. They go everywhere. Don't worry, these things are normal. Look on the bright side; the further they run, the more exercise they get and the more energy they expend. The further apart they are, a lot fewer kinder collision accidents can happen. If they look like they are having FUN then what more do you want? At the end of each round of the game patiently address any issue that will facilitate learning. Games can be confusing. After several versions of the game your kids will get better. Have FUN with your students. The bonding you achieve with them through play will carry over into every aspect of the school day.

Suggested Assignment:

Plan to play Like Totally It and one other game from this lesson for ten to fifteen minutes. Be sure to allow time for compliment nominations at the end of the game. Repeat doing these games as often as you like.

Lesson Six:
CREATIVE PLAY

Introduction

Implementing the philosophy and rules found in the Healthy Play Curriculum will help you successfully teach basic social skills for your class and children. But that's just the starting point for using play as an effective learning tool in school. To maximize learning of both social skills and academics, let's focus on a continuum of three basic game concepts. Understanding these play dynamics will open exciting doors to bring play into your whole day's curriculum.

We humbly acknowledge that Spencer and I have not invented the wheel. The basis for our continuum comes from particular concepts presented by the New Games Foundation nearly 30 years ago. However, we have greatly expanded, updated and reworked the original concepts to be more accessible for behavioral and academic applications.

There are three categories in our continuum of game activities. The continuum starts with something that we call "Creative or Innovative Play." That's the first basic idea. This lesson will explore how you can modify and change game activities. We want you to discover how Creative Play will allow you and your students to advance the learning potential in each and every game you play at school.

Exploring Creative Play

Creative or Innovative Play begins with the understanding that all games are made up. Yep, every game has been made up. The games weren't here in the earth's core when the planet was formed. Moses didn't climb the mountain, get the Ten Commandments and a complete rule book of all games, including the special card games supplement as a bonus for his efforts. The rules for games are not hidden in our genetic code. Every culture makes up games and games are usually made up by people wanting to have FUN.

Knowing this fact is a powerful tool; it empowers you and your class to use imagination and creativity to make learning any subject more enjoyable. There are games for math, spelling, geography, science, etc. If you can't find what you need, then just make up your own.

It is useful to understand that there are really only six types of games. The first game type is "Follow the Leader." Everybody plays this game. Just moments after you were born, you started playing one of the best Follow the Leader games ever invented. The game is called "Smile." Mom or Dad held you in their arms and they put pleasant smiles on their face. In a short time, once your eyes could focus, you learned to smile back. Then the real fun began because you quickly discovered that your grandparents, siblings, uncles, aunts, cousins and all sorts of other people knew how this game works. Advanced Smile involves noses, eyes and goo-goo noises. But, Follow the Leader doesn't stop there. By the time you're in kindergarten you play this game with others when you skip, jump, wave your arms and turn summersaults in succession. By middle school, Follow the Leader determines the shirts and shoes you buy, the songs you like and the movies that are a must to see. We keep playing Follow the Leader all our lives. For adults, it's the cars we buy, where we go on vacation, but mostly, we evolve our Follow the Leader games into the laws we want.

The second basic kind of game is "Tag." The world's most complicated form of Tag is called Baseball. Baseball is nothing more than Tag. The baseball is "it." You knock "it" somewhere and you run to base, where you are safe. Anything with a base where you are safe sounds like Tag to us. And, if you get tagged with the ball before you reach base, you're out. That's the rule somebody made up. Other rules make Baseball a more complicated form of Tag. Foul balls count as strikes. Well, they count as strikes unless it's your third strike and then they don't count as a strike unless you were trying to bunt. If this happens, then a foul ball does count as your third strike. Whew! Those are rules that PEOPLE made up to have FUN. And, when working in elementary school, we can make up the rules the way we want to have FUN. Our goal is education, self esteem and values. Different ideas can be made up which meet these needs.

The next basic game is "Keep-Away." They say that the American attention span is dwindling, but we don't believe it. Each year Americans can watch a 12-hour marathon of Keep-Away on New Year's Day. That kind of attention span is awe inspiring. In the fall, Americans watch three hours of Keep-Away every Monday night, formally calling it Football. Football is really no more than a complicated version of Keep-Away. But, that's all football is, a big game of Keep-Away. Basketball is also Keep-Away, but you dribble the ball. Hockey is Keep-Away on ice. Soccer is Keep-Away, but you kick the ball. Once you get the idea that there are only a few basic types of games, you can see where people's imaginations take over to make games better and more interesting.

The fourth kind of game is "Capture." Chess, checkers, and cards are typical Capture games. Here, a bigger or more valuable piece usually captures something smaller. The values of kings and queens associated with the chess pieces or cards were made up to reflect the medieval world the people lived in. What if cards represented foods? A glass of milk might capture a candy bar. Bread could move further than soda pop if they were based on the RDA guidelines.

"Logic Puzzles" are the next basic style of game. These activities are based on intellect. An important part of the overall Healthy Play curriculum is using a wide variety of activities. By doing this, we highlight all the different talents students possess. In your class you will have kids who are good at running and jumping. Other students will be whizzes at solving puzzles. Some children will be imaginative and creative while others may become your rule developers. At every grade level, we've seen future diplomats and doctors at play. Solving Logic Puzzles using cooperation and teamwork will let all the students stretch their minds and learn while having FUN.

The sixth kind of game is "Accumulation." Whoever gets the most of something is the winner. Monopoly must be the ultimate Accumulation game; if you get all the hotels and all the money, you've accumulated the most, and therefore you win. Most of our video games are just point-accumulation activities, but often with a lot of graphic violence. Even video games could be made better if they at least made the students do the math to add up their own scores. What we like to do in HP activities is accumulate people. When you've accumulated all the players in the game, everyone wins. The more the better, and with this format, students' feelings won't be hurt because they are never eliminated from the game.

The basic premise behind the concept of Creative Play is that all games are made up. So we can simply change the rules, titles or other features of any game to meet the needs of the individuals playing. Let's use the following scenario as an example of how we can use a rule change to meet the needs of a particular individual. Imagine you're working with this class and one child is the class scapegoat. None of the other children want to include this child in any of their games. He's got "a way high cootie-factor." The game we're playing is called SAFETY HAVEN (page 248). To keep from being tagged "it," children need to hug and hum with another child. As you might imagine, no one wants to hug the scapegoated child. Nobody wants to touch this cootie-filled kid, much less hug and hum with him. But, you happen to notice that this ostracized child is one of only three children who are wearing the color purple this day. You stop the game momentarily and announce a change in the rules. The children are instructed that, "Now in our game of SAFETY HAVEN you're only safe hugging and humming with somebody who is wearing the color purple." Instantaneously, the children rush off to seek safety with the new "safe" children to avoid being tagged "it." Without much thought, our scapegoat child quickly becomes their safe port in the storm. The child becomes included in the game by his peers. It didn't take six months of intensive psychotherapy to accomplish this. The teacher just used good judgment and creativity.

Or you might want to reinforce the number "five" for your kindergarten class. So during SAFETY HAVEN you change the rules. You are now only safe hugging in groups of five children. Now you have a kinetic and visual way of reinforcing your children understanding the number five.

Once you accept the concept that the games can be changed, new vistas appear for the use of play in your educational curriculum. These are but a few examples on how you can use the concept of creative play to meet the various needs of your group of children. There are many other ways, such as the following, to make games much more successful by using the concepts of Creative Play.

Keep Safety the # 1 Focus

The number one way to make games more successful is to keep the game safe. The one rule that I wish I had growing up back in my childhood town of Wappingers Falls is that, "hard tags just don't count." You remember those hurtful tags? Bam! Those kinds of tags often knock people down or bring tears to their eyes. Well, they no longer count! And, not only do they not count, if you tag hard and just happen to hurt or knock somebody down, you'll have to stay with them according to Rule # 1. You're out of the game until they feel better and can play again. Combining hard tags with Rule # 1 becomes a very powerful tool and we really encourage all teachers to change to safer styles of tagging.

Reward Teamwork to Foster Cooperation

You can reward teamwork with bonuses or praise. You can even alter traditional games. Let's say you are playing a traditional game of basketball, but you want to create a greater sense of cooperation and sharing with your group of students. Imagine we have our two teams. Both teams have been told, "Hey, if you guys can all share the ball where everyone gets a chance to play and make a basket, your team will get a 50 point bonus." Team One says, "We don't need your stinkin' 50 points." Team One has Jasmine, Jorge, Al, Roger and Madison. They're one really hot basketball team and Jasmine just happens to be the school's best basketball player. The kids at school say she'll be the next Michael Jordan. This is how Team One's kids play: every time one of them gets the ball, it goes automatically right to Jasmine because Jasmine is their hot-shot player and high scorer. Clearly, in their minds, if Jasmine gets the ball, she'll make all their points, and they'll score higher than Team Two. It doesn't seem to matter that no one but Jasmine really gets to play on their team. True to form, Jasmine performs well and has scored all of Team One's 36 points.

Over on Team Two, we have Cathy, Alex, Salim, DeMarcus and Erin. Team Two buys into the 50 point bonus and adopts the attitude that says, "Let's go for the 50 points. Let's try really hard and share." And so they go about playing well and share the basketball. DeMarcus is a really good basketball player. Alex, Salim and Erin are also pretty good. In fact, they have all made their baskets and need only Cathy to make hers to get that 50 point bonus. But, for Cathy to make a basket she has to stand just on the right spot of the court. The sun has to be behind her, and the wind can't be blowing too hard. In fact, Venus has to be aligned with Mars for Cathy to make a basket. Team Two still wants that bonus and will have to help Cathy by providing her a perfect set-up shot. All of the sudden, DeMarcus gets the ball and passes it to Cathy. Her team roots her on, "Go Cathy, get that 50 points." Oh, the pressure. Because she is not known for her basketball skills, this is the first time Cathy's had a basketball in her hand for the whole school year. In fact, having a basketball in her hands is so rare that she momentarily stops the game as she ponders what the word "VOIT™" might mean and why basketballs are so bumpy. Returning from her daze, she shoots, but the ball doesn't make it anywhere near the hoop. Still, she had the ball in her hands and it was real exciting. So the game continues a little longer. This time, teammate Erin gets the ball back to Cathy. Cathy gets it. Having the ball twice in her hands may actually qualify as practicing now. Wow, she's had the ball twice within a five-minute time frame. "Go Cathy, get that 50 points," shout her teammates. She throws. There it goes, bouncing off the back board. Third time, teammate Salim sets it up. And, it is the perfect setup for Cathy. Cathy throws it up towards the hoop, and the ball appears to move in slow motion. From an unidentifiable source we hear the theme music from Chariots of Fire, whoosh, the ball gloriously goes in. Suddenly, Team Two, because they decided to play cooperatively, is now winning 60 to 36. And the child who is often ridiculed for poor skills becomes the hero, the 50-point player. Creative use of scoring, team rewards and praise become other ways to foster cooperation.

You could have also reinforced sharing and cooperation by having the following rules: A basket doesn't count as a score unless everyone on the team touches the ball. This would encourage inclusion and passing the ball to others. Or, you could allow for a one-point score to anyone who gets the ball to touch the back board even if the ball doesn't go through the hoop.

Have Multiple "Its"

Another thing you can do to improve total participation and excitement is to have multiple "Its" in a game. If there's just one person chasing after another person, your game of Tag becomes quite boring for most of the participants. Kids are ego focused. They want the world to revolve around them. This is not good or bad. It is just where they are at developmentally. As Charlie and I have seen throughout this country, all kids want to be playing, all the time. Our research and our experiences as parents and brothers and sisters supports that children can't become nurturing and compassionate until their ego needs are gratified. Let's accept, respect and honor this. When you have multiple "Its," everybody stays involved. Ego needs are gratified and then children can start to focus on higher level learning like sharing and being compassionate.

In fact, having multiple "Its" makes it easier to be equal for players of differing abilities and disabilities to play the same game together. A child in a wheelchair becomes equal with chair-less children in a game of LIKE, TOTALLY IT TAG. With so many people tagging, the playing field expands into a joyfully chaotic arena where "mercy tags" for the physically challenged are eliminated. With multiple "Its," the superstar athlete is often humbled as another child with less athletic skills can tag her. No one needs play up or down to another. In most of the games we will teach you, we will use the multiple "It" concept. We recommend at least one "It" for every 5-8 people.

When using multiple "Its," you may need to come up with identifying markers so everyone will know who is "It." We like to use bandannas. We like to play down their power as "gang colors" and just turn them into simple reminders of whose "It." If "colors" are too provocative on your campus or in your neighborhood, you can easily substitute some other cloth towels cut into strips. Use anything you want: bandannas, paper towels, stuffed animals, balls, bean bags, torn up sheets, whatever works for your budget, or school culture.

Alter the Game Speed

Imagine a game of LIKE, TOTALLY IT TAG. Maybe the children are becoming so excited that some have become reckless and others end up not feeling safe. Creatively change the speed of the game. Instead of running, players are now instructed to move heel to toe. This means that children have to slow down to carefully and sequentially touch the heel of one foot to the toe of the other as they move through the playing field. We might have them jump on one foot. The game slows down, becoming safer, and still maintains excitement.

Maybe the game time is going too fast. A traditional round of LIKE, TOTALLY IT TAG usually lasts about 30-seconds. Walking heel to toe instead of running makes your 30-second game now last 2 minutes. Change the rules to make the game safer or more enjoyable.

Add More Bases

You might want to add more bases to your games. Let's alter the traditional game of Kickball. Imagine seven bases instead of four. Keep in mind, long, long ago some guys were probably drinking beer and wondered, "How many bases should we have?" They made up four, but that doesn't mean elementary school kids need to be stuck with that. When there are seven bases even less talented players can get on base. As the teacher, isn't that what you really want to have happen? Give every student a chance to run around and get healthier. In fact, in SEVEN-BASE KICKBALL the bases are not spaced evenly apart. We usually make first base very close to home. At school, we do not have to play by the same rules professional athletes do.

In HP Kickball, we eliminate all the problematic rules to make the game more fun for the people playing. Foul balls are boring and waste a lot of time. So foul balls now count even if you kick the ball behind you into the backstop instead of out towards the outfield. And, who says you have to run to the right? Maybe you could opt to go the other direction around the bases. There are few things more fulfilling than seeing a child who never gets on base score a seven-base home run because the ball just tapped their foot and they faked everyone out by running to the left instead of the right. All any adult or child wants is to feel successful when they are at play. All the students want to feel that everyone in their class is their friend and that they are not going to feel humiliated or intimidated. When you alter traditional games it is important to use the voting process as often as possible. We also encourage making only one change at a time. It can get too confusing if you make all five changes to a game at once.

In school, you will constantly take advantage of the flexibility Creative Play offers. Let's say two students had a disagreement over who was safe or out at 6th base. They used Rule # 2 and came to the peaceful conclusion to have a "Do over." This meant the player needed to return to 3rd base to start over. However, while they were arguing, the next batter ended up on third base. The question becomes, can you have two runners on the same base? Why not? Which is the greater learning experience from the kickball game, who wins the game or supporting two kids who learned how to resolve a conflict the right way? It makes sense that you could/should change the rules to support more important learning.

The most exciting aspect of Creative Play is when the kids take over the process. We had just finished working at a school where we taught some fifth-grade students SEVEN-BASE KICKBALL. The kids' eyes and minds went wide open when they discovered the freedom to make games better. By the next week when we returned to the school, we discovered they had already invented their own game of "Double Pitch Kickball." Two pitchers simultaneously pitch to two kickers, and both players kick their own ball and run opposite directions around the bases. The base runners must coordinate their base-running strategy so that they can touch hands at second base and at home in order to score. If either base runner is tagged out, then both of them are out. And because the kids made up the game, they wanted to play again and again.

This is an example of what every teacher should let their classes achieve with Creative Play. Let the students own this process by trying out their new ideas. These fifth graders had immediately begun to use HP concepts to establish how to make up rules they all would follow. This event bonded this class together with a vital sense of cooperation toward their common goal. This was a real, hands-on, action learning experience that didn't come from reading about self-esteem or peer mediation. The game was just the FUN vehicle for useful curriculum.

Change the Number of Balls in a Game

When we play soccer with the Healthy Play curriculum, we usually use three or more NERF™ or Palos Sports Special RuffSKIN™ balls. There's so much more action going on for everyone when you add more balls. With only one ball, it's usually only the gifted soccer players who get to play and run around. Occasionally, some of the other children get to play, but they're pressured to turn the ball back over to the best players who will do the scoring. In general, the majority of the students just stand around during the game. Not any longer.

With multiple balls in play, the "superstar" players tend to congregate around one ball trying to offset the other team's best players. But now there is a second ball waiting for the average players to try their best. There's even the third ball. Students who almost never get a chance to play are now actively kicking and passing a ball to other classmates. Every student now gets to develop a stronger heart, lungs, muscles and better coordination. Given a chance to actually play, all students have an opportunity to develop their bodies and improve their skills.

When there are three or more balls in play, there is more action and a lot more scoring. We also recommend two goalies on each side that are constantly being rotated throughout the game with other players on their team. A hidden benefit of so much action coupled with frequent goalie changes is that no one can follow the actual game score. The teacher can begin accenting the point that the class is just playing for FUN and doesn't really need worry about scoring. The majority of students will see the point.

Innovative or Creative Play is often contrary to the modeling and goals we see in our adult culture. As a society, we try so hard to pressure our kids into team sports at the earliest possible age. In reality, kids have not matured enough for these highly developed team games. As educators, we need to look to people who are knowledgeable about child development like E. Erikson and J. Piaget. Their models show that children aren't ready for team sports until nearly middle school or even high school. At the appropriate developmental age, children can master in weeks what they have been pressured into trying to do for years. Their maturation process must move beyond the very self-centered, ego-focused period of their life before they can actually achieve success with team concepts. This egocentric period of life is not a bad thing. It's just part of being a child. At ages 5-11 they are rarely part of a team. They merely wear the same color tee-shirt as everyone else. In elementary school settings, it is important to acknowledge that each and every child just wants to play with the ball. "My turn" is their focus. Put extra balls out there and every student will be included.

Change the Boundary Size

Let's return to the game of LIKE, TOTALLY IT TAG, which we mentioned earlier. Here every player in the game is "It." Envision that you are going to play this game in a space of half a basketball court. Thirty students will freeze almost everyone playing in less than 15 seconds. By doubling the space of the game and playing on a full basketball court, the game will last 30-45 seconds. The added space also means the game is much more physically active. There is now more space to run. Pretend you want to play this same game on the football field. The children have lots of space to avoid being tagged. There will be lots of long-distance running for the players. The game can now last a long time or maybe too long. Players who get frozen early could be stuck standing for minutes while the others run around. This could be boring. On the other hand, if every student in the whole school played at once, you might find the football field is the perfect balance for the number of people, playing space and the time needed for the game.

Boundary size allows you and the class to control the amount of action. Use this dynamic to promote safety in games. You and your students now have the freedom to make up rules that are good for the PEOPLE.

Expand your creativity. Boundaries don't have to be squares, rectangles or circles marked by lines or cones. In Arizona, where the temperatures often reach 100 or more degrees, one teacher found a great solution for their Tag game. The shaded area of two big trees became boundary for their playing space. Students eagerly complied with these strange boundaries. More importantly, the teacher imaginatively used the game for a science experiment. Student groups were asked to predict and followed up on their postulations as to when the playing area was going to be at its maximum size based on the sun's position and the amount of shade. They also measured the temperature difference between playing in shade or sun. This academic exploration of boundaries also meant they had to use various math skills. Try having your class calculate the number of square feet in different size playing areas. As often as possible, involve practical cross-over academic learning experiences in your games. These concrete examples make sense to young minds.

Change the Focus of Scoring

At almost every, no, at every school we have visited there are classes where scorekeeping has become a major problem. The conflicts and arguments about scores have led many exhausted teachers to give up playing completely. Totally abandoning all play is not an effective learning solution for children at school. As always, your first approach should be to use your class posters to point out why the class is playing. Sometimes this works immediately, but more than likely, this refocusing on the social skills concept of play may take weeks or months. Your next tool to deal with constant scoring arguments is Rule # 2. Another option is to ban announcing the score out loud. It's okay to keep the score to yourself but don't say it out loud. If you say it out loud you will miss some or all of the next day's play. Some teachers have banned scoring for the whole school year, and students very quickly seem not to miss it. They just like that they still get to play and can now do so without headaches from constant bickering over the score.

One of the more imaginative solutions to scoring that we have developed is something called the single-digit score. With this concept, a team's score can never exceed a single-digit number. Therefore, a "9" becomes the best score either team can ever achieve. Once your score goes to a number which is 10 or greater you reduce it back to a single digit by adding the numbers together. Example: A score of 10 becomes $1 + 0 = 1$. A score of 23 becomes $2 + 3 = 5$.

This really changes game strategy. If you were winning 9 to 5 and you score that 10th point, your score changes and now you find you team losing 5 to 1. The kids will quickly see this new challenge when someone like Skippy, the class home-run hitter, is up to bat. Bases are loaded, but all of a sudden, everyone wants him to make an out. Being competitive has new tactics. Or, maybe Skippy is the kid who always makes the out. Now his team is grateful that it's his turn because he will keep their score right where it is at 9. Single digit scoring presents new possibilities for everyone and a lot less pressure on the score. You may find there are more tie games and you're practicing math.

Another scoring solution is to play games where the ultimate score is pitting the whole class against itself. This is like playing the whole class against time. Games like MAGIC SHOE (page 129) can be easily timed. If yesterday the class did the game in One minute and 43 seconds, can the class improve today to do it in less time?

Encourage Others to Offer Suggestions

Make everyone feel comfortable offering suggestions or ideas. In class, every student has valuable ideas to contribute from time to time. Play is a place where children should feel free to practice sharing their notions without fear of being laughed at by their peers. Initially, "put-downs" by some students may occur. Be prepared to immediately use your class peer-pressure system to establish an environment which allows everyone the freedom to be heard. If problems persist, you can use the arguing rule to discuss with a specific student that hurting someone else's feeling is not part of why the class plays.

We've talked about voting as a means to make rule changes that empowers the whole class. But majority "wins" is not always the only healthy alternative in a democracy. Use games to reinforce this learning. Try modeling minority rights in your games. "Tomorrow, let's try the rule change the other way and then we can see if we like one way better than the other. Maybe both ways will be just as good, only different." Don't be afraid to try ideas which you (the teacher) know probably won't work unless they are obviously unsafe. Even though you are trying to involve everyone, always use your good discretion to veto any idea you know could be harmful to the students.

Help children get comfortable with trying ideas where they get to experience the outcome of their decisions. When you begin trying different options you are actually using the scientific method of learning. When a classroom community views failures as successful learning experiences, there will be no stopping their potential to use imagination and creativity. This is the potential carry over you can achieve in your academic subjects when you safely practice these concepts during play.

Creative Play Games:

PEACE PATROL AND GREMLINS
(Second grade and up, 10-40 players, a basketball court with painted lines, bandannas or markers to identify the gremlins)

How It's Played
This is a classic battle between the forces of the noble "Peace Patrol" and the mischievous "Gremlins." Play occurs on a basketball court with painted lines. Gather your class in a circle formation in the center of the basketball court. Choose one Gremlin for every six players in the game with a minimum of two Gremlins and a maximum of four. Everyone else is a member of the Peace Patrol.

The object is for the Gremlins to freeze all of the Peace Patrol by tagging them. The goal for the Peace Patrol is to rescue each other every time one of them is frozen. Give each Gremlin a bandanna or marker so that everyone will know who the Gremlins are once the action starts. The game starts by having all the Gremlins meet in the center of the basketball court and count from twenty down to zero (stand close to the Gremlins as they do the countdown as you may be surprised to hear how many students make errors). The Peace Patrol members will scatter themselves all over the rest of the playing area. To make the game much more challenging, all players (both Gremlins and the Peace Patrol) must stay on the painted lines and can only move or run around when they are touching a painted line with at least one foot. After the game has begun, the Gremlins spread out moving along the lines of the court and begin tagging

Peace patrol and gremlins

and freezing members of the Peace Patrol. Once tagged by a Gremlin, a Peace Patroller cannot move. To let other members of the Peace Patrol know they need to be rescued, a frozen player waves one arm over their head and calls out, "Save Me!" When explaining this, have all your students put one arm up in the air and say, "Save Me. Save Me. Save Me!" Unfrozen members of the Peace Patrol will hear their alarm and following the lines, will come to their frozen classmate's rescue. When rescued (gently tagged) by an unfrozen Peace Patrol member, the once-frozen Peace Patroller is free to run and save other frozen classmates.

If a Gremlin misses stepping on a line while chasing a Peace Patroller, that Gremlin must count out loud to 20. During this counting process the Gremlin loses his ability to freeze Peace Patrollers. However, when a Peace Patrol member misses stepping on a line, they become frozen and must stay that way until rescued by another hero. Peace Patrollers do not have to count to 20 when

frozen, but should be encouraged to call out, "Save me!" to be rescued. The painted lines are very important and provide a great opportunity for giving feedback about playing fair. It's often useful to
ask your class if they will help you play fair by reminding you to
be frozen if they see you miss stepping on a line. Now expand this
to remind the group that they can remind anyone to be frozen for
missing a line.

A round of PEACE PATROL AND GREMLINS typically lasts
from three to five minutes. Generally, you can judge it's time to
start a countdown when the four Gremlins begin to look tired.
Multiple rounds should be played to allow all the children the opportunity to experience saving their friends. This time, to pick the
replacement Gremlins, have the students who were "it" the first
time give their bandanna marker to someone, other than the
teacher, that helps them with reading, math, spelling, art or homework. Let the students know that they will have to tell everyone
what this person does to help them with a subject at school. Gather
the new Gremlins in the center of your group. Have the person
who picked each Gremlin state what subject that Gremlin helps
them do better. Feel free to add some verbal praise supporting that
this person is good with math or spelling. (As you can see, even
choosing who is going to be next, is actually more important than
the game. Giving kudos to peers is now one of the values that the
game experience brings to everyone's attention. Be creative and
think of many different qualities the kids can use to pick their replacement: someone kind, respectful, plays fair, responsible,
shares, etc.)

THE GIFT OF THE GAME

Everyone in this game gets to experience what it feels like to be a
knight in shining armor, Superman™, Wonder Woman™, a police
woman, a fire fighter, a parent, a nurse or doctor, but most importantly, a good friend. To feel like a hero is to be the rescuer and receive all the gratitude while doing something helpful for another
person who needs your assistance. These are wonderful feelings

that most people, and especially children, don't get enough of. Being helpful is incredibly empowering and nurtures a child's desire to be compassionate. Children learn that being helpful is what human beings do for each other. Learning how to give as well as how to receive becomes the cornerstone for healthy "relatedness" and wards off antisocial behaviors. The Healthy Play curriculum has identified these specific games because they reinforce positive behaviors. Recognizing the classmates who saved you in the game will be frequently mentioned in your end of game compliment sessions.

TRIPLE TAG

(All grades, a large playing area, no equipment, any number of players)

How It's Played

Set up boundaries for your playing area. All players are it and may tag any other player. What makes this game different from "Like, totally it" tag is that kids must be tagged three times before they're frozen solid. The first time a student is tagged he must hold the spot where he was touched with one hand. The second tag forces him to use his other hand to hold that spot. (Now that both of his hands are occupied, he can tag players with his head, elbow, or body. Feet or knees may *not* be used for tagging because of safety concerns.) The third tag freezes that player solid.

Play continues until only a few players are left unfrozen (about six). At that point, have everybody who is frozen yell out a five-second countdown to indicate that the game is coming to an end.

The Gift of the Game

What's in a name? Plenty! When we first observed this game on playgrounds, it was called hurt, wounded, and dead or hospital tag. It was clear the players tried to make the game live up to its name. The game was played in an aggressive style, and children did consciously try to hurt one another. In fact, if you want your children to play like gladiators or reenact scenes from the local ER, have them play hospital tag. We suggest instead that you play triple tag. It's the same game, but the name conjures up playfulness and not scenes of mass destruction with wounded bodies scattered on the playground. Names have power. Names of games can suggest expected behaviors.

Names also can help groups of different ages buy into the activities. For instance, there is a game called Noah's ark, which involves kids mimicking an animal (for example, hopping like rabbits) to find the partner who shares their same animal name. It really is a delightful game. When we play it with church groups and young children, we play it as Noah's ark. However, when we play it with teenagers and adults, we play it as the mating game. Ooh! It's still the same game, but the mating game sounds less childish to teens and adults. They're more open to your suggestion of this game. In fact, don't tell older kids that BROKEN WHEEL (page 99) is an advanced form of duck, duck, goose. They might become resistant to this game with that information. Older children would miss out on a fun activity because they were turned off by the name of the game. Never forget that "naming" is important and sets the tone for desired behaviors.

ENDANGERED SPECIES
(Third grade and up, 15 or more players, large playing area or grass or a basketball court, identifying bandannas or markers)

How It's Played
Use a large playing area about the size of a basketball court or larger if you're on grass. Gather your class in a large circle. Have your class identify the name of an endangered species (such as a panda, whale, tiger or condor) for the focus of the game. Let's pick Pandas for this game example. Choose two "Trappers" and give them the identifying markers and have them go to the middle of the circle. The Trappers' goal is to capture the Pandas by gently

tagging them with their hand. A captured Panda has been caught and can no longer run around. Luckily, the other Pandas can work together in teams of two or more to free their trapped friends. Two uncaught Pandas must hold hands while encircling the captured Panda. They now raise their arms up and down once, yelling "Panda Free!" This breaks the spell of the Trappers' freeze and allows the Panda to roam free to save other caught Pandas.

There are many strategies in this game for both the Trappers and the Pandas. The Trappers can guard the captured Pandas, but this has a downside because the free Pandas will just stay far away and not get caught. When the Trappers look tired or when they capture all the Pandas start the countdown to end the game. A new round of endangered species is chosen with new Trappers. Continue using creative positive attributes to determine the new Trappers. The game begins again.

Students may want to offer different rules to the game. Most frequently, they want to change the rule of allowing a Trapper to

Endangered species

trap you when you are trying to set the panda free. Again, do not make a unilateral teacher decision. Bring the issue to the group's attention and have a vote. See which rule the students like better. Always be ready to send disagreements to the side of the game. Say good things to kids playing the right way.

THE GIFT OF THE GAME

This is one of the best activities we know to blend learning with fun and build a more cooperative school community. In most of schools where we have worked, classes of similar grade levels do many learning projects together each year. To maximize the values taught in ENDANGERED SPECIES, try planning one of these co-operative projects the week when you will be teaching your environmental curriculum. Have each class pick a different endangered species to study and make a large mural poster stating all the facts critical to this animal's survival. Share your posters with the school by placing them in the hallway and plan a class time to look at the other classes' posters. Simultaneously, during the week, play your class version of the game during your regular activity period.

Here's where the real fun happens. At the end of the week, meet with all the classes involved and play each class's ENDANGERED SPECIES version of the game (using pandas, condors, tigers and other species). Be sure to allow a really big space and adjust the number of Trappers to the size of the group. Before you start playing with the other classes, make sure to briefly discuss FUN, PEOPLE and the 2 RULES. Make all the classes respond to the chant of "Why do we play..." The GIFT comes from students practicing saving another individual during the game. This is obviously a very nice experience to share with your class. However, it is so much more significant when the students begin to practice these behaviors in their larger mixed classroom communities. By interacting with many different classes, the connections are quickly made that saving everyone is important. All the classes need to work together for their mutual benefit. Playing and learning together can break down unnecessary barriers which occur between classes. This makes the total school environment more livable for everyone. In the Healthy Play curriculum students learn to play with each other, not against each other.

MAGIC SHOE
(Kindergarten to second grade, indoor or outdoor walking space, no equipment, any number of players)

How It's Played
This is a great game to begin developing trust and cooperation in younger children. Have each child take off one shoe (ooh, it stinks!) and balance it on top of her head. Each MAGIC SHOE should be balanced on its owner's head, so she can move around. Players then practice walking around trying to keep their shoe from falling. Now have everyone line up across one side of your playing area. The object is for students to walk about 25 feet to the other side without having the MAGIC SHOE fall off their heads. If it does fall, the child becomes frozen. But that's no problem. Any other unfrozen child can come over and help by stooping down and picking up the MAGIC SHOE and giving it back to its owner. (At first you can allow the student who is doing the helping to hold their shoe on their head while they bend down to get the other person's shoe. After a while, you might want to vote on the option to do it without hands or a choice to do it either way.) Once the shoe has been replaced on the head from which it fell, the frozen player can move again. To make the activity more challenging, try to see how fast the group can help everyone get to the opposite side. If this proves successful, try going over and back. Can the class beat the best time they've ever done? Can they walk backwards? How about with their eyes closed? Make up lots of new rules. Bring in your academics. Here is a chance to talk about seconds and minutes. It's a chance to practice subtracting the total of one race from the other to see exactly how much faster you did your time.

Another wonderful variation on this game is to play it with two

Magic shoe

teams. Divide your class up using the Double Divide method (see following paragraph). Place each team on opposite sides of the basketball court. Instruct your kids that this game is not a race against each team, but instead a race against time. The task is to complete the walk to the other side in as few seconds as possible. Both teams can assist not only their own team members who have become frozen due to falling shoes, but the opposing team members as well. Talk about building cooperation.

THE DOUBLE DIVIDE:

Step one: Have everyone in class pick a partner. Children without partners put a hand in the air and look for others who aren't partnered. Save yourself from being partnered until the students are all matched up. This way, on days when you have an even number of students you will not get a partner. On the days when the total is an odd number, you will get a partner.

Step two: Let the partners choose between two items. For example, you might pick Vanilla or Strawberry ice cream. Every partnership now must have one person choose to be either Vanilla or Strawberry ice cream. Now you ask for all those students who picked Vanilla to raise their hands. Quickly check to see that each partnership has one hand up. Have all the Vanilla partners go to one side of the play area. Have all the remaining Strawberry partners go to the other side. Like magic, you will have two equal teams chosen without captains.

THE GIFT OF THE GAME

We like this game so much because kids like it a lot. This is one of the silliest activities that adults experience at our trainings, and at first, some are reticent to walk around with shoes on their heads. But kids understand the pure silliness of taking off that smelly ole shoe and placing it on their heads. Children won't hide their willingness to believe in their shoe's magic power. To play activities that adults may feel extra silly doing is important to model with your students. Many aspects of the Healthy Play curriculum are purely focused on the teacher bonding with the children. Enjoy and stay open to the delight of innocent beings. They have much to teach us.

SPELLING, GEOGRAPHY, MATH TAG

(Any grade level. It's played outside as a running tag game on a basketball court size playing area or as a sitting down activity in your classroom. You will also need some questions from any subject your students are studying and the answers.)

How It's Played

This is the ultimate application of using creative play dynamics while supporting academic learning. You will need to prepare a list of questions on a subject you are studying in advance of playing this game. Let's use this week's 25 spelling words for the initial game. Determine how many students you have in the class and then figure what 40% of that number is (You have 20 students so 40% will be 8. In this game we are using a much higher percentage for picking the number of multiple "ITs"). The number of people IT in your game will be 8. Make 8 copies of the correct spelling words for the week.

Gather your students in a circle in the middle of the basketball court to explain the game. Randomly chose 8 students to be IT and give them a copy of the spelling words. They can look at them and study them as much as they want. Determine a secret word which will start the game. Allow the students who are not IT to move away. Start the game.

In SPELLING, GEOGRAPHY, MATH TAG the object of the game is for the people who are IT to chase and tag someone in their class. Once tagged, both players stop running and the person with the spelling words can pick any word on the list they would like the person to spell. If the person spells the word correctly, they can run away and the person who is it must try to tag someone else. If the person misspells the word, the person who is IT must verbally spell the word correctly for the other person to hear. (You can quickly see how many of the multiple learning styles are involved in this game.) They then give the spelling list (the marker in this game which identifies who's IT) to the person they tagged. This person is now IT and must try to tag someone else.

Play this game for approximately five minutes. You might let your students know that you will play this game twice more this week. If your kids are competitive at all, we bet they'll practice their spelling words before the next game.

The reason for such a high number of people being IT in this game is to maximize the number of people who are reviewing and learning the spelling words. If eight students tag eight other students then sixteen out of twenty students are actively involved. The simple game of tag now has the potential for academic review on every subject you teach. Naming all the bones of the body just became a tag game. Presidents, capitols, sentences with punctuation errors, math problems are all tag games. Taking your students outside for a quick break meets their physical, social and academic needs.

In kindergarten, you don't need lists for the kids to read. Use bandannas to make many students IT. If you are studying different letters and words that begin with that letter the game becomes, "Tell me a word that starts with the letter "C'? "How many fingers am I showing you?" Have animal pictures and then students will need to state what animal it is. Use a smaller space to make sure you can overhear that the students are saying the correct answers. In the kindergarten version, it doesn't matter if you get the answer right or wrong to determine who is the next IT. The person tagged is automatically the new person who is IT. Kinders just like being IT.

THE GIFT OF THE GAME

A fifth grade teacher told us of his experiences using SPELLING, GEOGRAPHY, MATH TAG with his class. On Monday he took his kids out to play and introduced them to the game. He played again on Wednesday. On Friday, the students insisted they play again. After returning to the room the students enthusiastically asked if they could take their test. The spelling test was taken and the students then requested he grade the test immediately. This was very unusual behavior for these kids. Until now there had been very little interest shown by the students in finding out what their grade was on any test.

There was a significant improvement in the grades, just as the kids knew they would be. He repeated the process with different subjects over the next several weeks. Each time the students were eager to take their test. Each time they wanted to know their grades immediately. They were so insistent that they volunteered to do absolutely quiet reading so he could grade them on the spot. What amazed him more was that the student's interest in seeing if they did well on a test transferred to all tests whether they played or not. His students were now interested and motivated to see how well they could do at school. It was a major change in their self esteem. By making learning FUN he had accomplished a level of involvement in learning his students had never shown before. This is one game he now plays every year with his students.

GHOST

(Kindergarten and up, any number of players, large playing area, no equipment)

How It's Played

Have all players form a circle holding hands. (Process any problems like hand squishing or arm pulling.) Pick four ghosts, place them in the center of the circle and have them pretend to go to sleep. The remaining players begin to walk clockwise around the ghosts while counting out loud the hours of a clock from one o'clock to midnight. At "midnight," players let go of each other's hands and run away from the ghosts that are waking up. Upon awakening, ghosts wave their arms high in the air while making ghostly sounds as they chase the other players. Each person they tag becomes a ghost who also has to mimic the sounds and arm motions of a ghost. The game is over when everybody is a ghost.

This game is so versatile. On Thanksgiving you can make everyone turkeys that run around catching everyone while clucking "gobble gobble." Or use your school mascot for another version of this game. During one seminar, which occurred on an election day, we creatively changed ghost to a game of presidents. Once tagged by a president, a player had to mock shake a potential voter's hand and make a campaign slogan, stating, "If elected I promise to ——." The laughter was tumultuous, and the campaign promises hysterical.

The Gift of the Game

Ghost is a great game to start every play session with. This accumulation tag game sets the tone for playing fair, using safety, and

Ghost

taking care of each other, and it involves all the players in an equitable way. Plus, you get to act real silly. If your children have difficulty holding hands, this is a great way to start practicing.

We've also found that most children want to be the starting ghosts
in the middle of the circle. We announce that we only pick those who
are being quiet and good listeners to be our starting ghosts. Wow! Instantly, the pleading stops and the waving arms relax. Suddenly it's
hard to find only four good listeners. Children learn quickly that positive behaviors are rewarded and that there is a time for silliness and
a time for being attentive. Their attentiveness is rewarded very
quickly with their silliest ghostly shrieks and actions.

WHO'S IN CHARGE?

(Second grade and up, ten or more players, indoors is fine, imagination is the only equipment needed)

How It's Played

Ever wonder who's in charge? In this game students will have a chance to find out. Have your group sit on the floor or in chairs in a large circle. Select one member randomly and have him move into the middle of the circle. The person in the middle now closes his eyes while you, the teacher, *silently* point out one person (and only one person) to be in charge. The person in charge is the leader of the group, and all group members must copy exactly what this player does. While the person in the middle still has his eyes closed, the player in charge starts the game by making some type of motion, such as waving. Quickly, all the other members start waving. Now the person in the middle opens his eyes and begins to try to figure out who's in charge.

At any given moment the leader can change motions, for example, from waving to patting his head. Quickly, other group

Who's in charge?

members see the change and copy the new motion. Now the person in charge (a silly person indeed) stops patting his head and sticks his tongue out. Everyone follows along. The person in the middle gets three guesses to try to figure out who the leader is. If the guess is correct, the two players exchange places and the game begins again. If after three guesses the person in charge has not been discovered, the game is halted and the great baffling leader is acknowledged. The person in the middle and the leader still exchange places and the game starts over. Encourage the person in charge to be very creative and use movements like clapping, shuffling feet, snapping fingers, making funny faces, moving in slooooowww motion.

Hints: To facilitate sharing, players can only be the leader once each time you play who's in charge. It is also very important that the members of the group not stare constantly at the person in charge. Have everyone look all around the circle constantly. When you first teach this activity, try to pick players who have the imagination and the confidence to initiate changes during the game. This game can be played again and again, and over time everyone will get to show his skills of being in charge!

The Gift of the Game

Compared to adults, children have very little power in their lives. In most classroom settings there is an established pecking order where some kids have power and others have none. The beauty behind this game is the sense of empowerment children experience when they are the leaders and everyone follows their direction. Even children who cannot identify the leader are not humiliated and left in the center of the circle. And, as a discovered or undiscovered leader, this child then steps into the center to try to figure out the new leader. This makes all the players just participants, not winners or losers. We also have had many teachers tell us that this game really breaks up cliques. Children who often sit together are quickly shuffled around the circle. Often the boys sit on one side of the circle and the girls on the other at the beginning of the game. Since the person who was the leader must eventually give up her seat to the person in the middle, the children naturally end up mixing and so learn physical and emotional tolerance toward others. This game also breaks down the cootie factor.

GIANTS, ELVES AND WIZARDS

(Fourth grade and older, the more players the better, a very large grass space, boundary markers)

We spent much of this lesson describing the impact of being on a team. This first game for older students will provide an opportunity for your students to challenge some of their preconceived ideas about team dynamics. It's a perfect time to use the double divide.

How It's Played

Set up a playing field that is approximately 60 feet across and 150 feet long. Make a mid line with a couple low cones at the 30 foot spot. Also mark the end-zone lines with cones which indicate the safety zones in the game. Have the players do a double divide to pick two teams. The object of the game is for one team to capture players from the opposing team enabling captured players to now play for the "other" side.

There are three options in GIANTS, ELVES AND WIZARDS and it is important to do group demonstrations of the correct positions. Have everyone become GIANTS standing tall with their arms stretched toward the sky. Now everyone become ELVES by crouching down and put their hands on the sides of their head to make big pointy ears. Finally, demonstrate that WIZARDS stand straight and wave their arms and hands as if they were casting a magic spell. Each of these figures has certain strengths and certain weaknesses. GIANTS beat ELVES. The ELVES beat the WIZARDS. WIZARDS beat GIANTS. Have all your students chant and role play the three options at least twice to help them remember what beats what. It's a grandiose form of "Rock, Paper, Scissors." Every choice beats something, but every choice also loses to something.

The teams separate and huddle where they vote on which one of the three options the whole team will be. We encourage the "thumbs-up" voting format. The majority will rule and decide what option will be played for that round. Even when it is clear which role will be chosen, continue the voting process so that everyone feels that their decision matters. Once the voting is over, make it clear that everyone on the team will act out the same chosen role. After the huddle, the teams meet on the center line, stretch out the line, face each other and then take one step back so that there is some space between them. Former partners, initially paired up with the double-divide, are not required to stand opposite each other. Pick one student to be the game starting monitor. When he sees that both lines are in position he will yell "Ready." At this point all players count out loud, "1-2-3" and then act like the character their team chose. Let's say Team X chose to be GIANTS, and Team Y picked ELVES. Remember, GIANTS beat ELVES. This means that Team X will chase Team Y and try to tag Team Y players before they can retreat to the safety zone behind their end-line. All Team Y players who get tagged become members of Team X. However, once behind your safety zone without being tagged, makes you safe. If Team X had chosen GIANTS, but Team Y was WIZARDS, then Team Y would chase Team X because WIZARDS beat GIANTS.

At the end of this round, newly formed teams regroup and pick a new character for their team. They are permitted to repeat the same choice as the previous round. The game can be played again and again. If both teams chose the same option, all the players are instructed to laugh, return to their huddle and pick another or the same option again.

Be ready for some confusion to occur in this game. It always happens. Spencer and I have played this game thousands of times and we still goof up. Some players on a team will do the wrong character. Others will forget which character is supposed to chase and who is supposed to retreat. Keep the mood light and laugh at the confusion. Use Rule # 2 as necessary and keep the game going.

Safety is important. Stretch your line out. Sometimes a student will fall and you don't want the others to trample someone on the ground. The middle of the group is the most congested area of play. Some students may feel more comfortable playing at the end of the line. Stretching the line becomes more important when one team has grown to 20 members and the other is down to six. Make sure the six people spread out evenly across the full width of the playing field. This will insure that the larger team spreads out as well.

We'd like to share another reminder about religious and cultural sensitivity that may come up with this game. The use of the "Wizard" character may not be okay for some people. Simply use Creative Play and change the game to bears, rabbits and dogs. Or, just create three options representing the different sizes of tall, medium and small.

THE GIFT OF THE GAME

GIANTS, ELVES AND WIZARDS is one of our favorite New Games Foundation activities as it has many important inherent lessons along with a ton of excitement and laughter. In many games, children bicker over which team they get placed on. Some children feel threatened if they are not placed on the same team with their best bud, or they become angry and resistant if they feel they are placed on the team they think will lose. The beauty behind this game is that though kids start out on one team they quickly end up on the other team. That's the point. You can end up going back and forth many times. During the after-play processing, children often say they played just as hard and tried their best on whatever team they played on. Lessons of tolerance, diversity and trying one's best instantly surface and can be explored. We also use this game to defuse kids' ideas that they need gangs. Children and teens that successfully buy into GIANTS, ELVES AND WIZARDS learn that they can and should count on all their peers, no matter which side of the playing field or "tracks" they find themselves on.

ANTI-WAR

(Grade one on up. Intermediates will play the multiplication version while primary students will do the addition version. A deck of cards for each group is required)

How It's Played

This game is played in table groups of up to six students. The dealer in every group passes out all the cards. Each player creates two equal, or near equal, piles with cards face down in front of them.

Card values are:

Ace = 1

2, 3, 4, 5, 6, 7, 8, 9, 10 = 2, 3, 4, 5, 6, 7, 8, 9, 10, (the values plainly stated on the cards).

Face cards (King, Queen and Jacks) = 10. Remove jokers.

Dealer says "Ready." Everyone counts up to three. On the count of three, players turn over their top cards. Starting with the person who is left to the dealer, players take turns multiplying the numbers on their own cards and announce their individual calculations. The person with the lowest score (product) wins and gathers up all the played cards, puts those cards at the bottom of his/her two piles and starts the next round by saying, "Ready." (Kids love that the lowest score is the winning one). If more than one player has tied with the lowest score, just those players will play another round to determine who has the lowest score who will get all the cards from that round and the previous one.

Eventually, someone will no longer have any cards. Not to worry! Just like before, everyone plays their hand and calculates their math problem. This includes the person who has no cards. That player will simply multiply zero times zero which will give them a product of zero. Of course, they will have the lowest score and will now get to be right back in the game as everyone will turn over their played cards to them. If more than one person has no cards then the whole group is instructed to come up with a solution which would enable all the people to play again. This will promote a sense of problem-solving, group consensus and inclusion. Play continues in this manner until the teacher is ready to end this lesson.

Rules for primary students:

Played the same way, but instead of multiplying, these students will do addition calculations to discover who has the lowest sum. Remove any cards which have numbers that the children have not yet learned to add.

Helpful hints: It is helpful to combine more that one deck to play this game. We have found that a deck and a half is about the right amount for up to six players. When you have decks missing cards don't throw them out. Just add them to your Anti-war decks and other Creative Spirit/Healthy Play card games.

GIFT OF THE GAME

Spencer and I often get the pleasure of being gifted with games. While traveling, (and it seems like we're always traveling), Spencer met a teacher who shared with him a version of the original game of "War." The difference in her "War" game was the making of two piles of cards and adding the numbers together. The person with the highest score got all of the others player's cards. This was a much more effective academic game and we were excited about collecting a new math card game.

That afternoon as we traveled very slowly in the Southern California traffic, we took the time to brainstorm how we could make this "War" game better. First of all, we weren't wild about the name of the game. The concept of teaching "War" is contrary to all the peaceful things we represent. For a while we tried calling the game different math related concepts; none of those ideas really felt right. Then we hit upon the concept of renaming the game "Anti-War." We could easily see ourselves teaching concepts that reflected the opposite of war, and this immediately changed the game. Now the lowest score would be the winner. That seemed like a fun wrinkle to add into the game. Then the epiphany occurred to us that we had just fixed the problem of eliminating children from the game. The change from the highest to the lowest score dynamic created solutions to students with no cards left and/or a zero score. This change meant that the person with the lowest score would always win and quickly would be back in the game. This factor enhanced the fact that the real purpose of the game was to practice adding. For that to happen, everyone needed to stay involved for the whole game time and this Creative Play rule change had just accomplished that.

Then it came to us that this game could be used for multiplying. Suddenly, Anti-War was a useful game for older students. We were now even more pleased with ourselves. The slow traffic had bogged us down with an additional thirty minutes, but gave us extra time to explore subtraction and division. Even if the traffic had lasted two more hours we couldn't figure out effective uses for division and subtraction. However, our success for what we did accomplish sure felt rewarding to us.

MENTAL MATH

(This is another wonderful addition, multiplication or subtraction game depending on the capabilities of the students playing the game. You will need a deck of cards for each group.)

How It's Played

This game is played in groups of three to six students at tables or in a circle on the floor. The deck of cards is placed in the center of the group face down. (Hint: Divide the deck into two stacks of cards when playing with a larger number of people so that all players can reach the cards easily). Each player will draw one card from the top of the pile and, without looking, place the card against their forehead so that all the other players can see their card but they can't. (If a player accidentally sees their card they discard the first card and draw a new card).

Card values are:

Ace = 1

2, 3, 4, 5, 6, 7, 8, 9, 10 = 2, 3, 4, 5, 6, 7, 8, 9, 10, (the values plainly stated on the cards).

Face cards (King, Queen, Jacks and Jokers) = 10

(Feel free to alter the game by removing cards with values that your students have not yet studied.)

Select a leader for the first round. The leader will look at the cards of the next two players sitting to their left (a clockwise direction) and total up the value of the cards. The leader will announce ONLY the total score of the next two players' cards. The person immediately to the left of the leader, who can clearly see the value of the card of the person to their left, but not their own, then has to determine and announce the value of the card that they are holding. The leader will validate if he has made a correct or incorrect calculation in determining the value of his card. Once the correct value has been guessed play continues by having that person who guessed their card's value determine the total of the next two players cards to their left. The game continues until the original leader gets a chance to guess his/her card. At that point everyone draws a new card and the new leader is the person to the left of the first leader.

GIFT OF THE GAME

Many of the best compliments and validations of our math activities have come from teachers who told us of how easily parents would enjoy playing these games with their children at home. Teachers used to report that parents were often not comfortable with helping children with homework assignments because they had insecurities about their own abilities to know the subject at hand, especially math. At family night, many teachers initially introduced some of the simpler math games like Anti-War and Mental Math. Just like the students discovered, parents too realized that when you make academics fun it reduces the anxiety that sometimes accompanying learning. The natural social connections inherent in these activities also fostered familial closeness and bonding. This is all such a win-win scenario.

We'd like to share another gift with you. One of our favorite teachers is Cindy Williams. We have known her for about ten years and have had numerous opportunities to visit her and the different classes she has taught. One of our problems is that Cindy is such an avid user of HP that we have run out of new games to teach her. Fortunately, the week before this visit, Spencer had just learned an addition game called, "Do you know what your number is?" He eagerly went to Cindy's class knowing he had a new game to share with her.

It took about ten seconds of actually playing the game before Cindy excitedly began exclaiming how great the game was. She went on about how it was a goal of this grade level to academically move students past adding up numbers on their fingers. It was now time for them to start learning to do math computations in their head. Finding techniques or tools to do that were not readily available. But, this new game was perfect for helping kids practice doing their math mentally. She was so happy! Then Cindy said, "You should call this game Mental Math." And so we have. Thanks, Cindy.

NINETY-NINE

(Players who can add numbers to ninety-nine, two to eight people per group, inside, deck(s) of cards)

How It's Played

Ninety-nine uses all the wonderful social skills of other card games, plus it's great practice for addition and memory skills. The object of this game is to force other players to play a card that makes the score go over 99 points. Each player wants to avoid playing a card that will push the score over 99 and end the game. Before starting the game, make sure everyone is aware of the following special card values:

Aces: 1 or 11 points
Threes: Hold the score
Fours: Reverses the direction of play and holds the score
Nines: 99 points, no matter when they are played
Tens: Minus 10 points (−10)
All picture cards: 10 points
All other cards (2, 5, 6, 7, 8): Their face value

The dealer gives each player three cards, and the players wait until the dealing is done before looking at their cards. The first player to the left of the dealer starts and plays any card. This now starts the score, which begins at zero. For example, if a king is played, the score would be 10. This player must remember to immediately pick up a replacement card from the deck before the next player starts his turn, or she must play with only two cards. The next player plays a 7 and says the new score, 17, then draws a replacement card. The next person plays an ace and announces the score is 28. (Remember, an ace is 1 or 11 points, so the score could have been 18 or 28.) The next player plays a 9, and the score automatically goes to 99. (Remember, nines are special, and you don't add just 9 to the score.) Here is where the game becomes interesting. Unless the next person has a 3, 4, 9, or 10 in his hand, the score will go past 99, and the round will end. The following player plays a 10, which is equal to minus 10 points, so the score goes back to 89. The next card played is a 6, so the score is 95. Now, a 3 is played, and the score *holds* at 95. Another 9 makes the score 99 again. A 4 is played, reversing the play to the right and keeping the score at 99. Next, another 3 keeps the score at 99, and this is followed by a 4, which reverses direction again and keeps the score at 99. Finally, the next player does not have a 3, 4, 9, or 10 and forces the score past 99, thus ending the round.

At this point you can shuffle and start a new round, or to play down anyone losing, you might just keep going this way:

Let's imagine that the score was 99, and you are supposed to play the next card. However, you do not have a card that will keep you from going over 99. In fact, your lowest value card is a 5, which would make the score 104. Using the rules of creative play, if you place a card making the value greater than 99, you are allowed to subtract 100 from that value. So 104 minus 100 is 4. The score now stands at 4, and the game continues without shuffling or undue attention placed on the person who went over 99.

"99" CARD VALUES FOR YOUNGER CHILDREN

Ace's = 1

9's = 99, no matter when they are played

All picture cards = Hold the values or score

All other cards (2, 3, 4, 5, 6, 7, 8 and 10s) = their face value.)

The Gift of the Game

This is a great chance to make math fun. It is important to allow all the players to add their own scores out loud, so that the fastest person in addition won't dominate the game. Every ten seconds, a player is validated by the group for properly adding their score. Players get more math practice by learning how to correct each other in a caring manner if an error is made. Obviously, you will not allow statements like "Hey, stupid, 33 plus 6 is 39 and not 41." Many students need practice in remembering details. Those with this difficulty will often find themselves with only one or two cards. (Maybe, if they practice remembering details in a game, they can transfer this skill to remembering to do some homework.) For many students, just practicing announcing the score may be the part of the activity that helps them progress in learning to speak up in class. It's never the score that counts. It's what you learn that matters.

DOWN TO ZERO

(Players who can subtract numbers from 100, two to six people per group, inside, decks of cards)

This activity is just the reverse of "99." In DOWN TO ZERO the score starts at 100 and players subtract the cards they play from the current total. Like the game of 99, all players start with three cards and they must remember to draw a replacement card before the next player finishes their turn or they will be down to only two cards. When the score reaches zero, players will play their safety cards (jacks, queens, kings and jokers) to try to avoid making the score go below zero. Eventually someone will run out of safe cards and force the score to go below zero and that will end the hand. Re-shuffle the cards and play again.

DOWN TO ZERO (OLDER GRADES)

SPECIAL VALUES:
Ace's = 1 or 11

2, 3, 4, 5, 6, 7, 8, 9, 10 = 2, 3, 4, 5, 6, 7, 8, 9, 10

Jacks and Jokers = 0 (zero points) and reverses the direction of play Queens = Adding 5 points to the total and reverses the direction of play. Kings = Adding 10 points to the total and reverses the direction of play.

DOWN TO ZERO (YOUNGER GRADES)

SPECIAL VALUES:
Ace's = 1

2, 3, 4, 5, 6, 7, 8, 9, 10 = 2, 3, 4, 5, 6, 7, 8, 9, 10

All picture cards (jacks, queens, kings and jokers = 0 (zero points)

(Feel free to take out any card numbers which students have not yet mastered subtracting. Change the total of the game to 25 or 50 if that makes the game useful for your age group

GIFT OF THE GAME
We taught Kay Ann four of our earliest math games and she used them daily during a school summer program. She noticed fairly quickly that all of the games were very effective in practicing addition skills, but that we did not provide any games for subtrac-

tion. The problem was quickly solved by using Creative Play dynamics to take the game of "99" and reverse a few card values. Now the kids could practice subtraction.

That was 12 years ago. No longer does Kay Ann need any help in using HP in her daily school curriculum. In fact, she usually has some advancement she can teach us when we visit her class. On my last visit, the students were studying math probabilities. To make the learning a hands-on project she assigned groups of students to invent games that could demonstrate probabilities. One of the groups had a whole bunch of those colored wrist bands. Each color was given a different point value and the number of each color varied (2 red, 5 yellow, 6 purple and 7 pink). Thus the probability was calculated on which color band and how many points you could achieve. Since each group did something special and different, as a class they had ten new games to play.

Kay Ann has also evolved the number of concepts in our program for the students to focus on. In addition to the chant of the two philosophies and two rules she has developed, "Whose responsibility is it for learning?" The class responds, "Ours." Play, classroom management and academics have been transformed into helping the children see that they are responsible for their own learning potential. If Spencer and I were to ever invent an achievement honor for teachers it would be called, "I'd want you to be my child's teacher." Our first nominee would be Kay Ann.

LOW SCORE

(Children who are learning or who know fractions, two to six players per group, inside, decks of cards)

How It's Played

Developing a stronger memory is a special learning factor in this social, card game. The following cards have special values:

Ace: 1 point

Joker: 0 points

King, queen, jack: ½ point

Two through 10: Their face value

The object of the game is to get the low score with four cards. The dealer deals four cards, facedown, to each player. Players *cannot* look at their cards. When all the students have received their cards, each player may now look at only *two* of them. This is the only free chance a player gets to look at those *two* cards. From now on, they must remember what their cards are without looking at them again. (They do not get to see their *other* two cards at this time.) Players can develop any pattern of placing their four cards facedown on the table to help them remember which cards they want to keep and which they hope to trade away. Now play begins. The remainder of the deck is placed in the middle of the players, and the top card is turned over, starting a discard pile. The person to the left of the dealer goes first and may either choose the top card from the discard pile, which he can see, or take the top card from the deck, which he can't see. Example: Player X knows that two of the cards in his hand are a queen worth ½ point and a 7, which is not very good. The top discard is a 5, which really isn't very good either but better than the 7. The player ignores the 5 and chooses the unknown card from the deck. He now looks at this card and decides if he wants to keep it. He picked an ace, which is only worth 1 point, and chooses to keep it. This player can replace the 7 with the ace, or he can risk keeping both the 7 and the ace and discarding one of the two unknown cards. (He can look at it before he discards it.) He chooses to replace the 7 and now must remember where he puts the ace because he can't look at his cards again. The 7 is now placed on the discard pile and play continues. The following turn he draws another ace. He now chooses to replace an unknown card, which turns out to be a jack. Oops, too bad. This jack is now a discard, which the next player thankfully accepts. Play continues until one person believes she has the lowest total score. At this point she'll say, "Low score." All players now have to turn over all four of their cards and add up their scores for the hand. If the player who called low score is the lowest, she receives the bonus of not having to add any score to their accumulative game total. However, if any of the other players beats or ties the score of the person who called low score, she not only gets her point total for the hand but must add a 10-point penalty to their score. All other players add the point total of their current hand to their overall score. If the cards run out and players stop taking the top discard, then the hand comes to an end, and all the players total their scores without either the bonus or the penalty.

To practice the most math possible during this game, have every player keep a score sheet on every other player. Make the game more complicated by making jacks equal ¼ point, queens equal ⅓ point, and kings equal ½ point.

LOW SCORE (YOUNGER GRADES)

SPECIAL CARD VALUES:

Ace = 1 point

2, 3, 4, 5, 6, 7, 8, 9, 10 = 2, 3, 4, 5, 6, 7, 8, 9, 10

REMOVE THE FACE CARDS AND JOKERS

(Initially you might play with only two cards. One known and one unknown)

The Gift of the Game

Aaahhh, fractions! Those demons of math that defy easy computation. This is a great activity to let students practice working with these numbers and mathematical concepts. First, whenever you are playing a game where a written score is kept, have every player keep everyone's score tally. The point is to keep all of the kids active during the whole game instead of sticking one player with score keeping. Second, this game really lends itself to rule changes. The original setup of card values is easy. Once the children master those number skills, start changing values, for example have kings equal ¾, queens equal ½, jacks equal ¼—or kings equal ½, queens equal ⅓, jacks equal ⅙ point. You can even say fives are worth minus 5 points. Now you'll be adding and subtracting. The wonderful thing is that students can share and help each other out with adding fractions.

NUMBERED CUBES

(Students who can work with whole numbers up to 5,000, two to six players per group, played at a table or on the floor, six number cubes [dice] for each group)

How It's Played

This popular game has been invented and changed by so many people it must be fun. It is a game for practicing when to keep the bird in the hand and when to try for two in the bush. Here is one set of rules to get you going, but we're sure you'll add plenty of your own personal touches to make the game better. The object of the game is to score over 5,000 points.

Scoring values:

    Ones: 100 points
    Fives: 50 points
    Single twos, threes, fours, and sixes: 0 points
    Three of a kind: 100 × the number on the dice
    Four of a kind:150 × the number on the dice
    Five of a kind: 200 × the number on the dice
    Six of a kind: 500 × the number on the dice
    1, 2, 3, 4, 5, 6 on the first roll: 1,000 points
    All six dice scoring: 250-point bonus, plus the player's turn continues (if he or she wishes)

The first player rolls all six dice and looks for scoring combinations. For example, two twos, one three, one five, and two sixes were rolled. The only score for this roll is the single five. It is worth 50 points. The player may end her turn or set the five to the side and reroll the other five dice. She rolls again and gets three threes, a five, and a six. The three threes are worth 300 points, and the five is worth 50. This roll she has 350 points, which she adds to the first-turn subtotal of 50 for a total of 400 points. She may end her turn and score the 400 points or risk these 400 points by rolling the one remaining die (the six). She can only score on the single die by rolling a one or five. *Failure to score will cost her all her points for that turn.* Let's say she rolls and gets a one. This is worth another 100 points, plus she earns a bonus of 250 points for scoring all her dice. Now she has a total of 750 points, and she may continue by rolling all six dice again. She does and gets four twos, a three, and a six. The four twos are worth 300 points and the three and six are worth nothing. The total is now 1,050 for the turn. She can quit or go on. She rolls the two dice and gets two twos. This does not score. She may *not* combine them with the previous twos she has rolled. Therefore, her score for all this effort is zero. She took too many risks. It is now the next player's turn and so on. Eventually a player will accumulate several turns' worth of points and pass the 5,000 mark.

The Gift of the Game

This game features plenty of math and lots of social interaction: taking turns, taking risks, practicing how to make decisions, and listening to others offer a lot of advice about what they would do if they were you. Again, make sure that every player keeps every other player's score.

One rule we've left out on purpose is how to end the game fairly when someone reaches 5,000 points. Should the game stop immediately? Should everyone else get one more turn after the score is reached? Maybe those people who haven't had the same number of turns still get their last chance. There are many possible answers, and it is a good idea to have the kids develop their own fair solution.

SLOW-MOTION TAG

(Kindergarten and early first grade, four or more kids, inside, no equipment)

How It's Played

Begin by having everyone sit close to each other on the floor. Ask all the children to move their hands in slow motion. Now begin picking things that can be tagged by the students in slow motion. The leader will say, "Slow-motion tag people's feet." Students gently tag only feet that are within reach. Players must always keep their bottoms on the floor, glued to the place where they are sitting. Sometimes they won't be able to reach people far away. When they have completed the first tag, move on to another slow-motion command. "Slow-motion tag people's elbows," or "Slow-motion gently tag people's ears." (This one always makes me giggle.) "Slow-motion tag things people are wearing that are green or red or blue." You can tag their buttons, their hair, their socks, and so on. This is a great place to begin positive safe touching before the students play any other tag games. Gentle tags create more friends than aggressive ones.

The Gift of the Game

Many a primary teacher has told us, "It's my whole year's kindergarten curriculum! It's all the tools of multiple intelligence learning in one game: auditory, visual, tactile, interpersonal, intrapersonal, and everything else. I just can't get over it! We'll practice shapes, colors, body parts, personal boundaries, motor skills, just everything! It's also much easier to teach young children how to tag gently than to reeducate aggressive tagging tendencies." It is exciting to see discovery occur at every age and to acknowledge that prevention is easier than intervention.

ADDING FRIENDS

(Pre-K, K and 1. There are two objectives to this pre-k and primary activity. The first objective is learning and/or reinforcing primary addition skills. The second is to give children an opportunity to learn how to move around a room quietly.)

How It's Played

Identify and name four areas in your room. Let's imagine that the groups were named Blue, Red, Yellow and Green. Randomly identify one child to be the "friend-maker" for the first few rounds. The friend-maker goes into the middle of the room, closes his or her eyes and counts up to 15 (with the teacher if necessary). Each child now has just 15 seconds to go to any of the four groups as quietly as possible. Instruct children that this is NOT a game of Hide and Seek to avoid their hiding under and behind objects. The goal for the friend-maker is to collect as many friends as they can and get them to sit at their feet. Here is how this is done. At the end of the count of 15 and BEFORE opening their eyes, the friend-maker says, "I want to add friends from the _____ group." Let's say the friend-maker said the "green" group. All the children who were in the green group go and sit at the feet of the friend-maker. The teacher asks a random child in the group how many children there are in the group of friends including the friend-maker. The child answers. The teacher always asks the group if they agree or disagree with the answer given. This way you can validate or correct the answer. The game continues and the friend-maker once again closes their eyes. Children can stay in their current position or reshuffle quietly to another group. During this round, new friends are usually added to the center position by the friend-maker and another addition problem is created for the class. Again the teacher will ask, "How many friends are there, now?" Older children can start to work on the difference between this new group and the last one. Now you'll have a subtraction problem for age appropriate kids to solve. If a friend-maker picks a group that has no children in it all the children at her feet are free to go off to new groups once the next round starts. Pick new friend-makers as needed to keep the momentum and invoke a sense of taking turns and fairness. By naming the groups to reflect geographical directions teachers can also use this game to introduce the concepts of north, south, east and west.

GIFT OF THE GAME

"Help!" the overwhelmed first grade teacher and her aide yelled out in unison when I walked through their door. I had walked into this room of squirrely first graders on the second day of school running around the room giggling and screaming their happy little hearts out. There was such absolute hyper-kinetic energy. You could have lit the city of New York for weeks if only you could harness it. "They have been like this all day and just are not responding to any limits. I don't want to have to yell at them to stop." In a quick assessment I could have taken them outside to dissipate their energy, but it was raining. Well necessity IS the mother of invention. On the spot, I came up with the game of Adding Friends. By turning walking into a game the students quickly bought into a playful way of calming themselves down. I then began to think that as quiet children were being accumulated in the center of the room by the "friend-maker" we were presented with an easy opportunity to help the children reinforce math skills while staying focused on the activity. I wish all games came to me this quickly. As an added bonus, later at our training, the teacher told Charlie and I that for the rest of the day many of her students continued to tip-toe quietly around the classroom being as if the game had never ended.

TWOS AND FOURS

(Outdoor play space the size of a full basketball court and played on grass is recommended. Second grade and up)

How It's Played

Among your student group, pick and create two pairs from four students. Have the students in each pair link elbows facing the same direction. When the game starts each member of the pair can use their free hand to tag others with. Each person that they tag links elbows with the student that tagged them. For safety reasons, have students face the same direction when they are linked up. When a group reaches four students linked up, that group has to split down the middle forming two separate pairs. Tagging continues until the game is over.

This is an activity that can reinforce simple concepts of division while reinforcing cooperation among pairs of children. Utilizing concepts of Creative Play, the teacher can change the game to help children learn and reinforce dividing by 3's or 4's, etc. To keep the game safe do not have linked groups go past 10 children total. The dynamics are such that the line of children can then become a "whip" and easily become out of control. Always remember to stop an activity before, or if, it becomes unsafe.

GIFT OF THE GAME

We all like the intense and highly stimulating "E" ticket rides. And, it is the same with many games that you'll share with your students. They tend to gravitate towards extremely active and thrilling ones. However, to have such activities played at an elementary school without any benefit of learning and coupled with a potential for injury makes no sense. For instance, I had always liked the thrill of the old New Games activity, BLOB. People linked up in a long line tagging others with the object of increasing the line in length with every person tagged. The end result was that the line could easily end up as a pretty effective whip if the game was not played cooperatively. If the line went too fast, people on the end often got whipped right off, falling down onto the grass. Though exciting, I have experienced it as a difficult game to initially play with elementary school students who lacked the cooperation to play it safely. BLOB is a game that we recommend working up to and only with highly cooperative children. The aggressive potential in the game of BLOB is why it is listed in the last lesson with the other Soft Aggression games, page 300. So what could I do with the forceful nature of this game? It is not always easy to maintain a high level of excitement for a game when you soften it. However, when I designed Twos and Fours I was pleased that it had an effective manner of chaining children together safely, especially those at the younger primary ages who possess less teamwork awareness. The many loud squeals of glee from all the students I've ever shared this activity with were my indication that this game was a hit. This was also a good reminder to me that not all the games I played with or created for children had to have the same level of maximum intensity to be effective. The added benefit that this game had of reinforcing math skills only added to its value.

ALL TOGETHER NOW

(3rd grade up, 6-40 players, no equipment needed, indoors or outdoors)

How It's Played

Participants are divided into three teams. Each group is given the task of developing their own "special identity" or cheer as represented by a physical movement and sound/(vocalization). The group must reach a unified decision (consensus) as to what their special movement and sound will be which will serve as their team's cheer to the other groups. Humorous sounds and movements are encouraged. It is not necessary for the sounds and movements to have any congruent connection with each other. The leader has each group demonstrate their motion and sound to the other groups. Led by the leader, the other groups then mimic the motion and sound they have just observed. The process is repeated until all the groups have shown off their special cheer and all the groups have copied them.

The activity leader praises teams "A", "B", and "C" for their unique identities but now poses the challenge that all the groups must now decide separately, and in secret, which of the three choices they think the other groups will choose to do "ALL TOGETHER NOW!" Each group huddles separately and selects one of the three options ("A", "B", or "C") that they will do. (Everyone on that team must do what their team has chosen; either their own original cheer or a new one from one of the other groups). The leader has the groups turn away from each other, jointly count to three, say the phrase "All Together Now," and then spin to face each other while demonstrating the cheer that their team chose to do. If all three teams selected the same choice then everyone has won. If the teams have chosen different cheers then they are "not together yet" and must re-caucus and try again, and again, and again until everyone does the same thing "All Together."

GIFT OF THE GAME

We love this game because the majority of people we play it with use creative play dynamics to resolve the problem of agreeing on one group solution. Usually the first couple of rounds of the game have the various teams doing the different choices which are available to choose from. Following the rules, they meet in their huddle and try to think what the other groups will try to do. Sometimes there is one group that wants to stick with their choice until the other groups do what they are doing. This could be a strategy of trying to be consistently predictable for the other teams to see. More often, there is an aspect of wanting to make the others follow their lead. This concept never impresses the other teams since the goal is cooperation and not dominance. Usually by the fifth or sixth round of the game, one of the teams decides they will combine all the dynamics of all the groups. This is the perfect use of Creative Play dynamics. Very quickly all the teams see the value of including everyone's ideas into a final solution. The game often ends by everyone doing all the possibilities. When it comes to creating a feeling of community in your class, what could be better than being open to including everyone?!

I KNOW MEDUSA

(5 - 30 players, a deck of cards)

How It's Played

The object of this "mystery" activity is for the players to discover the identity of one or more among them who are Medusas. The Medusa, or Medusas, has the power to turn other players into stone by winking at them. A deck of cards equal in number to the amount of players, including the predetermined "Medusa" cards, such as the ace of spades and/or one-eyed jacks, is needed. Each player takes one card, face down, and passes the rest to the others until all cards are handed out. No one is permitted to see another's card. The people with the identifying cards become the Medusas for that round. The players start to walk around and slowly mingle within the play area. If a Medusa winks at a player, that player counts silently to three and then becomes a frozen statue. Dramatic and humorous freezes are highly encouraged. If at anytime an UN-FROZEN player, acting as a great detective, thinks they know the identity of a Medusa they shout out, "I know Medusa!" Before they announce who they think the Medusa is, they will need another person to collaborate with who will state courageously, "Me too!" This collaboration cannot come from any frozen players. The collaborator, and not the initial accuser, announces the identity of a person who they think is a Medusa. The initial accuser will either agree or disagree with the collaborator regarding Medusa's identity. If they don't agree they announce, "I disagree" and the game continues. However, if the initial accuser agrees, two things could happen. If the accusation was an incorrect one, both the accuser and collaborator become frozen statues. But, if the accuser and collaborator were right and the identity of a Medusa has been correctly discovered, all the people frozen by that particular Medusa become unfrozen and are free to move around in the game again. Game continues until all the Medusas are discovered or if the Medusas turn everyone into frozen statues.

GIFT OF THE GAME

After a follow-up training, Don came up to us quite excited and shared that he couldn't wait to do his unit on the Greeks with his class of students. He explained how the unit talked about all the different gods and their various powers. Finally he said, "Just imagine a whole class of 30 students standing there frozen like stone. It'll be so quiet." I mean, people like this game, but usually not with this level of enthusiasm. Sure enough, about three weeks later we got an email describing how much fun the class was having playing the game. Firstly, we both love getting an email or a phone call about you using HP with your kids. Don't fret that we don't have time for such interruptions. Call us! It always makes our day. Secondly, it was a nice confirmation that changing a game to foster further academic use was a good idea.

This is another old game that has been around in several versions. The two most common names for this game were "Assassin" or "Killer." Even with our healthy beliefs about Soft Aggression games, there was no way we were going to play murder-titled games. In our first edition of Learning to Play, Playing to Learn we tried to rename the game and called it "I Seek Justice." It's a good name and conveys the message that good citizens will catch the wrong doer's of the community. But, we never heard back that anyone played the game under that title. Since Don's call, we started promoting the game for use during Greek Mythology studies and have heard of other teachers using this version of the game.

FOX IN THE MORNING, FOX AT NIGHT
(Kindergarten and older, 10 or more players, large open playing space, boundary markers)

How It's Played
The class is asked to stand shoulder to shoulder on one of the wider boundary lines of a large, playing field, which becomes the "forest." Choose one to four children to be "Foxes" and ask them to go to the middle of the forest. Tell the remaining children on the boundary line that they are bunny rabbits who want to go to the other side of the forest where a delicious carrot patch awaits them.

But, before they can cross from one side of the forest to the other, the bunnies must first ask the permission of the Foxes. They do this by chanting in unison, "FOX IN THE MORNING, FOX AT NIGHT, MAY WE RUN WITH ALL OUR MIGHT?" The Foxes have to respond with, "YES, YOU MAY AND YES, YOU MIGHT, AND IF YOU RUN IT WILL BE ALL RIGHT!" The chase is on! The bunnies must run to the other side of the forest without being tagged by a fox. Reaching the other side of the forest without being tagged means you are "safe" and can munch on some imaginary carrots. However, bunnies that were tagged are automatically turned into immovable fox-helpers. They aid the foxes by reaching out from their immovable places and attempting to gently tag remaining bunnies during subsequent rounds as the bunnies run to the opposite side of the forest after chanting and receiving permission from the foxes. The round is played until three or four bunnies are left. They could become the foxes for the next round or you can pick new foxes randomly.

We encourage you to change the dynamics of the game once it is successfully underway to keep it stimulating and to make it interesting for children who have others skills besides being able to run fast. Allow the foxes to huddle before the chanting begins and decide how they and the bunnies are to move through the forest. Instead of running, they could choose to have the whole class jump, skip, walk or sing as they move from one side to another. The foxes will also have to move in the same manners that they instruct the bunnies to move. They will cue the bunnies on how everyone must move by changing their part of the chant and filling the desired action in the blank: "YES, YOU MAY AND YES, YOU MIGHT, AND, IF YOU _____ IT WILL BE ALL RIGHT!"

THE GIFT OF THE GAME

Many teachers and school monitors have used FOX IN THE MORNING successfully during recess when there are larger numbers of children of multiple ages and fewer adults, per child, to monitor them. There is no doubt that with a larger number of players, manageability becomes more of an issue. But, there will come a time when the school is ready to share individual classroom successes of Healthy Play activities with multiple classes or even whole schools. This game lends itself to being played easily with larger numbers. Also, if the mode of movement is changed creatively and often, many children of all abilities can play without boredom setting in quickly. The chanting or singing brings to children the beauty, fun, sense of inclusion and power to be found in singing. We need to help set the foundation for the upcoming generations to join in unison with their own "Give Peace a Chance" or "We Are the World" chants and songs.

ARE YOU A GOOD LEARNER?
(Kindergarten and up, 10 or more players, an inside space, stable chairs)

How It's Played
Players arrange their chairs in a circle with about one foot of space between chairs. One person is selected to be the first leader. This player does not have a chair and moves to the middle of the circle. The leader then selects one of the players sitting in a chair and then greets him with a hand shake and the phrase, "Are you a good learner?" The person in the chair must respond (in a very loud voice so everyone can hear), "Yes, I'm a good learner, and I like PEOPLE who_____." At this point, the sitting player uses his imagination to identify some attribute that several or all of the other players sitting in the circle might have; for example, people who are wearing something green, who are wearing shorts, who brushed their teeth today or who like ice cream. Once the attribute is stated the action truly begins. All players possessing the given attribute (that is, those who are wearing green) must leave their current chair and find another place to sit, which was vacated by another person having this same attribute. Pushing or shoving are not proper behaviors for good learners, so competition to find a chair cannot be rowdy. At

the end of the chair changing, one person will be left without a chair and this person becomes the next one to start a new round by asking the question, "Are you a good learner?"

We have developed a rule that players are allowed to be in the middle only once during the game. Children will often want to be the center of attention and will play in a way that lets them to be the remaining player after chair ex-

Are you a good learner?

changes. When this happens, have the child who has set-up or inadvertently found themselves in the middle twice select another child to take their place.

THE GIFT OF THE GAME

The positive association, affirmation and actions of being a good learner are highlighted as students play this activity. It is essential that children practice announcing that they are learners. This game publicly helps children state to their peers that the concept of being a good learner is alive and well at their school. There has been a noticeable trend among some children that being educated or smart as not a "cool" thing to be. Hopefully, this announcement of being a good learner can have at least a small effect enabling those children to see that being smart is something they should aspire to be. This activity also includes everyone as equals and promotes opportunities to practice caring and sharing while they are involved in mild competition. This moderately active game is perfect for the leader to process positive behaviors in a contained setting. Everyone gets a chance to laugh, have fun and live the good values that happen when being a good learner is put into action.

Safety tip: To avoid children possibly getting shoved out of the way as they rush towards the same chair, enforce a "Chair Tapping" rule. Whoever taps or tags the chair first, with their hand, is the player who gets to sit in the chair. This rule effectively diminishes aggressive behaviors, softens the game and makes it even more enjoyable. Always use safe and sturdy chairs.

COSMIC MOTIONS

(Third grade and up although modifications can be made for younger children. 8-30 players, inside or outside space, several Palos Sports RuffSKIN™ or spongy Nerf™ balls and other objects: be creative)

How It's Played

After the big bang all the stars, planets and comets wandered the universe and our solar system without purpose. Finally, they have come to your classroom where you can put the cosmos into its proper motion. You will soon establish the orbits (repetitive patterns) of the objects that we have in our solar system. Form your students into a circle and have everyone raise one hand. Having a hand raised in the air just means that the student has not yet had the sun tossed to her and is waiting her place in the orbits of celestial objects. To start the game, the teacher calls out the name of one of the students with her hand up and gently tosses her our sun (a yellow ball). It is important that you and your students not only call out the receiving student's name but also clearly identity the object/planet/sun you are tossing. Once your name has been called off you are now permitted to keep your hands down for the remainder of the game so you can easily catch balls tossed to you. That player who has received the sun now calls out another person's name (someone who has his hand up) and throws the ball to him. Hand raises are just used at the beginning of the game to establish a constant pattern of who will toss to whom. Remind children that they must always remember who they threw the ball to because that becomes the permanent order and identifies the person that they will always throw to. Have students continue throwing the sun (the yellow ball) until everyone has caught the ball from someone. When the last person catches the ball, the teacher now raises her hand and the ball is tossed to her completing the orbit. She then tosses the ball repeating the previous pattern. Practice the tossing order at least one more time making sure all students throw to the same person they threw the ball to the first time. Remind them to always call out people's names and then identify the name of the celestial object they have in their hands before throwing to the subsequent student.

Now you're ready to add a planet (a different colored ball). Start the sun (the ball from the first round) going around the circle. After it made two or three orbits, add the planet. If that planet's orbit goes well, feel free to add another planet. Now try something different by adding a comet. The comet (often a Frisbee™) gets handed around the circle from one player to another in a clockwise direction. Now add a moon. It gets passed around the circle in a counter-clockwise direction.

Black hole! Take a brief pause from passing the star, planets, comet and moon around the circle and identify your black hole (a distinctly different ball). The black hole gets passed in reverse order around the circle. Reverse order is when players toss the black hole to the person that they received all the other stars and planets from. Practice this reverse direction at least once to make sure everyone knows where to toss the black hole. Now put all the other objects back in motion.

Hint: It really helps to call out the name and establish eye contact with the person to whom you are throwing the ball, so they are ready to catch it.

Special rule: If planets collide, don't worry because your group belongs to a "no-fault solar system." No child has to run into the center of the circle to retrieve their ball where they might be bom-

Cosmic motions

barded by a planet if a ball goes out-of-orbit. (Remember this is a game of COSMIC MOTIONS and not Dodge Ball.) As an out-of-orbit ball gently rolls to any individual in the circle, they'll just pick it up and simply put it back into motion by throwing them to the person they normally throw to. When a wayward planet is accidentally tossed to the wrong person, just have that person place the planet back into orbit by tossing it to who they usually toss to. Try bouncing or rolling one or more of the objects.

THE GIFT OF THE GAME

Mastery over skills, especially seemingly difficult ones, such as juggling, is a sure way of increasing anyone's self-esteem. To perform this activity, cooperation must be nurtured and self-control maintained. If your group is only able to juggle one or two COSMIC MOTIONS item(s) the first time they attempt it, consider that successful. The children will enjoy greater success each time they play this game. Additionally, this game emphasizes and promotes levels of cooperation of your group. But, there is more that can be gleaned from this activity. Children can have their academics reinforced kinetically through COSMIC MOTIONS by juggling the celestial bodies of the solar system, the names of presidents, the names of continents and more. We even know of a massage school that has modified this activity to help their students remember origin and insertion of muscle groups.

Charlie and I have always enjoyed this game because it provides name recognition. We encourage any game which has this attribute for the following reason. As we travel around the country conducting our program at multiple schools we've noticed a disturbing phenomenon. We could go into classrooms months after the beginning of school and there frequently were children that didn't know the names of many of their fellow classmates. Our observation was that if a student is that invisible they often feel alienated from their peer group. Feelings of alienation are not only socially debilitating but also weaken academic competence.

We learned of an extremely creative way that a fifth grade teacher in Moreno Valley, CA uses this game. She informs her class that anytime throughout the school year when they get a new student they will play the game of Cosmic Motions within 15 minutes of that new student's arrival. Can you just image what happens when some anxious new student who has been uprooted from her old hometown enters this classroom in the middle of the semester? She is enthusiastically greeted with many welcomes from happy potential friends who are absolutely delighted that she has just shown up because it means they get to play a game. They bound quickly and within mere minutes she is learning many of her classmates' names and they hers.

SILENT BALL

(All grades, any number of players, one ball or more if desired, indoor or outdoor area. Obviously, a quiet activity)

How It's Played

Usually, we don't like "elimination-type" activities, but the multiple values found within this game makes it such an overwhelmingly successful experience that we had to include it. It helps students solve problems, learn patience and self-control. Additionally, we were able to come up with an idea that eliminated the elimination. (See below)

Make sure you explain all the rules clearly and answer everyone's questions before you begin a round of SILENT BALL. Start with all the players standing in a circle. Have everyone count down: 3, 2, 1, 0. Once you reach zero nobody (teacher included) is allowed to talk at all...not a peep! Play begins by throwing the ball to any player you wish. If the throw was good and the catch was good, then play continues. There are three ways to have someone's role change from being an active "ball-tosser" to becoming a non-tossing "sitter" in SILENT BALL. The first way is when the throw is inaccurate or too hard or when it involves some other factor that the group decides is a throwing error. The player who makes a throwing error must sit down where they were standing. The second way to change from a tossing to a non-tossing role is when the person who was thrown a perfectly catchable ball drops it. In this case, the player trying to catch the ball must sit down. The third way is whenever players speak out loud, laugh or make sounds, they too must sit down. This even occurs when someone wants to ask a question or get a clarification. If you break "silence," you must sit down. Players who end up sitting down must remain silent and cannot catch the ball.

As expected, there are many times when a judgment by the group is required to indicate if the thrower or the catcher has made the error. A silent consensus process must be used to work out this problem. Some groups point elbows at the person they think made the blooper. Majority rules. Be creative with your judgment technique. Players who are now sitting are still eligible to participate in this judging part of the game as long as they remain silent.

Since this game does remove players from part of the action, it is very important to keep the play moving. Make throws and catches progressively faster or more challenging, so the children make more blunders. Add another ball, have them stand on one leg or catch with only one arm to make it even more difficult. We recommend playing until no less than five or six players are left. Multiple winners create a greater positive reward for the group. Clarify any rules between games and re-start the activity with everyone. One possibility is that sitting players who talked can be briefly timed-out from the next game to help them recognize their need to control their behavior and play fair. After the games are over, you might want to process any frustration the children experienced.

As we mentioned earlier we came up with a solution to the elimination factor. Instead of having students sit when they committed a tossing or catching error, have them walk one brief lap around the outside of the circle. When they return to their original place they can once again become active players in the game. We suggest that you bring the two non-throwing options up to a vote by your students. We have never ever experienced adults or students that voted to sit down. They will always vote for the short lap and quick return to the game. Voting will also help students own the rules of the game.

THE GIFT OF THE GAME

For years, SILENT BALL has been used by teachers as a diversionary activity on rainy days. But, this game can be so much more. What has been exciting for us to see is the transformation in thinking when teachers realize that games are potential classroom management tools. The quiet calming effect of SILENT BALL can be used therapeutically at any time on any day. Teachers are now playing a single round of the game before reading or when the class returns from recess when the kids need to settle down and control their behaviors. Instead of trying to bribe the class with, "If you're quiet for the next four hours, we'll get to play a game of

Silent Ball," we now see teachers assessing the temperament of the class and using an activity like SILENT BALL to quickly achieve positive behaviors. The power struggle to gain control of the class has been replaced with FUN, and the class can then move forward to the next academic task.

OVER, UNDER & AROUND KICKBALL

(Third grade and older, six or more players, large outside playing space, a soft Palos Sports RuffSkin™ or NERF™ soccer ball)

How It's Played

There may not be a better game invented for total team-work than this one. Begin by setting up a long, straight, boundary line. Divide students into two teams using the double-divide method. Have one team scatter themselves across the playing field. The other team will form a straight line about three feet back from and parallel to the boundary line. The first person in line gets to kick first and that player's original partner (from the double divide), who is now on the other team, gets to be their personal pitcher. After the pitch, the kicker may kick the ball anywhere in front of the boundary line. At this point, the real action starts.

The team in the field (the whole team) scurries over to the location where the ball was kicked. The objective at this point is to form a single file line and have the first person in line pass the ball OVER his head to the next player, who passes it UNDER his legs to the third, who passes it OVER her head, then UNDER, and so forth, until everyone on the team has touched the ball in this sequential pattern. Any errors in the OVER-UNDER sequence must be corrected before the ball gets passed any further. When the last player receives the ball, the team in the field yells, "Stop."

While all this commotion is happening in the outfield, the kicker is busy trying to score runs by running circles AROUND her team of players who are standing in line. (The first few times you play this game you might find a few players running off in a traditional Kickball manner around nonexistent bases. Utilize a gentle sense of humor as you remind them that they are to run around their team and not bases.) The "at-bat" team chants the score each time the player finishes running AROUND the whole team. When the other team yells "Stop," the player running AROUND her team is finished and goes to the end of their line. The next player is now up, and their double-divide partner is the new pitcher. In OVER, UNDER & AROUND KICKBALL there are no outs of any kind. Balls kicked behind the boundary line are simply replayed. An inning is defined by everyone getting a chance to kick. Teams then switch places, and partners pitch to the player who pitched to them. We've generally found it best to begin by keeping only individual scores. If your class can handle team score-keeping, then you can add up everyone's runs, or use the single-digit scoring method.

THE GIFT OF THE GAME

We were playing a traditional Kickball game with a group of fifth graders when a typical problem came up. Three players on one team kept hogging the ball and all the plays. Several kids started to look disgruntled so we brought the game to a halt, sat down and talked. Quickly, several students said they didn't like being left out of the game. Aha, the game wasn't fun. We had come to one of the golden rules of play and decided to see if we could make things better. The class processed their difficulties and frustrations and made a rule that you couldn't run more than four steps with the ball before you had to throw it to someone else. This worked well and the teacher praised them for solving their problem. The students learned a strong lesson in cooperation. However, feeling her class would benefit from additional practice regarding teamwork-oriented skills on the following day she suggested trying another Kickball game: OVER, UNDER & AROUND KICKBALL. The next day they did and it solved all those feelings of being left out of the action. The kids bubbled as they shared praise for their new found teamwork and strategies. Each child felt as they were a part of the game. They made connections between this new game and how they tried to improve the game they played the day before. Her students were excited knowing that they had learned a new Kickball game which was so inclusive.

HILLBILLY TAG

(All grades, ten or more players, identifying markers, large playing space)

How It's Played

Set up boundaries. Choose several players to be it (one for every six to eight players with a minimum of two its), and give each of them an identifying marker. In this tag game you can choose to run around trying to avoid being tagged or to link up with another player to be safe. Linking up is done only in groups of two by interlocking arms at the elbow with the players facing in the *opposite* direction (the classic swing-your-partner square-dance move). When two players are linked up, they are safe from being tagged by one of the its. Since players who are linked up each have an available arm, a third person can join on one of the open sides. But when he does, the player on the opposite side must unlink. Players can also choose to unlink at any time.

The its try to tag players when they are not linked up. When a player is tagged, he becomes it, and the identifying marker is passed to him by the previous it. This game has lots of potential for creating new rules and again is an excellent source for giving positive praise to everyone.

THE GIFT OF THE GAME

This is probably Snoopy's favorite game because it's like dancing. The simple action of the swing-your-partner moves makes everyone laugh and feel good. The real gift, however, comes from using this activity to promote safe physical contact between peers. Hillbilly tag is a step beyond hand holding and the logical step before hugging, which is done in safety haven and detectives. The fast-paced action of having multiple players who are it forces the remaining students to seek refuge with anyone who is close enough to link up. Again, in this game, children practice saving and helping each other, which is far more useful than elimination or intimidation.

Schools can use this activity to mix classes together without the negative effects of pitting one class against another competitively. When your goal is to make your whole school a peaceful community, you must put your words into concrete actions that the children can perform. Let their creative spirits soar while they dance and play tag.

PSYCHIC NUMBERS
(First grade and older, any number of kids, anywhere, no equipment)

How It's Played
Divide the students into groups of three or four. Have the group choose a psychic number from one to fourteen. (Let's say they picked nine.) Each player uses one hand and the group counts, "One, two, three." Upon saying, "three," each person displays from zero to five fingers. The group counts up the total number of fingers shown and sees if they totalled their psychic number. Once accomplished, they choose a new number. The group can use both hands and try for larger psychic numbers. Another version is for one player to secretly think of the psychic number and only tell the group whether their total is higher or lower than the desired amount. After three attempts using their fingers, players try to guess what the psychic number is.

THE GIFT OF THE GAME
Teachers often request activities children can do in small groups. They also need short activities to help kids stop fidgeting behaviors when they're standing in lines or waiting between other activities. Psychic numbers is such an activity, and it reinforces addition, subtraction, and multiplication skills.

One principal showed us her lunch line of children who were all playing psychic numbers. She said, "Last week, before our school's Healthy Play training, our lunch line was disruptive with children hitting and teasing each other. Today, with minimal encouragement from our monitor to play psychic numbers, there is laughter and learning.

"When we first planned to use psychic numbers as a lesson, it took three times longer than we thought it would. At first, the students didn't understand how to make their numbers, and it seemed like a real mess. But after demonstrating by writing the numbers on the board, sure enough, someone in each group caught on. Things went like wildfire as the students took over and patiently explained how to play the game with each other."

Teachers often state, "We play psychic numbers almost every day. It's so great when students do the teaching and the learning, and it carries over to their other math work in class." Aren't the minds of human computers really amazing?

MICROWAVE POPCORN

(Kindergarten and first grade, any number of players, indoors, imagination)

How It's Played

Have children sit on the floor on their bottoms. Start the game by pretending you are going to make popcorn. Have the children pretend to go to the pantry by opening an imaginary door and looking inside at what's there. One person might see a box of cereal. "That might taste good, but it's not what we're after," you say. Another might see a jar of peanut butter. "I like peanut butter, but we'll put that back for now." Finally, you spot the popcorn. You pick it up and pretend to put it in your microwave oven. Have everyone set the timer and push the start button. At this point, everyone becomes a kernel of popcorn ready to be cooked. Have them start by wiggling a little bit as they pretend to get warmer. Then wiggle faster. Wipe their foreheads because they're really getting hot. Fan off their brother and sister popcorn kernels. Begin to sizzle as they rock back and forth even faster. It's time to pop! Stand up and start jumping up and down while saying, "Pop, pop, pop!"

For even more fun, try making caramel popcorn by pretending to pour caramel over the popping corn, and when one person touches another, the two stick together by holding hands and so on until the whole class has made a giant caramel popcorn ball. After the game I always like to pretend to eat some of my microwave popcorn.

THE GIFT OF THE GAME

This version of Terry Orlick's Sticky Popcorn is a delight for the players. In all imagination games everyone is equal. Imagination, or "pretend," games hone creativity and camaraderie. Pretending to retrieve items from the pantry or from a refrigerator keeps the kids attentive and focused.

Microwave popcorn is another creative game that aids in crowd control. Children need to learn how to become excited without hurting each other. When standing up and sitting down on the floor, many young children often step or sit on other children. They need to become aware of their physical space and boundaries. Learning how to "pop" together without hurting another child during the caramel pouring is valuable. You may want to model how to "stick," jump, and sit down together with one of the children prior to the game. Also, we encourage you to have the children successfully practice this skill before playing subsequent rounds of microwave popcorn.

ROLLING LOGS

(Kindergarten to second grade [older people like it too], two or more players, soft playing surface, no equipment)

How It's Played

This activity is based on Terry Orlick's Log-roll game. Pair children up and have them lie on their backs on the ground. Their feet should touch each other so that they look like one long log. The idea is to roll over in unison, so their feet don't come apart. Now try two, three, four rolls. Change partners often and repeat log rolling. Next try touching hands and rolling. Ready to make it more fun? Try crossing legs or arms. Now make bigger and bigger giant redwoods by having two players touch at the feet and another player touch at the hands. Build the numbers up until the whole class is attached. Give lots of praise to the children working together.

THE GIFT OF THE GAME

It was a wonderful spring day when I accompanied a third-grade class out to the field, intending to play deep-sea diver and giants, elves, and wizards. It was pleasantly quiet as we walked out in a nice, orderly line. All of a sudden, four or five kids sprinted forward and began rolling in the grass. Quickly the whole class followed, and so did I. Kids really respect you when you join them in what they are doing. We continued this unstructured fun for a good while, and then I changed my agenda and taught rolling logs with incredible success.

Excitement and boundless energy are part of children's lives. I felt blessed that I was able to suppress my adult urge to demand control and allow these students the freedom to express themselves in an unpredictable but appropriate manner. It also felt good to have developed a wide repertoire of activities over the years so that I could playfully restructure the children's energies into an enjoyable team-building experience.

SPOONS

(All ages, six to ten players per deck of cards, indoors at tables or on the floor, playing cards, some spoons or similar safe objects)

Hint: Many games with cards do not need to have complete decks. If you've caught the feeling of why we play (to have fun!), then it doesn't matter if you're missing some cards. The game will still feel fair to everyone, and you won't have to compulsively count decks all the time. This also saves on expenses.

How It's Played

Up to ten players seat themselves in a circle or oblong shape. Spoons are placed in the middle and spread out so that everyone can reach them equally. There will be one or two fewer spoons than the number of people playing the game. Three cards are dealt to every player, and the remainder of the deck(s) stay with the dealer. After everyone has been dealt his cards, all players may look at their cards. The object of the game is to get three of a kind— that is, three kings, three sixes, three twos, and so on. Play begins with the dealer looking as rapidly as possible, one by one, at the cards remaining in the deck. If the dealer wants a new card from that deck, he or she just keeps it and discards another card from his or her hand, placing it facedown in front of the next player. If the dealer doesn't want the card, it is passed face down to the next player. (Each person can only hold three cards in his hand at a time.) Successive players look at the cards now being passed around the table, one at a time, and decide whether to keep them

Spoons

or pass them on. Eventually, someone will get three of a kind. At this point, they have permission to take the first spoon. This should be done as sneakily as possible, because if any other player sees a spoon being removed, she can quickly grab one, too. Once one player with three of a kind takes a spoon, then everyone else is allowed to take a spoon, regardless of the cards they hold. Eventually, all the spoons are taken, and one or more players are left without spoons. (We suggest having two or more spoons missing, as it shares the impact of not getting a spoon among multiple players.) These people are given an imaginary letter from the group, beginning with the letter S. If they eventually collect enough letters to spell out "spoon-sized-frosted-fruity-shredded-total-mini-wheats," they are eliminated from the game. (If this ever does happen, you've probably been enjoying this game far too much for any one day.)

THE GIFT OF THE GAME

This is one of the all-time great social games. It focuses on taking turns, being patient, being hurried, being confused, developing strategies to get the people with the fewest letters, and laughing. It offers a lot of room to make special rules. A favorite incident of mine occurred when two players simultaneously grabbed the same spoon and hung on tightly. With their hands in midair above the table, one of the other players wondered aloud who was going to get stuck with the letter. Without a moment's hesitation this girl (who will probably become a very successful lawyer) said, "Oh, he gets the letter. I'm holding the spoon part, and he's only holding the handle." Even he couldn't question this logic and accepted his letter without further argument. This is what we love about using a variety of games, which highlight different people's talents.

BITE THE BAG

(Any age, two or more players, indoors, one tall paper bag for each group of six players)

How It's Played

The name of the game says it all. All you have to do is bite the bag. Ooohhh, gross! The object of this game is to stand on one foot, bend over, bite a grocery bag, and pick it up off the ground. Allow players as many chances as they want. Failure is frequent, but innovation is incredible as people contort themselves into bizarre poses as they try to defeat the bag. Once everyone has tried to bite the bag, the next step is to rip about three inches off the bag and start the process again. Keep making the bag shorter and shorter until no one can pick it up.

Hints: The reason we suggest so many bags is so that players do not have to bite an area where someone else has bitten. Also, as the bag gets shorter, you may want to station yourself as a spotter to help overenthusiastic players from nose-diving into the ground. Always remind players that the bag is worth about a penny, but the dental work if they crash on the ground is likely to cost hundreds of dollars.

THE GIFT OF THE GAME

One of the things that we like most about this game is that it favors shorter and more flexible people. The overwhelming lesson from such a funny game is to reveal that all games are this silly. Basketball, baseball, football are really no more important than bite the bag. We are constantly amazed at the ingenuity of players who try their hardest to move on to the next lower level. This is another game where players can make up as many rules as they want. It's their game.

RANDOM NUMBERS

(Second grade and older, any number of players, indoors, a deck of cards *without the tens, kings, queens, or jacks*)

How It's Played

Students are each given four cards, and the leader selects two. Each card represents a digit in a two-digit number. Aces are equal to 1. For example, one player receives a 1, 3, 5, and 9. The leader, either a student or the teacher, has a 7 and a 4. The leader chooses the random number of 74. (You could have chosen 47 instead.) The player must now arrange her cards face up in any order to make two, two-digit numbers. The player adds these numbers together to come as close as possible to the random number. The first player could make 95 plus 31 for a total of 126. Not very close. Try 59 plus 31. That's 90, which is better. Try 19 plus 35, which totals 54. That's too low. Finally try 59 plus 13. This places her close, at 72.

Every student tries to come as close as possible to the leader's random number and is allowed to check her answer with her peers. Redeal the cards and select a new target number. Once the addition of random numbers is mastered, you can play the same game doing subtraction. Math is fun.

THE GIFT OF THE GAME

One of the more exciting things for us is to return to a school where teachers have been using creative-play dynamics and find that the teachers want to teach us new activities that they have discovered or created. Random numbers was one such game. It's especially satisfying to see many teachers feeling so empowered that they search for useful academic games and then share them with their faculty peers. This exchange of games also adds wonderful spontaneity to our trainings while we and our participants gain new knowledge, which we can then pass on to others. To paraphrase some ideas from Arlo Guthrie, "Can you imagine hundreds of teachers playing games with their students every day? Why, they might think it's a movement." And, that's just what it is. Everyone has something to share.

PENGUIN WALK

(Kindergarten and first grade, any number, indoors and/or outdoors, no equipment)

How It's Played

Young children adore this simple follow-the-leader activity. Have the children form a line with one child directly behind another. Inform the kids that we are all going to become penguins and go for a walk. Choose one child to demonstrate to the others how a penguin looks. That children will role-play the classic penguin look and movement: Arms held stiffly at their sides with hands pointed out at ninety-degree angles. The movement is a slow, gentle waddle. Also, point out that penguins make no sounds. You now find yourself in possession of a controlled line of happy penguin children that you can quietly take anywhere.

THE GIFT OF THE GAME

Accompanied by our good friend Yosi Prince from the Ministry of Education in Israel, we arrived for our initial visit to a first-grade class at Lynn-Urquedes Elementary School. We were greeted by the teacher, who said that her class couldn't stay in line together without yelling, touching, or hitting each other, let alone play outside without aggressively invading each other's boundaries. Yosi had seen us in action implementing our activities with various classes but was curious how we would be able to address a class that couldn't even form a manageable line. Setting up the class for the penguin walk turned the process of lining up into an act of enjoyment instead of intimidation. Having to keep their hands by their sides and off each other and having to keep their mouths closed created a playful atmosphere. The teacher praised the class for their new ability to form and walk in a line. The children, even at this young age, experienced a successful group activity with little redirection from the adults. This spirit of cooperation carried over to more challenging games, which also were successful.

Hint: If the children are quiet and in line but still want to bump into each other, just remind them that "Penguins just don't bump into each other." It is our experience that children want to be mindful penguins. We've gone to schools and seen multiple penguin lines, and it is such a joy to see the children enjoying even the most mundane experience of walking through a hallway quietly.

FRIENDSHIP FREEZE

(Kindergarten through second grade, any number of players, indoor or outdoor space with room for the players, no equipment)

How It's Played

Popular in the primary grades, this activity helps make everyone feel special, and it provides a safe way to learn and practice appropriate touching. Children are asked to form the famous Creative Spirit "clump" by standing *loosely* together while still a group. You instruct the group that whoever can answer yes to your questions or statements is to raise his hand. The children who do not answer yes must find a child with his hand raised and gently hug him. Once they are hugging a friend, they remain frozen in that hug until the next question is asked. You should allow two children, one who is willing to hug and another who will be comfortable being hugged, to demonstrate to the whole class what a healthy, friendly hug looks like. The questions or comments should celebrate the ordinary things about being a human being, such as: "Raise your hand if you have an older sister. Raise your hand if you did your homework last night" or have a puppy, or like vegetables, or have smiled today, and so on.

THE GIFT OF THE GAME

This game works on multiple levels. Young people need to learn what appropriate touching looks and feels like. They must learn that there is a vast and wonderful area of touching between erotic and violent touch, both of which are too often presented by the media as the only types of touching in our society. This activity is a wonderful tool for teaching those lessons. With this game, children find themselves easily mixing with their classmates while learning all the things they share in common. They can celebrate being special in being ordinary. Teachers may choose, from time to time, to highlight situations that may make some children feel different or uncomfortable. This can help them to get beyond feeling stigmatized. For instance, you might ask children who have a stepparent to raise their hands and receive hugs. Often they see they are not the only ones with this family dynamic, and they get rewarded for just being who they are. Remember we cannot give just lip service to the statement "People are what is most important." We must show that we celebrate all people for all that they are.

GUESS WHAT WE ARE
(Primary grades, four or more players, inside or outdoor playing field, cones or dividers)

How It's Played
Divide the class into two teams, and place the teams on opposite sides of a playing area. One team jointly agrees on an animal, a person, or a thing that they want to be. They will soon present their new role to the other team. Once a decision has been made, the whole team must move toward the other team, playacting the thing that they have chosen. The other team shouts out loud what they think the opposing team is. When the players meet, the second team greets the first with an identifying handshake or pat. Teams switch roles for the next round. For example, team A decides that they want to be lions, so they crawl on all fours while mimicking roars. Team B shouts out their guesses, and when team A finally reaches team B at the dividing line, they extend their hands and greet the lions of team A, "Hello, Mr. [or Ms.] Lion. Glad to meet you." Team B now must choose an animal, a person, or a thing and present it to team A.

THE GIFT OF THE GAME
The game of guess what we are provides hours of enjoyment when we play it with young children. We've also found that it is especially effective in classes where children have multiple challenges

(handicaps). For children with limited cognitive and verbal skills or limited mobility, many games can be difficult. This advanced version of Terry Orlick's delightful unknown animals gives challenged children a game that meets their needs to have fun and be accepted. All children, regardless of ability, can either imitate or identify puppies, kittens, snakes, thunder, waterfalls, and more at their own communication level. This activity is also a fun way to mobilize fine and larger muscle control, and it can be worked into a physical-therapy routine.

ENDSWITH

(Grade three and up. An Atlas, pencil and paper)

How It's Played

This is a wonderful game to help students practice their knowledge of geography. ENDSWITH can be played by an individual, in groups of two to five playing separately in class or even as a whole class in a team format. The game can be played with participants having access to maps and books or can evolve into a game played via players' memory without aids.

Begin by determining the geographical boundaries for the game. It could be the whole planet earth, a specific country, continent, state or even the universe. (This flexibility allows the teacher to make the activity meaningful to the content being taught in their class). Decide what geographical locations will be acceptable answers in the game, i.e. continents, oceans, rivers, mountains, countries, states, cities, national parks, etc. Now identify the first location to start the game and you're ready to play.

The last letter (what it ends with) of a location determines the sequence of the game. If the game started with TucsoN the next location must start with the letter N because T-u-c-s-o-N endswith the letter N. The next place might be NebraskA which endswith an A. The following location must start with the letter A and could be AlbuquerquE. Now you need to think of something that begins with an E and so on. Once a place has been named it cannot be used again in that game by that individual or team.

Scoring options:

To make the activity more exciting, especially when playing as teams in your class, you might want to have the following scoring options:

The simplest method is to give one point for each place identified by a team or individual.

A more advanced option awards one point for each place that starts with the letter A.

Every place that begins with any other letter; B, C, D, E, etc. through Z is worth five points. Every place NOT used by any other team is worth three bonus points each. (Hint: keep the time of the game very short if you are comparing lists to find unique places NOT used by other teams.)

Examples of what the game might look like:

You've divided your class into four teams. The geographical boundaries are the whole planet. Any location listed on the map is an acceptable answer. It's an open map game. The starting place that all teams will use is TucsoN. The time for the game will be three minutes. Each team will make a written list of their places. Spelling must be correct for any place to count towards their score. At the end of the three minute time limit the game is stopped. All teams simultaneously send one member to the board to write their ENDSWITH list down for everyone to see. The lists are then scored for the 1 point "A" words and 5 points for any other letter words. Lists are compared and 3 point bonuses are given to places NOT used by any other team.

GIFT OF THE GAME

Endswith is an old game called "Geography" I first played when I was in fifth or sixth grade. I must admit, my friends and I got pretty competitive playing this game trying to know the most places so we could outlast each other. We developed all sorts of strategies for making things difficult for our opponents like making as many answers as possible end with an "A." This was countered by learning at least a hundred places that started with "A." Then it moved on to finding places that ended with "X." Phoenix was a good start, followed by Appomattox, Essex, Saint Croix, Bordeaux, Dreux and Robaix. You get the picture, study France. This was countered by learning places mostly in China and Mexico that started with "X." What I recognize now is how much learning I did while having fun. It wasn't even part of school time. Play and learning were part of any long drive in the car or a boring rainy day. Endswith makes world geography fun to learn. If they didn't keep changing all the countries names I'd probably still know all of them.

"42"
(Decks of cards for each grouping of students)

How It's Played
We invented this game for making math practice more fun! This game is slightly more difficult than one of our other favorite math games, "99," in that there are multiple calculations to do with each card drawn. However, students will increase addition and subtraction skills while finding learning enjoyable.

Before play begins remove any jokers from the deck. The game can be played with two to six players in a group either sitting at desks or on the floor. You do not need a full deck of cards and/or you can have more than one deck. We also recommend while initially learning any card game that everyone shows their cards face up for the first couple of hands. This will make it easier for you, the teacher, to walk around to several groups, see how they are doing and answer questions quickly. Additionally, the more resourceful students in the groups can cooperatively mentor and help each other learn the game. Once the group masters the game they play with their card values hidden from other players.

Card values are:

Ace = 1

2, 3, 4, 5, 6, 7, 8, 9, 10 = 2, 3, 4, 5, 6, 7, 8, 9, 10, (the values plainly stated on the cards).

Face cards (King, Queen and Jacks) = 10

The goal of the game is to collect exactly "42" points with the cards in your hand.

A dealer is selected and the cards are mixed up. The dealer then deals five cards to each player and places the remainder of the cards in the middle as the draw pile. Each player looks at all five cards and adds up the points in their hand.

Example:

Juan has a 2, 5, 7, 8, and queen for a total of 32 points.

Ashley has an ace, 3, 5, 9 and a jack for a total of 28 points.

Susan has a 2, 4, 10, queen, king for a total of 36 points.

Jason has an 8, 8, jack, queen, and a king for a total of 46 points

Play starts with the person to the left of the dealer and moves in a clockwise direction. Since Juan dealt, Ashley is first. She draws the top card from the draw pile and looks at it (it's a king and worth 10 points). Since she only has 28 points she decides to keep the king and chooses to discard her ace. Now she has a 3, 5, 9, jack, king for a total of 37 points.

Important: players may only hold on to five cards in their hand so must always discard a card for every card they choose to keep.

Susan now draws a 5 and discards the 2. Her new hand is 4, 5, 10, queen, king for a total of 39 points. Jason draws a 9 and discards a jack. His new hand is 8, 8, 9, queen, king so his total is now 45. Juan picks up a 7 and discards the 2. His new hand is 5, 7, 7, 8, queen for a new total of 37. It's Ashley's turn again and she picks up an ace. This doesn't really help her so she discards the ace and her score will remain at 37 points. Jason draws a 6. If he calculates correctly (8, 8, 9, queen, king) and discards the 9 giving him the following value: (6, 8, 8, queen, and king) his score will be "42". If he discards one of his 8's (6, 8, 9, queen, king) his total will be 43. If he discarded the queen or king his total would be (6, 8, 8, 9, king) 41. However, since he chose correctly he wins the hand and becomes the "42 Mentor". As the "Mentor" he can help any or all players desiring advice on adding or subtracting their card totals.

Play continues until a second player reaches "42". This ends the hand and the player to the left of the previous dealer becomes the new dealer and play starts again. If all of the cards in the draw pile are used, shuffle the discard pile up and use these cards to create a new draw card pile. It is perfectly fine for players to use pencil and paper to add and subtract their scores. The eventual goal is for all students to be able to figure out their scores in their head. Since the purpose of the game is to practice math, we discourage students using calculators. The one exception to using calculators is when the class is studying the use of the abacus. This would be a perfect game to practice calculating on an abacus!

GIFT OF THE GAME

This is just one of those silly moments where as the inventor of the game you get to share a little of your personality. Hypothetically, I could have picked any number for the total a player needed to win the game. I avoided 21 on purpose so kids wouldn't go home and said they played "Black Jack" at school. Otherwise, any number could have been chosen. But, for those of you who have read The Hitch Hikers Guide to the Galaxy you know I could only pick "42." This number is the final result of the eon's long experiment done by the mice to answer the question to "the meaning of life and everything." Yep, it's 42. What a perfect opportunity this game gave me to share this knowledge with those that didn't know that answer. Over the years it has been fun for me to find a student or teacher who knew this piece of literary trivia. It gives us a special little bond with each other and a chance to explain this fact to everyone else in the group. Okay, you probably weren't impressed with this fact, but then, you probably didn't read the book.

DIVIDE AND CONQUER
(Deck of cards for each group of students playing)

How It's Played
Divide and Conquer is another perfect way to allow students to practice math skills while having fun! Before play begins, remove any jokers and picture cards (kings, queens and jacks) from the deck. The game can be played with two to six players in a group either sitting at a table or on the floor. Like most of our card games, you do not need a full deck of cards or you can have more than one deck. Have all players initially show their cards face up. This way all the players in a group can help each other learn the game co-operatively. Having everyone in your class show cards face up also makes it easier for you to walk around to several groups and see how they are doing. Once the group has mastered the game they can play with their cards hidden from the other players.

Card values are:
Ace = 1

2, 3, 4, 5, 6, 7, 8, 9, 10 equal 2, 3, 4, 5, 6, 7, 8, 9, 10 respectively as shown on the cards

The goal of the game is to eliminate all the cards from your hand by finding cards that divide into each other without any remainder. A dealer is selected and the cards are mixed up. The dealer then deals five cards to each player and places the remainder of the cards in the middle as the draw pile. Players may look at their cards but cannot make a play until it is their turn.

Example:
Jamal was dealt a 2, 5, 7, and 8. Amani was dealt an ace, 3, 5, and 9. Madison was dealt a 2, 4, 6, and 10. Daniel was dealt a 5, 6, 8, and 9.

Play starts with the person to the left of the dealer and moves in a clockwise direction. Since Jamal dealt, Amani is first. She draws the top card from the draw pile and looks at it (it's a 10). Amani now has an ace, 3, 5, 9, and 10. She checks to see if any two cards divide into each other. The ace, valued at 1, will divide into any card she has and so she will save it for another turn. Amani also has a 3, which divides into the 9, and a 5, which divides into the 10. She chooses to discard the 5 and 10 and announces "10 divided by 5 = 2." This completes her turn and leaves her with the ace, 3, and 9.

Madison now draws a 6, which gives her a 2, 4, 6, 6, and 10. She sees that the 2 will divide into the 4, 6, 6, and 10. Her 6's also divide into each other. Madison chooses to discard the two 6's and announces that "6 divided by 6 = 1." Madison is left with a 2, 4, and 10.

Daniel draws a 7, which gives him a 5, 6, 7, 8, and 9. None of his cards divide evenly into each other and he is therefore unable to discard any cards this turn.

Jamal draws an ace, which gives him an ace, 2, 5, 7 and 8. He's played Divide and Conquer before and knows how hard it is to get rid of 7's so he uses his ace to divide into the 7 for his play. Jamal announces "7 divided by 1 = 7" and he is left with a 2, 5, and 8.

Play returns to Amani who draws a 3. She now has an ace, 3, 3, and 9. Amani makes her play by saying 9 divided by 3 = 3. This leaves her with an ace and a 3.

The game continues until one of the players has divided and discarded all their cards. The first player to "divide and conquer" becomes the Mentor for any or all players in the game that would like some help. The game continues until a second player is able to divide all their cards and discard them. This ends the hand and the player to the left of the previous dealer becomes the new dealer and starts a new round. If all of the cards in the draw pile are used, shuffle the discard pile up and use these cards to create a new draw card pile.

This activity is far more intellectually active than having a computerized game keep score and totals for the players. Additionally, people-interactive card games teach patience, cooperation, mentoring, communication skills and numerous other healthy behaviors. It's essential to realize that you are not just teaching games. You are teaching many valuable and transferable social and academic skills. And most importantly, you're making school and learning fun!

GIFT OF THE GAME

We were doing a follow-up training in a Tucson school and were also showing the classes the different math games. My class had recently learned division so I choose to play Divide and Conquer with them. Some students got paper and pencil out so they could do the math work while others did not need to. Still others looked pretty confused which is to be expected when you teach a new game. The game progressed in each group and eventually someone got rid of all their cards and became the mentor. This was a wonderful moment to watch. The kindness and gentleness of the mentor was remarkable to see as he patiently helped his classmates learn the game. In another group, a girl shared her strategy on which cards to play first. Each hand demonstrated similar helpfulness by every one of the students who became mentors. I was convinced. Kids can sure make great caring one-to-one teachers with their peers. In reality, the mentoring activity was much more important than the simple division exercise this game was initially developed to accomplish. I only wish results like this showed up on standardized tests.

Modifying Favorite Traditional Games

SEVEN-BASE BASE KICK BALL

(First grade and up, fifteen to thirty-four players, outdoors, a Nerf soccer ball, seven identifying markers for bases)

How It's Played

The first alteration we suggest for traditional kick ball is to eliminate the three-out rule for each inning. This rule places too much pressure on one child to succeed or face her teammates' anger for ruining their chance to have fun. A more equitable inning is based on letting every player have a turn to kick. This could mean a team might make nine outs in a row and the other team might make nine home runs without making any outs. Once everyone on a team has had one turn to kick, their inning is over. What's really important is letting all the players get a chance to play in each inning.

The second variation is to expand the number of bases. Five, six, seven or more bases make the game much more exciting. And you can place them anywhere. You can even try making them unequal distances from each other. Another variation allows the runners to go either way around the bases. Players coming from opposite directions could both be safe on the same base. Maybe your class would prefer that players running in opposite directions can't be on the same base. Try both. The next change might be to eliminate foul balls. They are boring and slow down the fun. Besides, it's easier to get on base if the player can kick the ball anywhere. Backward kicks toward the backstop are a good way to get on base.

Some groups let players throw the ball at the base runners to put them out. A good, safe modification of this rule is to disallow any out where the throw is too hard. We also don't allow students to throw balls at a player's head or below the knees. Throwing at players' feet can make them trip and fall. Heads are vulnerable, too, so we don't count tags that hit a player's head. Safety is always paramount. Only use Nerf or other soft balls. Keep teaching that people come first in all games.

THE GIFT OF THE GAME

For older students this is *the* game that will break down the barriers and let everyone play and have fun. Their eyes will be focused intently and their mouths wide open as you shatter the written-in-stone notion that there is only one way to play kick ball. You've got to lead this discussion of rule changes to believe it! And once the doors of innovative and creative play have been opened, your class will never play the same again. This game is a must.

Seven-base kick ball also lets children realize that no one wants to be the target of a hard rubberized ball thrown aggressively. Children quickly come to appreciate the kid-friendly nature of softer spongelike balls. In fact, at some schools where we taught enthusiastic students seven-base kick ball, they wisely opted not to play it again until the school provided softer equipment. Once the softer balls were provided, teachers reported that the children played this game frequently. Children really don't want to get hurt.

BASKETBALL

(Third grade and older, four to sixteen players, basketball court)

How It's Played

We've found that those children who love basketball will practice dribbling, shooting, and other skills as often as they can. Other children become increasingly removed from this game if they aren't so committed. Often adults or their peers don't give them a chance to practice or play. A great way to get kids to share the ball is to have a bonus of fifty points if *everyone* on the team scores a basket. Soon everyone on the team will be included, and the players will develop strategies to help that person who needs ten shots to make a basket. As a consequence, this person will get better. What excitement when the team cashes in on the fifty-point bonus!

Another idea that fosters teamwork is having all players on a team take a shot before anyone else on that team can shoot a second time. This continues for the second shot, the third shot, and throughout the game. Here are some other scoring ideas. Every player on the team must touch the ball before a shot can count. Try giving points for just hitting the backboard, allowing a double score if the ball rolls around the hoop and comes out. Add your own creative changes. Another possibility is to deemphasize the dribbling rule. Encourage those who can dribble to do so. Encourage the rest of the class not to worry if some players carry the ball occasionally or all the time.

THE GIFT OF THE GAME

My men's group was celebrating a member's birthday with a picnic in the park and a game of basketball. One man brought his female significant other. Two of the men brought their young daughters. Now, my men's group is composed of your typical sensitive new-age guys, in touch with their own and others' feelings. But put a basketball in their hands, and some revert back to their traditional male conditioning. You know: Score at all costs, and competition is the name of the game. Just as in elementary school, the teams were divided into the boys versus the girls. To even out the teams, the girls' team asked me to became an honorary girl. The average height on the girl's team was about 4 feet 11 inches. The boy's team average was about 6 feet 4 inches, and they were aggressive players. It seemed likely this game would exclude or patronize the young girls. I quickly proposed that before a basket could count, the ball had to be passed and touched by all members of the team. My buddies, who were afraid of losing membership in the new-age sensitive-guys club, agreed with this idea. Automatically, the younger girls became equally important and necessary, and they were included in all plays when the girls' team got the ball. In fact, as an honorary girl (and certainly not the best-playing "girl" on my team), I also played more than I expected because of this inclusive rule. After the game, my male friends commented on how the game opened up for *all* the players and how much the youngest child's skills had improved. They saw that this benign rule change allowed that child to participate and practice and thus improve more than she would have in a traditional game of basketball. The guys still won that game, but we *all* left feeling satisfied, regardless of our gender, age, and size. We all felt exhausted but joyful at a chance to play and celebrate with our friends.

VENNIS
(Third grade or older, four to thirty-six players, a volleyball court with net)

How It's Played
One of our favorite volleyball adaptions is a game we call vennis. It's both volleyball and tennis with the major rule change being that the ball is allowed to bounce. Some groups like to allow only one bounce each time the ball comes over the net. Other groups allow one bounce between each hit. Begin by letting players practice while they learn to play more skillfully. Change the serving rules so players receive unlimited serves until they get the ball over the net. Let them serve closer to the net if that makes the game more successful and fun. Some players take a long time to learn this skill, so after three attempts, we let them throw the ball over the net. Another change is to allow more than three hits. At least once each game, every player on the team must volley the ball before hitting it over to the other team.

Scoring options can really change the game. Try playing for a cooperative score, wherein both teams try to reach a combined number of successful volleys back and forth across the net. Another idea is to score points based on the number of players who touch the ball (maximum of three) before they knock it over the net. Each time the ball comes back to your team, you must start over. In this game, either team can score, regardless of which team serves the ball. This last idea helps players focus on just playing and not getting hung up on the score. After both teams have served, have the serving players rotate to the other team. All of a sudden, fate can move you from the team that has the low score to the team that has the higher score. But watch out, because six rotations from now you'll be back on your original side. Have fun!

THE GIFT OF THE GAME
My all-time favorite game of vennis was played with some children and teenagers in the psychiatric hospital where we both

worked. It was during Christmas recess, which made hospital life even more difficult because these kids were not happily enjoying family, friends, gifts, and good food at home. At 10 A.M. we went out for the one-hour morning recreation period. One of the kids suggested that instead of allowing just one bounce between players, we should try two bounces. We also agreed to have an unlimited number of players hit the ball before knocking it over the net.

The first serve and subsequent volleying took almost three minutes to resolve the play. Players and teammates ran through the open gates of the fenced court to retrieve errant balls before they could hit twice. Balls hit over the net but out of bounds were chased down and carefully hit back to their side of the net, where they tried again. One volley must have lasted nearly ten minutes before the ball finally bounced three times. The game lasted two hours and forty-five minutes. We all gave up out of complete exhaustion and total satisfaction. The final score was 2 to 2.

THREE-BALL SOCCER
(First grade and older, the more players the better, at least three Nerf soccer balls, soccer field or large playing space)

How It's Played
Probably the best thing to do for soccer is to add more balls to the action. (Again, we recommend nice, soft sponge balls because they are so people-friendly.) Playing with three balls really increases the excitement, and if you use five, almost everyone scores a bunch of goals during the game. You'll actually have people trying to keep track of the score, but unless the game is videotaped, there is no accurate way to keep track.

Another useful addition is to have more than one goalie. Anytime a goalie gets tired of playing that position, he may choose anyone on his team to replace him. Usually, with multiple balls, people in the field get so tired they need a rest and will want to be a goalie.

Three-ball soccer

THE GIFT OF THE GAME

I had taught Mrs. Swanson's fifth-grade class three-ball soccer the week before, so this week I was planning to teach over, under, and around kick ball. To my pleasant surprise, the kids had used some of their class money to buy three Nerf soccer balls. When I arrived, the students could barely contain their excitement, as they had plotted to use their three balls and my three balls so we could play six-ball soccer. Even more enjoyable was when the teacher said to me, "Watch how they've decided to pick teams." She announced, "Find a partner who you think has similar soccer skills." Without manipulation or squabbling, the students quickly found appropriate partners. The class completed the double divide and had teams with amazingly equally skills. Kids know how to be honest about their abilities. They just don't want the consequences to be failure, humiliation, and loss of esteem.

Additional Processing Techniques:

One of the greatest sources of wisdom came to us not from any guru, teacher or book. This piece of sage advice came in the form of the common railroad-crossing sign: Stop, Look & Listen. What great advice. Stop! Take the time to notice the world around you. Stop, and truly look at what your world offers you. Listen to what it tells you. Listen to your heart and feelings. Awareness of self and others is the key to growth. If there is this much wisdom on a railroad-crossing sign, imagine the pearls of wisdom hidden within children and responsible teachers. The follow techniques are designed to help you cement positive behaviors with your group of children beyond the Nomination for Compliments taught in the earlier Time to Play section:

See, Hear and Feel:

This technique helps children become more aware of their inner feelings and asks them to identify positive things they either saw, heard or felt while playing. Children will quickly say that they heard laughter and saw everybody having fun. This is great as it publicly acknowledges the joy they've found and can achieve again. Soon they'll be able to identify more profound feelings. Verbalizing that one feels "happy" can evolve into, "I feel joyous being accepted and part of our group," or "I feel safe that our class can play together without hurting each other." It is this acknowledgment of one's feelings that creates the self-awareness that motivates behavior.

Compliment Tag:

Have you every tried to get a verbal response from your group of kids and gotten only that incredibly silent and empty void instead? Sure you have. It's so quiet that you wonder if these are the same kids who were just screaming with joy mere seconds ago. Kids clam up sometimes. But, we have an answer. Utilize the permission granted in the concepts of Creative Play and turn your processing into another game. We play "Compliment Tag" and it goes like this: I'm "it." I start by giving someone a compliment and that makes him or her "it." He or she in turn, being "it" (the leader of the current round) has to tag, figuratively or literally, another person "it" by giving them a compliment and so on. As the teacher, you may want to focus your compliment on a child who is often overlooked or for a difficult child who did well. For example:

TEACHER: "I want to compliment Jason for staying with Israel when he fell. (Everybody applauds.) That makes you it, Jason. Who are you going to tag with a compliment?"

JASON: "I want to tag Lucy with a compliment because she plays fairly. You're it Lucy." (Applause.)

LUCY: "I want to tag Skippy with a compliment. He was able to play two out of our three games. He is really trying hard to play without hurting anyone." (Applause.)

SKIPPY: "I want to tag Jeremy with a compliment because he is my friend and reminded me that I was tagging too hard." (Applause.)

Why IS Play Valuable and Necessary in School?:

I tend to utilize this processing technique for use in grades four on up when I want the older students to begin taking responsibility for their behaviors and also define for themselves why play is not only enjoyable for them but how it will help them socially and with their academics. When children can clearly see the connections between the game activities and their well-being along with academic performance the teacher has facilitated successful learning opportunities. They will concretely, linearly and possibly abstractly start to see how positive behaviors become self and group motivating filled with rewards both personal and productive.

Creative Play Summary

Creative Play is the first of three game dynamics that will allow you to utilize play more effectively in your daily curriculum. It provides a freedom to change any game, at any time, to meet the learning and social skill needs of your students. The wonderful thing about Creative Play is that it will remind you often that you get to be a creative and innovative person. Working with children requires a sense of fluidity to respond to the ever changing needs of your students. You are blessed not having to work with static widgets and instead have surrounded yourself with amazing evolving beings filled with potential, life and a high capacity for joy.

Being creative in play is relatively simple because play is relatively simple. There are only six game types in the world and all games are just variations of those few types. The HP philosophy and rules will keep you focused upon the right direction when utilizing play and the situations of your students will gift you with many opportunities to flex your creativity.

Creativity allows you to make activities better so they have significance at school. Keeping safety a number one priority is probably the most primary thing you can do to make any game better. Changing aspects of the game to include everyone only further enhances a game's worth. You can have multiple "Its," reward teamwork with bonuses, add more balls and/or bases and allow everyone to offer ideas to foster a very inclusive effect. Experimenting and changing the size of the playing field or the speed of the game will grant freedom to meet specific needs. Eliminating scoring problems also has a powerful influence on making games more student-friendly.

Being open to creative processing techniques will only enhance all possible gains available. In fact, the after-games processing is essential in increasing and cementing positive behaviors. Without processing, you will not garner the full benefits of the Healthy Play program. Without processing, you will not give students a chance to easily wind down and they might return far too stimulated to the classroom making learning difficult. The strength in processing is providing an opportunity to utilize positive actions as a chance for praise and appreciations. We encourage teachers, counselors, after-school and Park and Recreation staff to always reserve four to ten minutes after activities for processing to transform these "really cool" games into true tools of behavior reinforcement and consequence.

Enjoy being in a profession that encourages creativity and innovation. Give yourself permission that not every one of yours, or your students' ideas, will be a gem or a keeper. That is perfectly okay! But, we imagine you will be thoroughly pleased by the large amount of creativity that you and your students will be able to generate. This creativity will only serve to make your job and the lives of your children more meaningful, joyous and productive.

Suggested Assignment # 1

Pick a new activity from this section of Creative Play games to play with your students for 20 minutes. After playing several rounds of the game try creating different rules: Number of "Its," speed or how you have to move, boundary size; either bigger or smaller or both, etc. After making one change, see if your students can suggest something different. Ask your students which version of the game they liked the best TODAY.

Suggested Assignment # 2

Over the next week, play at least three different activities from this Creative Play lesson with your students and try two new processing techniques.

Ponder the following questions to yourself:

Over the course of this week, are you, as a teacher, becoming more comfortable with facilitating games? Have you creatively initiated any game changes that were not mentioned so far in this course? If so, what were those changes? Do your students seem to have an easier or more difficult time with playing well with each other? Reflect upon which students of yours have been able to benefit from the HP approach and why? Reflect upon which students you've identified that will need more time to come aboard.

Lesson Seven:
TRUST and
COMPASSIONATE PLAY

Introduction

It doesn't take a rocket scientist to notice that most of our Western culture game activities and sports seem designed for the highly skilled few who play to win by defeating others, often through intimidation.

The goal of our book as it relates to effective classroom management curriculum is to assist us all to become educational advocates and active elders of our school communities, so every student can benefit from all the values identified on the "Why do we Play?" and "What is the most important part of all games?"

posters. Remember those posters? We hope that you have not taken them down to make room for your Halloween decorations. They provide a concrete foundation and reminder of the values your students want to embody when they play and throughout the day. They are your students' values. Let the poster values be a source of praise and may their answers continually guide them towards becoming mindful, happy and socially connected people. No matter where Charlie and I travel conducting the HP program, the poster values are consistent. Children uniformly give the following answers and benefits: they play to have FUN, to make friends, to feel good, silly and accepted. The most important parts of all games are the PEOPLE as well as sharing, playing fair, and being safe. These are all worthy values. However, the only way to achieve these values is by fostering compassion amongst all the participants. The only way to forge compassion is through creating trust in oneself and others.

Trust exists on multiple levels, but it is clearly seen on two. There's the physical level and then there's the emotional level. On the physical level the issues are: "Can I trust myself not to put myself in any kind of situation where I am going to get hurt. And, can I trust all the other people I am playing with to respect my body?" On the emotional level we ask: "Can I trust myself and others to protect my self-concept."

(Spencer talking:) I'd like to disclose a little bit of personal sharing. In a galaxy, far, far...excuse me. Years ago, I had a work-related injury that resulted in two herniated disks and a hyper-mobile sacrum. I was in a lot of pain and definitely limited in terms of my mobility. The first reaction I had was immediate withdrawal from almost any kind of physical activity because I was certain I was going to re-injure myself. And I was sure that everybody else was put on this planet to exacerbate my pain. What was even more devastating for me than this physical component of my pain was the emotional component. I was 33 years old at the time, and I was used to riding my bike about 8 to 12 miles a day, working and playing daily with teenagers (and keeping up). Before my injury, my concept of self and my identity were those of a physically and emotionally healthy adult. Yet, all of the sudden, my self-concept was changed dramatically and my trust of self and others decreased exponentially. I was unable to rejoin in physical activity until I could meet my trust needs.

Now, I relate this story, not because I want the reader's empathy or sympathy. I am a fairly healthy and active person again. But, I bring up my past pain history to make the point that this fear of self and others; these issues of trust are pieces of emotional significance that I continue to bring to all game activities even though this injury happened years ago. On some levels, trust issues of the memory and fears surrounding my physical and emotional pain remains to this day.

Children universally seem to naturally bring trust issues to game areas. They think, "Gosh, I'm the last one to be picked. I'm just not good enough. I just feel too clumsy." As they feel these thoughts, they invent defense mechanisms to avoid play. As they avoid, withdraw, isolate or act out, they often bring trust-defeating baggage to their play spaces. Eventually, these negative behaviors will spill into other spaces throughout the school day. As they get older, they will continue not only to bring trust-defeating baggage to their play spaces but to their work spaces as both teenagers and adults. We adults, having lived through these experiences and their consequences know this all too well.

Total trust and genuine compassion can never be achieved unless we address personal, emotional and group social factors compassionately. Values like kindness, caring, sharing, being able to be silly, allowing for failure, tolerating and appreciating that failure, protecting everyone's self-concept and eliminating teasing are so important. These are all vital ingredients in creating a trustworthy game and a safe learning environment for personal, group and academic growth. The HP curriculum provides a naturalistic system for fostering a personal and communal sense of compassion in your classroom and out on your playground.

The 5 C's

Sometimes we play games or activities that we think are safe, trust-worthy and compassionate because they just were the games we grew up with. But, upon further scrutiny we can see that many of these games actually produce an opposite effect. Simon Says is a perfect example. We think it teaches the concept of following rules. However, because it has that horrible component of eliminating children from the activity if they goof up one of Simon's com-mands it actually reinforces poor behavior. Since no child wants to be kicked out of Simon Says, when they goof up, they will lie and manipulate about their action to stay in the game. So when you look carefully at the traditional way of playing Simon Says we can see that it actually promotes teaching children how to become bet-ter liars and manipulators. So much for the innocence behind that traditional game, eh?

There is a method that we use to examine if an activity will fos-ter or break down trust and compassion. Many decades ago the New Games Foundation came up with a wonderful formula that helps educators identify whether a game that they playing with kids is a safe, successful and ultimately a trustworthy one. The for-mula is called, "The Five C's." A safe game, a trustworthy game, which will build compassion, is one that's contained, cushioned, controlled and played with a sense of caring and community.

A trustworthy game is contained.

You know exactly where the boundaries are. You know exactly where you need to be to play the game. If you are not ready to play the game, you can move outside the boundaries. And, you are al-lowed to do so in a manner knowing that no one will humiliate, ridicule or intimidate you for not playing. This freedom to decide when to take a healthy risk is an important one. We must encourage children to develop a sense of "personal readiness." When is it okay to join in an activity and when is it smart to avoid participation? Personal readiness allows for increased awareness of oneself, others and the immediate environment. Children will have many challenges placed in front of them throughout their lives. As educators, let's help them practice making wise decisions. Giving and practicing choices will facilitate healthy risk taking and learning boundaries. So, often invite a child who is reticent to play an activity to join but do not power-struggle with them to do something that they are not ready to do.

A trustworthy game is cushioned.

Your activity is played on the most appropriate and safest space. Unfortunately, in our travels to multiple schools around the country, it is clear that most playground spaces often have glass, rocks, sprinkler heads and other objects that are really dangerous to kids. During school off-hours, many campuses become prey to individuals who may not respect community property. We need to help the children and staff re-own their campus. Additionally, we want them to re-own that they are worthy of being safe and can take personal responsibility to see that this happens. Turn that responsibility into a game before playing any of your scheduled activities. Create an Eco-walk. Get all the kids to line up, shoulder to shoulder. Then instruct that they walk from one side of the playing field to the other side observing, pointing out and, if appropriate, pick up items that look unsafe. Once on the opposite side, the teacher and students deposit unsafe items into some kind of trash receptacle.

Another aspect to think about when we look at cushioning a game is that we do whatever we can to make a game safer. For instance, our local Tucson, AZ ABC affiliate, KGUN 9, news stated that in the 1995 playing season for Little League, there were a reported 160,000 injuries that resulted in trips to an emergency room. CNN reported that in 1993, there were over 115,000 injuries for organized children's baseball leagues including four deaths. The deaths occurred when a child was hit in the chest with a hard ball and went into cardiac arrest. Four deaths. Wow! So should we stop playing organized baseball games? The answer is quite clear. No. Baseball is a great game when played safely. So how could we make this particular game a more safe, a little more "cushioned?" Since most of the deaths were related to cardio-vascular problems when someone was hit with the ball in their chest, one of the coaches or parent present should be identified as being able to perform CPR. Playing with effective yet softer balls might help. More protective gear and slide-away bases are other worthy items and ideas to consider.

We are not guaranteeing that by using the games outlined in this book that you and your students will be free from injuries. No one could make that guarantee. Accidents may always happen. However, we can make a significant dent in injuries resulting from purposeful acts of aggression and violence by enacting the HP philosophy of play and games advocated in this book. As responsible educators and elders of our school communities, who have been entrusted with the care of our children, we must remain diligent in creating safer environments for our children. Using foresight, good common sense and correcting mistakes are ways that we can make activities have a greater sense of safety, trustworthiness and cushioning.

A trustworthy game is controlled.

It is really important that we, as teachers, counselors, parents and elders not be afraid to stop any activity if it gets out of control. Our idea for educational systems is that we don't have to play any game for the full four quarters or because there's 20 minutes left. We can stop any activity as needed. We focus on key socializing aspects way before we focus on scoring or winning.

Taking permission to stop a game when acting out occurs facilitates a wonderful learning opportunity for children to explore what they need to do to bring the game back in control. Teachers that stop unsafe activities really focus on improving social skills. If we just let games go until the end of the allotted time, ignoring any acting out, we are missing the point of what we can really teach and learn during those activities. So, it is incredibly valuable to not be afraid to halt unsafe games, bringing the kids together, listening to their solutions and getting their input. And, if they can't come up with input, or, if they are unable at that time to practice the input, then it's time to stop and move on to something else until the children can focus on potential solutions. Remember that with this concept comes the awareness that Healthy Play is all a process. No magic pills or immediate long term solutions. You are going to try solving your game's problems today, and if doesn't work out today, you'll come back again to it tomorrow. You might find yourself saying something like, "In three more days, let's try solving this problem and play this game again. It seems apparent that we're just not ready for it today. We've been unable to make this activity fun. And, we must always play to have fun. So, let's try again in three days." If you haven't stopped a game within the first three days of utilizing the HP curriculum, then you either have the most angelic kids that you have ever wished for and deserve, or, more likely, you have been too timid to stop an unsafe activity.

It has been our experience that some teachers may become reticent to stop an unsafe activity because they might feel that by doing so their students won't like it or they won't like their teacher. Absolutely, it is nice when your students like you, but please don't let any insecure feeling get in the way of a more important learning opportunity. You are their teacher, not their friend. Don't confuse being friendly to your students with being their friend. You have a responsibility to your students by being consistent and will stop and take charge when an activity becomes unsafe. By modeling compassion and appropriate action your students will be able to count on you.

Additionally, take yourself out of the role of being the only one who is doing the problem solving when problems occur in the games necessitating the cessation of the activity. Don't fall into the trap of giving children the easy or obvious answer just because it is clear to your adult awareness. If you do this, then you will soon become a prisoner of children always coming to you for all their answers. Being overzealous in over-teaching so a child can be forced to "do it right" has its hazard. I try to remember one of child psychologist, Jean Paiget's quotes, "Every time we teach a child something we keep him from inventing it himself." Let the kids participate and facilitate problem solving. You are in an excellent position to delegate responsibility to your students. This way, they can practice learning these skills in order to become healthier children and successful adults when they grow up.

And finally, a safe game, a trustworthy game, is one that is played with a sense of caring and community. Once again, we are trying to develop social skills to help students invest wisely into their, moral, social and human capital. We are trying to bring people together at a very young age and teach them the skills that they are going to need to learn to be successful children, adolescents and adults. To do this we need to create a compassionate and trusting environment.

We have a friend who is a therapist and when asked what she felt about therapy, her chosen profession, she said, "Therapy? I don't believe so much in therapy. What I believe in is caring communities, because, if we had a real sense of community, of belonging, in areas where we lived, worked and played, we'd probably need a lot less therapy. The greater a sense of community one feels as an accepted member, the less they will feel a need for therapy. If we really practiced true family values and created caring and nurturing communities, I could easily find myself out of a job. I would never just do therapy. I help create community."

This mixed up world can be repaired. But, to do so, we must take action and engage wholeheartedly in acts of loving-kindness. Can you imagine what it will be like on your campus when any child who becomes emotionally or physically hurt quickly finds that the nearest child is there with a genuine, "Are you okay?" and stays with them until they feel better? Our Rule # 1 will make empathy and compassion flourish. Any students who are having a disagreement, conflict or problem find they can easily and peacefully resolve that problem utilizing Rule # 2. There will be no need to retaliate cruelly at the bus stop later when no adult is present. When we take action towards mindfulness we create compassionate communities. And when we do, through compassion we create trust.

100% Trust

Although we have placed "Compassionate Play" second in the Healthy Play continuum of game activities, in many respects, it embodies the first and most basic of the classifications. Compassion and trust concepts really begin for your class the moment you develop the two posters on, "Why do we play?" and, "What is the most important part of every game?" By doing this exercise, your class has empowered and trusted you to help them achieve the values they have listed. It will be important for them to see that there is a serious personal accountability inherent to having FUN during the school day. Your students must be able to trust and learn from your leadership.

In our seminars, the initial activities we do are the most important of the whole training. These games must establish that trust and compassion will be actualized for every person attending. There will be no learning or enjoyment if these dynamics are not present. We always begin by doing an activity called, the iPod™ of the '50s (page 233). This game is clearly visually bizarre and therefore presents quite a personal challenge. It involves having a person wrap a string around their index fingers which is attached to an oven rack. Their fingers are then placed in their ears. The person also bends over slightly so that the oven rack doesn't touch their body. At this point, we call on the other participants to come forward and lightly hit the oven rack with their keys, pens, notebooks, coffee cups, etc. to make sounds that only the person plugged into the oven rack gets to fully hear and appreciate. The person plugged into the oven rack actually hears the most wonderful musical tones and chimes. Their willingness to take a risk and trust that they will be safe is absolutely rewarded.

What really is involved here is not just playing the activity, but establishing trust. The first volunteer, who often doesn't know all other participants, Charlie or I, must take a personal risk by becoming the central focal point of this activity. If we were to betray their willingness to try this activity in any way, the training experience for everyone would be severely damaged. Fortunately, we take play very seriously. We'd never intentionally embarrass or humiliate anyone in order to get a cheap laugh. Respect is always acknowledged and anyone can choose not to participate without repercussions. By successfully demonstrating this most awkward looking activity, all the participants can begin the process of trusting that their experiences, during our seminar, will be safe and that Charlie and I, as their facilitators, will be compassionate. A total trusting environment can often start with just one person. The same is true for creating a compassionate school. It only takes one person who takes that first healthy risk to become the change agent for all others establishing a trusting environment.

The second game of our seminars is just as essential. Playing Rumpelstiltskin, (page 231), accomplishes the task of individual name recognition. There is nothing more important for membership into any group than having your identity known by the other group members. The obvious carry over for your class is that it is essential for students to know each other's names. We don't mention this "obvious" comment lightly as we are frequently surprised that even in November, late into the school year, many children still cannot name everyone in their class. Trust and social skill development begins by having an identity.

Many trust programs or curriculum advocate doing really exotic things. They have people balanced high on top of telephone polls with ropes, climbing walls, and other daring feats. Creative

Spirit's Healthy Play curriculum does not advocate these experiences for the typical school setting. We believe children's trust skill development needs to be much more basic than this. We feel that before children are exposed to the "high wire act" they first must master simple things like appropriate touch and boundaries. Almost every class has difficulties with students just holding hands. Kids also need to learn not to punch or push each other when standing in lines. Fierce name calling and put-downs is rhetoric far too easily used by so many children. Before we can teach them exotic activities, we believe they need to practice giving truly meaningful praise to each other and tolerate simple tasks like holding hands or not pushing each other. Additionally, people can get really hurt doing those exotic "trust dives, falls and lifts" if someone doesn't remain focused or if participants don't take their responsibilities seriously. We have heard too many of those painful stories to advocate those activities, especially with elementary school students. Keep your trust issues and activities focused on practical age-appropriate issues.

Practicing trust and compassionate behaviors will begin with implementing the caring for an injured student Rule # 1 every time. Daily modeling will occur as the children use Healthy Play dynamics to develop safety rules which value PEOPLE as the most important part of the game. There will be rules like; hard tags or feet tags just won't count. We will not use hard rubberized balls in games like Kickball or Dodge Ball. Maybe Dodge Ball, played traditionally is an unsafe game and should not be played at all. But, if you do play it with students, head shots should not be allowed. However, if someone does get hit in the head with the soft Ruff-SKIN™ balls that we'd advocate, they are automatically safe. Additionally, the thrower of the ball must check them out to make sure they are okay. These simple behaviors develop compassion. Players who forget to do this need to sit out of the game for a brief time to remember what's important. This is the type of basic school curriculum that we have observed most children need to practice to facilitate a compassionate campus.

For trust to be present...it must be 100%. Anything less than 100% causes doubts. We realize that we are all human, but still, it is very important that we truly strive for this level of perfection. The example we use in our seminars to demonstrate the value of 100% trust works like the following:

Let's examine the trust concept of honesty and relate it to the educational grading process. Pretend you are in an average class of fifth graders. It's a typical class and the kids often spend time wondering and gossiping about their teacher. One day you explain to them that you have decided to become an "A" quality honest teacher. The best grade one could get in school is an "A." Being an "A" quality honest teacher certainly must be better than being a "B" or lesser quality honest teacher.

So, from now on we will grade honesty just like everything else at school. An "A" quality honest teacher will tell the truth 90% of the time. To provide your students with their first trust exercise you announce that you will now tell them 10 personal facts about yourself. Nine of the facts will be true. One fact, and only one, will be a lie. This way you will be 90% honest. It will be the task of each member of the class to determine which statement is the lie.

Here are my (Charlie's) 10 facts:

1. I have lived in seven decades.
2. My favorite color is bright yellow.
3. I usually don't match my socks and just put on what ever color of stripes I get.
4. My wife's nickname is, "Goldberry."
5. I was born in Buffalo, New York.
6. I went to Arizona State University to become a nurse.
7. I enjoy playing Rolling Stone songs on my guitar.
8. My pet dog's name is Hoover.
9. The name of my son is Forrest.
10. I enjoy playing chess.

At this point, the class can raise their hands and speculate which one of these facts is actually the lie. Someone always challenges my socks. But, it's been over twenty years since I bothered to match them. Unmatched socks make sense. They make a more colorful pair. You don't ever waste time sorting them after doing the laundry. It's cost effective. When I get a hole in one sock all the others still match it just fine. Next guess.

Usually, people don't believe I call my wife, "Goldberry" until I recite the several poems written by J.R.R. Tolkien about the wonderful woman of the woods who lived with Tom Bombadil. Quoting poems about your wife makes you a romantic. Not making her sort sock makes you easy to live with but weird. Yes, we call our dog Hoover. She is really the best cordless wet or dry vacuum you could ever want. Drop some popcorn or spill some milk and all you do is call, "Hoover," and it's quickly sucked up. I was born in Buffalo in 1949 so that's seven decades and eliminates those truths. I am a RN who went to ASU. An ideal afternoon would be to play chess with my son Forrest while wearing my favorite bright yellow tee shirt. That completes the nine truths.

The lie is that I play guitar. Only in my dreams did I ever play rock and roll guitar. I'm not even good at air guitar.

If you use this demonstration, don't give away the truth until everyone guesses what they think the lie is. The average group of students will challenge at least five or more things as being lies. Even though you were a 90% honest teacher, a typical gossipy group of kids would be questioning your credibility over 50% of the time. Your 90% credibility now stands at 50%. So, ultimately, instead of being viewed as an "A" quality honest person they would now have to give you an "F" in honesty and trust you as such. And, therefore they might never really be sure if they could figure out correctly when you are lying or telling the truth. They would always have to wonder about every fact you told them even though you are honest 9 out of 10 times. The trust factor of honesty seems to erode exponentially when it is betrayed or hidden. Trust is also easier to lose than to gain.

Horse-play, like fake fighting, also erodes trust quickly. We try to point out that fake fighting often leads to real fighting and violence. "Oh, we're just goofing around," is the typical response from most children. So to demonstrate our point we use this following example:

Pick a child and ask them if they could be serious with a demonstration. If they can, proceed. If not, find a child who can. Remember to always reward the other child for their honest response. State to the child that you've picked, "Let's pretend that nine out of ten times, I'm going to come up to you and I'm going to give you a big smile and a nice handshake. Every time I see you, big smile, nine out of ten times. But, if I were to tell you that one of those ten times, I'm going to punch you in the teeth real hard, and it just might be this time, would you feel safe to shake my hand right now?" An honest child will wisely state, "No, not at all. I couldn't trust you or your smiles. Odds are you could hit me anytime."

Once again, that's how trust works. Trust can deteriorate quickly. A Russian-roulette version of trust will only set up an atmosphere of paranoia and fear. As much as humanly possible, we should keep trust as high as 100%. Using play, and our philosophies regarding play, gives you wonderful opportunities to practice 100% trust and compassion with your students. The great incentive in teaching social skills through play is that students want to play. They will modify their actions so they can be in the game.

When lining up to go out to play and you see some kids are pushing each other never hesitate to reflect that those using assaulting behaviors are not taking care of the PEOPLE. Then have the offending students leave the line to have their disagreement. Once they've resolved their conflict they can now join in at the end of the line.

Often in games where children are instructed to hold each other's hands you'll hear the following. "Ewww, I'm not holding a girl's hand." You might even see children zoom off to the other side of the circle to hold a friend's hand or the hand of someone who is the same sex. In older grades, homophobic feelings might cause same-sex hand holding to become an issue for some students. The scape-goating that occurs in all of these scenarios is damaging to those it is perpetrated against and also to those committing the offensive behaviors. If, certain girls or boys refuse to hold each other's hands, have them step out of the game until they can take the exact place where they started without problems. Don't stop the game for those who can hold hands appropriately.

Crushing someone's hand or pulling their arms is not being cute or funny. But, some kids like to torment their peers by doing just that. Children engaged in these kinds of actions are being aggressive. These acts by children need to be immediately addressed. You will not be able to develop real trust as long as children are allowed to scapegoat their peers in front of others or the whole class. When their actions or words convey such scape-goating, your leadership and quick intervention is necessary.

This concept of 100% trust is most effective when it is transferred to the whole school community. When you are walking on the school grounds give kids frequent praise for doing kind deeds. Regularly say things to the whole class like, "I want to thank Skippy for the way he settled his argument at lunch without fighting." Give your students incentive to gain your recognition for demonstrating positive values.

On the other hand, if, as you're passing down the hall and you see kids mock fighting, state, "Are you caring for the PEOPLE?" This forces the child to briefly think about their actions. It is much more effective than just saying, "Hey, break it up," or, "Stop!" If a first grader falls on the way to the bus, the next kid doesn't get to race over them to get the window seat. Bring that child back to do the caring helping them remember that they were closest to the injured child. Acknowledge behaviors that need challenging. All students must learn caring and shared responsibility for everyone and throughout their campus. Caring and acting responsibly are not just the jobs of the teachers and school elders.

Games that promote Trust and Compassion:

In this section of the play dynamic continuum we'll focus on activities which specifically have strong trust and compassionate play elements to them. That doesn't mean that the other activities presented in this book don't focus on trust. Every game, as well as every action, during the entire school day has an effect on the trust level of the students, teachers and staff at your school. What we want to do here is highlight specific game and activity resources you can use to help your students practice learning more about responsibility and compassion.

You will find many compassionate and trust building games presented in this lesson. Pick the activities you believe your class is ready to try that are also age appropriate. Trust games have a natural component which involves students progressing into higher and more sophisticated levels of trustworthy behaviors. It is possible that not all of your students will be ready to do every one of these games. Perhaps your whole class might not be ready for a few of these activities. Some years, you may do more of these activities than others. Work with each class individually. It is important that you use your good judgment to choose the games that the children are ready to handle. However, we have come up with the trust activities that uniformly work for a great majority of students and have included them here. Enjoy!

RATTLESNAKE TAG

(Kindergarten and older, 15-30 players, inside or outside, a rattle or shaker)

How It's Played

Begin by having everyone stand, hold hands and form a circle. The people holding hands define the boundaries of the playing circle and become the "safety net" for this game. Their importance should be strongly emphasized. Now, randomly choose two players to play inside the circle. The two players in the middle decide which one of them gets the rattle. The object for the player without the rattle is to try and tag the person holding the rattle. But, she must do so with her eyes closed. The player with the rattle keeps his eyes open but must constantly shake the rattle to let the other player know his approximate location. The person with the rattle tries to avoid being tagged. The game begins with the two players standing far apart on opposite sides inside the circle. Before any action is to take place, the player trying to catch the person with the Rattlesnake Rattle closes her eyes and spins around one or two times.

One person will be chosen to be the "safety-net monitor." This person will give various commands to the safety-net members. To help the person in the middle of the circle who has her eyes closed, the "safety-net monitor" may give commands to the group such as, "Take one giant step in" or "Take three baby steps closer." This helps facilitate compassion for those players having a more difficult time tagging the rattle holder while maintaining the challenge for those who find this playful task easy. A safety rule for this game that we want to share with you is that the person with the rattle can not purposefully lead the other person who has their eyes close to bump up or crash against the safety net. The rattle holder may not get down on their knees to avoid being tagged. If either of these actions occurs stop the game and process trust and safety issues. Another rule is that the safety net must always have its members hold hands to form a consistent soft wall to gently prevent the player with their eyes closed from ever going outside the circle. So many kids get excited watching this game and will start squealing or shouting out locations of the person holding the rattle. You will have to remind the safety net that they must remain quiet throughout each round of the game so the person with their eyes closed can hear the rattle being shaken. Additionally, for many people it's scary to move around with one's eyes closed. Many players may need to open them to check out where they are. This is a perfect

Rattlesnake tag

opportunity to support safe play, personal care taking and de-emphasize arguments about "cheating." A player must acknowledge the opening of their eyes by just saying, "Oops." When this happens, the game is temporarily halted until the person without the rattle closes her eyes again and spins around one time. Use your good discretion for younger students who may not want to close their eyes at all. That is totally fine. However, for children who get too disorientated by spinning around with their eyes closed simply eliminate this feature. Never have children spin around more than two and $1/2$ times with their eyes closed.

THE GIFT OF THE GAME

This is a great trust activity to start with because the inherent level of trust that this game requires is so very basic. Can the children hold hands, especially kids of the opposite sex? Can the person with her eyes closed trust that the "safety net" won't let go of their hands so that she ends up helplessly going beyond the boundaries and into a dangerous or humiliating situation? Can the person with her eyes closed open them due to discomfort or fear without being ridiculed as a cheater? Will she be able to count on the safety net to move in, making a tag easier as needed? Can anyone in the class trust everyone for their emotional and physical safety?

This activity facilitates, encourages and acknowledges trust and compassionate behaviors. Children in the "safety net" are asked not to play unless they can hold hands firmly to protect the two in the middle. In fact, built into this game are immediate verbal rewards for children deemed most trustworthy by their peers. Each round, the person who will have her eyes closed selects the person that she thinks will be most trustworthy to be her own safety-net monitor. Students will tend to pick the child that is not the fastest or strongest but the one who is the most trustworthy. It is the safety-net monitor's job to assist and protect the person with her eyes closed. He protects her physical safety by stopping the activity when members of the safety net are not standing up or holding hands. He protect his buddy's self esteem as he asks the safety net to keep taking baby or giant steps in, so a tag occurs way before the child in the middle can either losses face or becomes dizzy. To be picked the safety-net monitor or buddy is an honor and most children feel proud to be thought trustworthy. To be trustworthy is a great attribute, yet many children are not often verbally or behaviorally rewarded and acknowledged for this essential quality. You, as the teacher, should model being the safety net monitor, to show your students how and when to move the safety net in to keep the game always safe, mindful and fun.

If you have a class where the boys and girls are quite separate and even hostile with each other, this activity quickly breaks down the gender barrier. Always announce that you want everyone to play, but the safety of the people in the middle is most important aspect of this game. Remind members of the safety net that they must hold hands to protect those in the middle even if it means holding the hands of a girl or boy. Start the activity with one boy and one girl in the middle. To enhance gender equity, when the tagging is done make sure that the boy and girl switch roles, so the tagger now gets to hold the RATTLESNAKE rattle. After each round, have the boy pick a girl and the girl pick a boy to replace them in the middle as they exchange their places in the circle for the next round. Before you know it, this circle that started out complaining and segregating boys on one side and girls on the other are now nicely mixed, joyously and cooperatively playing. Remember to additionally instruct children to pick only those who are good listeners, who are well behaved and who haven't yet had a turn.

Unless you have a lot of time, you will probably not be able to let all children take a turn in the middle. To facilitate giving everyone a chance and to shorten the time playing this activity you might not want to have the two children in the middle of the circle exchange roles before picking others to replace them. Or, you might want this to be the place where children can learn and practice the skills of delayed gratification. To do this, however, you must acknowledge before the game that everyone may not get a turn in the middle this time. Perhaps, at recess they will have their turn or maybe tomorrow when they play this game again.

You must always stress the importance of everyone's role, including those trusting members of the safety net. Be sure to model and highlight compliments to members of the safety net for their faithful behaviors. We have had many teachers and counselors report that this was the game that broke through that goofy boy/girl barrier. This is because everyone must hold everyone else's hand. There are no exceptions if students want to play. We've seen dozens of kids refuse to hold hands and we've asked them to step out of the circle and watch the game. This is not punishment. This is just the safe expectation of appropriate behavior. By the second round of the game, most students have conquered this acting out and have warmly joined the whole class. This intervention demonstrates how the constant practice, which occurs during play, begins to change how your whole class will interact.

Finally, we like how this game models acceptance and support of an individual's fears. Players are given permission to open their eyes when scared without fear of being labeled a "cheater." You can almost feel the relief in your class when you, the teacher, state,

"It's sometimes scary to move with your eyes closed." Children may then learn to verbalize their fears and understand that others will help them through them. Modeling permission to be scared or uncomfortable is so important. This acceptance of normal human feelings and behavior allows children to practice honesty and personal responsibility. These are, by far, more valuable skills to practice than just chasing people with their eyes closed.

PERSONALITY
(Fourth grade up, groups of 6-15 players, indoors, writing pad or chalk board)

How It's Played
Players sit in a circle. Six people per circle is a good number, but groups can have a few more players. One player is chosen as the leader for the first round. Another player is chosen to be the scribe who will keep track of questions and answers. The leader silently thinks of any one of the participants in their own circle. The object for the participants is to try and guess the person the leader is thinking about. They do this by asking the leader abstract questions which will allows the leader to describe the positive essence or personality traits of the secret person.

   The players each take a turn asking their questions as the scribe briefly writes down their questions and the responses. Questions should be phrased, "If this person were/was a _____, what/which type of _____ would they be?" Participants are encouraged to be creative with their questions. The questions should be broad in concept to give the leader many options for response. **Example:** "If this person were a musical instrument (or an animal or a breakfast cereal or a country of the world), what/which kind of _____ would they be?" Note that these are not direct questions like "What color hair does the person have?" Nor should the questions go after "favorite" likes of the person picked. This is important as people may want to initially define the person by their favorites. Try to discourage this. The activity is not called "Favorites," it is called, "Personality."

The leader then must answer the question with a positive and truthful answer based on his own perception of that person's personality. After the six questions have been asked and answered, the scribe reviews the data out loud for the group. Then, each student makes a guess of the identity of the person that leader has described. (It is critical that the leader not disclose the name of the secret person until all players have had their turn at guessing.) The scribe writes down the player's guesses and then tallies them creating a record of guesses. The leader then discloses the identity of the person that they were thinking of. At this point, the leader describes how each of his answers pertain to positive personality traits of the secret person. For example: "When you asked what kind of animal this person would be, I thought of an "otter" because Kaylene is always so playful and happy." After all the answers have been described, a new leader and scribe are chosen and the game goes on. Multiple repetition of this activity will help gently move children from concrete answers to more abstract ones. Don't worry if it takes a bit of time to get there as it will be well worth it.

THE GIFT OF GAME

Kids can be the kings and queens of put-downs. Getting them to give or receive compliments is sometimes as difficult as nailing Jell-O to the wall. PERSONALITY addresses this dilemma by helping kids give sideways compliments to others until they learn how to deliver them directly. Since this game takes some abstract thought, you probably can't play it with young children. Even some adults have a difficult time with abstract thought. Think fourth grade and up. Remind yourself and your students that you are going for questions and answers that describe what the leader thinks best represents or describes the person. This is not a game where you describe a person's favorite likes. For example, I was the leader who was secretly thinking of Charlie. Someone asked me, "If this person was a color, what color would they be?" Now I know Charlie's favorite color is bright yellow, but bright yellow doesn't make me think of Charlie's personality. Instead, I answered, "This person would be the colors of the Arizona sunsets." Later in the game when I gave my reason for this answer, I said, "Charlie, who is so diverse, couldn't be just one color, he had to be many. And, I see both the colors of the Arizona sunsets and Charlie as majestic and magnificent." Trust me, there was a bright smile on my buddy Charlie's face to hear himself described so positively and thoughtfully. This game works well with people's first impressions but shines when done repeatedly. Players grow in intimacy each time this game is played. On the Child and Adolescent wing of the psychiatric facility where Charlie and I met, PERSONALITY was the most popular game during our community meetings. Once the children and teens experienced the warm feelings of giving and receiving compliments and learning how positively others viewed them they didn't want to stop playing this game. The outcome, answers and comments were often so touching that we went through lots of Kleenex with all our happy tears.

VARIATION: REVERSE PERSONALITY

Playing this game backwards creates a game called REVERSE PERSONALITY. For younger grades and for classes where children have difficulty saying nice things about other students you might want to actually start with this version first. Every player is given a piece of paper and pencil. As a group, players come up with six generic questions that could abstractly describe every player. Questions should be phrased, "If I were a _____, what/which type of _____ would I be?" Participants are encouraged to be creative with both the questions and their answers. The questions should be broad in concept to give players many options for responses as they answer the questions about themselves. Ex: "If I were a cartoon character (or a creature in the ocean, a type of movie or an object in the kitchen), what/which kind of _____ would I be?" Like the regular version of Personality, make sure that you do not utilize direct concrete questions like, "What color shirt do I have on?" Players write down answers to the creative questions describing themselves. The students are instructed to describe only positive personality traits or descriptions of themselves. Honesty and personal compassion should be stressed. Once the students have completed answering the six questions about themselves they write their name at the top of their papers and hand them in to the teacher or counselor.

Randomly, the teacher or counselor will pull out a Reverse Personality sheet of paper and read out loud the questions and answers without indicating who wrote those responses. "This person thinks of themselves as a panda bear for the type of animal. The color is blue. When asked which cartoon character they'd be, they replied Cinderella. Type of food was Mexican. And, when asked what kind of ice cream they would be, they said, 'Rocky Road.' Who do you think it is?" The other players have to guess who the author was by pointing to that person. Or, the kids could tally up their guesses for the secret identity behind this round of REVERSE PERSONALITY. After everyone makes their guess, the identity of the author is revealed and the page is given pack to the originator. The student author then explains the rationale behind each answer that they gave. The gift that many kids soon discover is greater insight about their peers while often realizing that many of them think alike and share the same qualities. They learn that their personalities are both similar and individualistic, that they are both part of the group and special individuals. Diversity issues are now being discovered in a playful manner facilitating empathy. You now have a box full of pre-made magic you can use all semester long.

Many teachers and principals have told us that our suggestion of opening every staff meeting with one round of PERSONALITY for staff sets the tone of the meeting as warm, validating and productive. The staff feels appreciated by each other, and group cohesion develops. This is so important because teachers, principals and most school staff work autonomously. Remember, the creation of a caring community supports and encourages acts of loving kindness.

COOPERATIVE MUSICAL CHAIRS

(Any grade level, the more players the better, inside, sturdy chairs)

How It's Played

We adore this "Musical Chair" variation developed by Terry Orlick. Begin by telling the players that we are going to play, Musical Chairs, but, in a new and improved manner. Since no one likes being eliminated in the traditional version of Musical Chairs, all the people in our version get to stay in the game, but the chairs still have to go. This means the game will have more people than chairs and the people in chairs will have to share sitting down by letting others sit in their laps or on their knees. Model how to gently sit on the lap of another person. Also, demonstrate how people sitting in chairs can spread their legs to let multiple people sit on each knee. As more chairs disappear, more and more players end up in sitting in people's laps or on their knees.

Have the group pick a song to sing and start marching around the chairs. When you, the teacher, stops singing the song everyone will be cued that it is time to sit down. Randomly pick some letters of the alphabet and have people whose names start with those letters remove their chairs and sing another song. I like to combine actions with singing, so with each round we might shake as we sing. Or, we might clap, snap our fingers, flap our wings or dance. To calm the children after each exciting round I tell them I will pick the quietest child to be my helper who will announce which action we will do along with my singing. Since everyone wants to be my helper they all calm down quickly. This lets me praise them often for their ability to be silly when appropriate and calm when it is called for. Sometimes you will find a few children who are not comfortable sitting in another's lap. NEVER force a child to sit in another's lap or on someone's knee. Let them watch the game or give them the opportunity to decide how the other students should move for the next round. They may be protecting themselves or there may even be a larger issue here. If there is a larger issue, make sure you are discussing it with your school's counselor.

What you will likely see is that when you stop singing, the majority of students will quickly find a chair or knee to sit upon. But, a few of your "Skippys" will be spinning around the inside of the circle seemingly unable to find very visible knees or laps to sit upon. Give them a to a count of three to sit down. If they have not sat down tell everyone to stand up and start the next round. If

Cooperative musical chairs

they still can't comply with the rules after another round, you, or a student, can use rule number two and have a disagreement with them regarding playing fairly. Keep removing chairs staying aware that you have always balanced safety with the fun of lots of people sitting in each other's laps.

THE GIFT OF THE GAME

No one wants to be kicked out of anything. For children, being kicked out of a game is equivalent to an adult being fired from a job. Doesn't feel good, does it? So why do we do it? Why do we need to play games that celebrate the one child who is always the fastest or the strongest? We don't. The smiles on children's faces when you tell them nobody will be kicked out of our game are joys to behold. With the rule that no one will be left out and there will be a place for them to sit down, children play this game less aggressively than traditional Musical Chairs feeling assured. Now there is no need to aggressively push another child out of the way to get a seat. Some kindergarten teachers use this game to reinforce numbers by having the children count the various numbers of people sitting in the chairs. Children also learn how to touch and support others in a gentle and safe fashion. Once you engage in one round of COOPERATIVE MUSICAL CHAIRS, you will never want to go back to the traditional way of playing it.

DETECTIVES
(First grade and up, 15 or more players, indoor or outside, no equipment)

How It's Played
Have your group make a circle and close their eyes. Quietly walk around the inside or outside of the circle and lightly tap a few players on the shoulder to become "Freezers." (Generally, pick one freezer for every six to eight players). Everyone else becomes a "Detective" and can now open their eyes as they begin to quietly walk around the playing area. The object of the Freezers is to sneakily touch the other players, thus freezing Detectives, without others seeing it happen. Once frozen, the Detectives become statues and remain still until they are saved. When another Detective gives them a warm sideways hug, the freezing spell is broken. The object of the Detectives is to figure out who all the Freezers are. They can't shout out the name of a Freezer, but it is smart to keep away from them.

Freezers are so sneaky that they can pretend to be frozen and quietly freeze you when you try to save them with a warm hug as they whisper that they are a Freezer. Oops! If two Freezers touch each other, nothing happens, and the Freezers can deduce that they just met another Freezer. After a couple of minutes, stop the game and have the Freezers raise their hands, so the Detectives can see how many Freezers they figured out. Play again, having each Freezer pick a replacement by tapping someone on their shoulder while everyone, but the former Freezers, have their eyes closed.

THE GIFT OF THE GAME

Like the game of SILENT BALL (page 168), DETECTIVES is an excellent transition game that can gently wind children's energies down, so they may return to the classroom ready for academics. We enjoyed discovering a tag game where the players walk instead of run. Excitement does not always mean speed and intensity. Joy and exploration of thoughtful, intuitive behaviors can happen at a relaxed pace. This is important for children to experience. Sometimes the world is clearer at a slower pace. People can observe more when they are attentive, curious and calm. Again, we adore games where the object is to rescue the players and not eliminate them. And, rescuing others through warm hugs teaches compassion and appropriate touching. This is especially important when the type of touching that is modeled for our children throughout most of their media programming is either violent or eroticized. With that kind of destructive modeling it is no wonder that children have a hard time tagging softly or can be inappropriate with their touching. This activity teaches appropriate touching done in a public setting which is healthy and connecting. For your pre-teens, this is a safe and appropriate way to let them explore age appropriate physical connections with their peers.

RUMPELSTILTSKIN
(Kindergarten and up, ten or more players, indoors, no equipment)

How It's Played
Ask participants to stand in a circle. Next select the challengers and have them move inside the circle. A good balance is to have one challenger for every six people in your group. This should allow for a dizzying pace of activity.

Instruct everyone to say the word *Rumpelstiltskin*. Have everyone repeat it again as fast as they can. (Speed is important.) Next, explain the commands *left, center,* and *right* to all the participants. The significance of these commands is that the players who make up the circle must now learn the names of the other players on their immediate left and right and, of course, remember their own name, which will correspond with the command *center.*

At the same time, individual challengers from the middle will approach any member of the circle and give *one* of the commands (*left, center, or right*) followed quickly by "Rumpelstiltskin." The player being approached needs to respond with the correct first name (based on the command given by the challenger) before the challenger finishes saying "Rumpelstiltskin." If the challenger finishes saying "Rumpelstiltskin" first or if the player being questioned gives the wrong name, then the challenger trades places with the other person and joins the circle. The other player now becomes a new challenger. If the person being challenged states the right name first, then the challenger remains a challenger and must try to find someone else to baffle. Players are moved about all over the circle and very quickly learn the names of many of the participants. Name tags are helpful.

THE GIFT OF THE GAME

There is nothing more simple or direct in promoting self-esteem than being recognized and called by one's own name. It is not uncommon for children not to know all the names of their peers in their own classroom even months after the beginning of the school year. If people in your class don't think it is important to learn a particular student's name, that student might find it difficult to validate her self-worth. Rumpelstiltskin changes all of that. Done at the beginning of the year, this activity creates name recognition, infectious laughter, and natural mixing.

Creatively and academically, this game has other great values. Let's say you want to teach your children the names of the original thirteen colonies, for example. Instead of having tags with individuals' names, have ones with the names of the colonies. You can repeat the names of the colonies on the tags as needed. Make sure that all the kids have one. Kids now have to say the name written on the tag to their left, center, or right. As they naturally are sent around the room, alternating between being a challenger or joining the circle, they begin to visually, linguistically, and kinetically reinforce their learning.

iPOD™ OF THE '50s
(Any age, two or more players, inside, an oven rack, a piece of string)

How It's Played
Take a five-foot piece of string and tie each end to one side of the oven rack. The first student winds the string around each of his index fingers so that the rack hangs about eighteen inches from his hands. Then he places his fingers in his ears. He bends over from the waist, so the oven rack is not touching his body. Then have the other participants gently strike the oven rack with any type of object they can find (car keys, pens, shoes, books, bracelets, soft-drink cans, whatever). Each object will produce a wonderful sound that will vibrate up the string to the listener's ears. What the "musicians" hear and what the person plugged in hears create two very different experiences. End your symphony with a gong: one person strikes the oven rack simultaneously with the heels of both fists, creating a deep and resonating note.

   Hints: You can have little children wind the string, holding a full-size oven rack, around their *whole* hand and put their hands over their ears. Also, you could substitute a lighter metal object, such as a toaster-oven rack.

THE GIFT OF THE GAME
If you ever attend one of our Healthy Play workshops, you will probably start off with this game. It's one of our favorites. It helps everyone start seeing that games really can just be for fun. If you can accept the risk of bending over with an oven rack plugged into your ears, then you are ready for anything. We encourage you to use this activity early on as you teach children the vast possibilities of having fun. If you are an educator, you might also use this ac-

tivity to discuss the science of sound waves.

BLUE MAGIC
(Third grade and up, an audience, and one "telepathic" assistant)

How It's Played
After telling your student assistant the secret of how this game is done (see below), return to the classroom and give the following speech:

YOU: I was truly amazed when I came to your class today, for I felt magical and psychic energies flow between me and my assistant. (*Like a wizard, wave your fingers toward your assistant as you make your favorite science-fiction special-effects noises.*) And, to prove that there is a telepathic link (*once again making your noise*) between me and my assistant, we would like to demonstrate our ability to perform blue magic! (*Have your assistant close her eyes and then ask another student to point to any object or person in the room. Make sure all the children know and agree on the object or person that was picked.*) I will verbally call off random items in the room, but when I get to the correct one, even though my assistant's eyes were closed, through our telepathic link, she will be able to verify that it is indeed the item or person that was chosen. (*Now have your assistant open her eyes and let her enjoy answering no to all the incorrect questions and yes to the correct one, to the utter amazement of her classmates. Since you and your assistant know the simple secret, you will be confident that your assistant will guess correctly. Those who do not know the secret will be amused and awed.*)

Encourage the children to guess how the trick is done, complimenting them on their "excellent guesses" until the real answer is exposed. They will come up with a great number of possible solutions, from a numerical component to secretive hand gestures. It will seem like magic. Continue to do this activity, balancing the frustration tolerance with the enthusiasm of the class.

The secret: Tell your assistant to answer yes to the following question after an object which is the color blue has been identified.

Example: Say the class picked the clock while your assistant's eyes were closed.

YOU: Is it the door *(which is the color brown)*?
ASSISTANT: No.
YOU: Is it Veronica's shoes *(which are the color yellow)*?
ASSISTANT: No, of course not.
YOU: Is it Marco's jeans? *(The jeans happen to be blue and this is your assistant's clue. Your assistant will answer no to this inquiry, knowing that the very next item you name will be correct.)*
ASSISTANT: No, it is not Marco's jeans. I get no psychic vibrations.
YOU: Is it the clock?
ASSISTANT: Yes, of course it is!

Warning: You can play green magic, red magic, purple magic, or even plaid magic. But, unless you want angry parents to storm the office of your school's principal or district supervisor, *never* call this game black or white magic. These titles bring up and may promote images of occultism. Names of games are powerful, and you can sway an innocent activity in the wrong direction by giving it an inappropriate title.

THE GIFT OF THE GAME

Nobody captures an audience like a magician. Someone who has mastered the seemingly impossible gets our attention. And this is important to remember when promoting ideas that break through resistance and complacency. The exciting thing about the activities that Creative Spirit promotes is their immediate marketability to the audience—in this case, children. Blue magic is a great bonding activity for your children who respond less to kinetic activities and more toward cognitive ones. This and other indoor activities help send the message that healthy-play values do occur inside the classroom as well as on the playground.

Experience has shown us that the greatest value comes from blue magic when youngsters take this logic puzzle home and play it with their families. Children report and experience a sense of satisfaction and excellence, and they feel special when they are able to stump their older siblings and parents. And they will. We were not able to solve the riddle behind blue magic right away when it was first presented to us. Family members who discover the secret have a chance to shower their children with praise for coming up with such a challenging and entertaining activity.

ACTING WORDS
(Third grade and up, any number of players, inside or outdoors, no equipment)

How It's Played
Select one player to think of a secret word. Then instruct this child, the leader, to announce to the group another word that rhymes with the secret word. For example: "My word sounds like *goat*." The group must attempt to guess the secret word. But to make a guess, they must put their guess into action by acting out their guess. One person might stand up and pretend to put on some clothes, miming the word *coat*. The leader will announce if *coat* is a correct guess. If not, another person might sit on the floor and begin moving her arms back and forth. "No, it's not a *boat*." A third person stands up and expands their cheeks and abdomen, and the leader states, "Yes, it's *bloat*." The child who guesses the correct answer is the new leader, and the game begins again.

THE GIFT OF THE GAME
It is clear how this game can teach children about words that rhyme and even homonyms. What isn't as evident is how this activity honors and celebrates skills other than being the fastest and

strongest. Everyone can play the simple roles for success in ACT-ING WORDS. We observed a teacher who used acting words creatively to manage a child who often sought attention by disruptive imitation of others. She appropriately set limits on these behaviors and encouraged this child's natural acting skills in the appropriate arena of acting words. The child got positive attention without putting others down. Another win-win situation.

PICNIC

(Fourth grade and older, the more players the better, inside or sitting down in the shade, no equipment)

How It's Played

Have players sit in a circle or around a table. Tell them that this is a logic-puzzle game. The goal is to figure out what items you can bring to get permission to go on a picnic. The players each take a turn and name an item they would like to bring on the picnic. For example: Charlie wants to bring chicken, and he gets to go. Tom wants to bring soda. He is told that this sounds delicious, but he doesn't get to go. Mary tries hamburgers, but she can't go either, even though hamburgers would be good to eat. Susan says she'll bring soda, and she gets to go. Why can Susan bring soda and Tom can't? That's the crux of this puzzle. The solution is that the players can only bring things that start with the first letter of their first names. Play logic-puzzle games in teams, so players can share answers and not feel alone if they can't solve the puzzle.

THE GIFT OF THE GAME

When you first introduce logic puzzles to your class, you should begin with this game. The logical pattern in which children use their names to solve the puzzle is generally easy to figure out and sets the tone for the logic puzzles that will follow. You may want to help a child who needs a self-esteem boost by letting him in on the secret so he can be your assistant (or "ringer").

A TRIP TO WASHINGTON

(Fourth grade and up, four or more players, sitting down, no equipment)

How It's Played

The goal of this game is to figure out what to bring so you can get one of the ten seats on the plane for a trip to Washington. Players take turns announcing what they want to bring on their trip. Example: Bill might try to bring a *suitcase,* but he can't start the journey. Paula might try a *hair dryer,* but it's too early for her to go with that item. Tom might try his *wallet,* and he gets to start the trip and gets the first seat on the plane. Actually, anyone could have started the trip to Washington if he had brought a wallet or a watch or a Walkman. The key to this game is to bring objects starting with the letters that will spell *Washington* (wallet, alarm clock, suitcase, hair dryer, ice cream, and so on) *in order.* Next, try traveling to Paris or Egypt or anywhere else you want. It is useful to write the correct answers on the board so people can see the pattern.

THE GIFT OF THE GAME

As you can imagine, this activity reinforces spelling as you have fun. Even when children solve the riddle to this my-rule game, they still want to play. So when you are teaching geography of the Middle East, play a trip to Egypt, Israel, Jordan, and so on. Young children especially like going home and stumping parents, older siblings, other relatives, and friends with logic puzzles once they know the solutions. It gives them a healthy sense of empowerment.

SILLY TILLY WILLY

(Fourth grade and up, four or more participants, inside or outside)

How It's Played

This is a favorite and quiet logic-puzzle game that will challenge students' spelling abilities. (It certainly challenges ours). The game starts by saying that you have a weird friend named Silly Tilly Willy. Now, Silly Tilly Willy only likes some things and really doesn't like others. The goal is to figure out what Silly Tilly Willy does and doesn't like.

Each player takes a turn saying, "Silly Tilly Willy likes ——, but doesn't like ——." The leader and those players who have solved the puzzle acknowledge whether another player has correctly stated Silly Tilly Willy's likes and dislikes. For example: Silly Tilly Willy likes to drive on the *street,* but doesn't like to drive on the *road.* She likes the *moon* and doesn't like the *sun.* Likes *trees* yet doesn't like *bushes.* Likes to *smell* things, but doesn't like *odors.* She's pretty weird! (The key to this puzzle is that Silly Tilly Willy only likes words with double letters and doesn't like words that don't have them.) The creative part of the game for the players in the know is to mislead others' logic by postulating items that seem to have some connection. A good example of this type of misleading connection would be that Silly Tilly Willy likes to gossip but doesn't like to tell secrets. Players in the know keep playing so they can both confuse and assist those players who haven't yet figured out the logic behind this puzzle. It is critical that people refrain from shouting out the answer when they solve this game. Have players test their ideas by whispering to the leader what they think the correct solution is. Again, when playing logic puzzles it is useful to have teams and/or to write the answers on the board. We've known this game to go on long after everyone knows the solution just because the players are having so much fun coming up with tricky comparisons of Silly Tilly Willy's likes and dislikes.

THE GIFT OF THE GAME

Boy, did we have to learn to spell better when we introduced this game into our workshop. At most of our trainings, Charlie and I are often being challenged on our own abilities to spell and/or correctly utilize proper grammar. We've even had to stop a training occasionally for a few seconds, during the Logic Puzzle section, to ponder if either of us really knows whether "Broccoli" really does have one or two Cs or Ls. Trust me, our spelling and grammar skills have had to improve. However, even as they do, another uncertain word eventually emerges to stump us and, once again, we'll find ourselves in the position of being ongoing learners. Too bad there is no real time Spell Check for our brains. Luckily, there are these wonderfully playful ways to learn.

ACTION/REACTION

(Kindergarten and up, two or any even number of players, inside, no equipment)

How It's Played

Pair up the players and have them stand about eighteen inches apart. Have the students face their partners with their arms held out toward their partner, elbows bent, palms touching their partner's hands. Have them slowly start the action by allowing their bodies to lean forward simultaneously. Then they increase physical pressure on their hands to break their forward momentum. Before they tire of holding one another up, start the reaction by gently pushing away from their partners until they are balanced standing up straight. As their trust grows, partners can move farther apart. After mastering two-people action/reaction, try groups of three or four. We do not advocate groups larger than four because the group becomes circular and the necessary tension for safely keeping balance is lost. In your class, you may want to have just a few students demonstrate this activity in front of the whole class, so you can be sure they are doing the action/reaction correctly. Remember, this is a game to build trust while having fun. Always highlight the message of safety and do not allow any aggressive pushing or teasing.

THE GIFT OF THE GAME

We all know those famous trust activities such as "trust falls," "trust dives," and so on. These are great games but rarely appropriate for an elementary-school setting. They are just too dangerous, and people often get hurt. Action/reaction is safe and appropriate.

Trust activities often bring up anxiety. When we do this activity in our workshops, we often model the type of acting out and anxiety that games like this can produce. As I explain this activity with a volunteer from our group, Charlie begins to channel our friend Skippy and places himself on all fours behind our trusting volunteer, coaxing me to push the volunteer over his back for a laugh. We temporarily bring the game to a halt to let Skippy know that we will *not* hurt any of the people and that his behavior is not going to make him any friends. In fact, I usually ask the other players if any of them feel that they would want Skippy as their partner for this activity. The answer is a solid "No!" Kids act out for many reasons, from getting a laugh to playing out their fears. We must recognize this and help children learn which behaviors will earn them the trust of their peers, so that they can successfully make friends. Stopping an activity is a great way to let the children know that we, as adults and dependable elders, will act responsibly and help them discover healthier ways to act.

I DOUBT IT

(Fifth grade and up, groups of three to eight players, either at a table or on the floor, cards)

How It's Played

The goal of this game is to be the first player to successfully get rid of all her cards. Have a dealer deal all the cards out. It doesn't matter if some players get more than others. Play starts to the left of the dealer, and that person must declare how many aces he has and place them *facedown* on the table. He may have zero, one, two, three, four, or even more aces if you are using two decks of cards, but he *must* say he has at least one ace. Bluffing is an essential part of this game, because you must *always* put down at least one card. Players will often have to declare having at least one of something they don't really have. When a student has to make such a play, he simply substitutes one or more cards that are placed facedown on the table and declares his bluff. Players should try to be as convincing as possible so that people believe they are telling the truth about how many cards they are trying to play. If everyone believes a player's response, his cards are left on the table and play continues. The next player must state how many twos he is going to play.

During any turn, anyone may challenge the honesty of the player by saying, "I doubt it." At this point, the card(s) being played are turned over, so all players can see if the truth was being told. If the cards accurately reflect the face value and number of cards claimed, the player who doubted the other's honesty must pick up *all* the accumulated cards on the table. This can sometimes be a hefty pile. If the cards do not correctly match the claim, then the player not telling the truth must pick up all the cards. The sequence of play continues ace through king and then starts over with an ace until somebody finally gets rid of all his cards.

THE GIFT OF THE GAME

It's great to have an appropriate place to put cheating. Have everyone acknowledge that this is one place and the only place where it's okay. You can use this effectively to redirect players in other activities where cheating is not part of the rules. We've played this game hundreds of times, and everyone has fun. As always, balance is the key to success. Players who try to cheat excessively get caught the most as their reputation catches up with them. This is a good lesson to show them that fact. We also like the way this game gives children practice in challenging statements they believe are false.

Discussion Gift: Picking Teams Randomly

Building trust is essential in creating a successful school experience for students. When trust is not present, human beings rely on the more primitive center of their brain and focus on self protection. It can become a major time consumer or constant distraction of what we could be thinking about. Being ever vigilant and defensive supercedes our attempts to utilize the higher functioning areas of our brain, those brain areas which are involved in learning. Trust provides us with sufficient reassurance that we can allow ourselves to relax and experience other aspects of life. Trust is actually the seed from which freedom grows and flourishes. The feeling of trust therefore becomes a necessary prerequisite for learning. In this lesson, we will continue to explore some of the dynamics in which play can help students develop a greater sense of trust. One specific area we will address is how teams are chosen. It is a dynamic which effects many students self concept and can impact their entire day at school.

Pick Teams Randomly.

Picking captains who pick teams; could the adults of this world create anything more psychologically painful for the majority of students' self-esteem than this process? We set up problems and failures before we even leave the classroom to play a game. The captains always pick certain peers first. These honored few, of course, think this method is great. They always get a big self-esteem boost for being popular or respected athletes. However, the last dozen kids picked often feel horrible.

In your school, do you pick teams for reading or math? How about spelling, science or art? What a change that would be. "Ooh, Ooh! We want Susie on our team. She never misses a spelling word. We'll all get A's this week." Of course, you don't do this. Then why should we treat the area of play so differently from other curriculum?

No child comes to class thinking, "I can't wait till 10:30 a.m. when we play Kickball and I get to be the last one picked because no one wants me since I always make outs." It's no wonder why so many children use defense mechanisms to avoid these negative experiences: Get sick, act out, make fun of someone else worse than you, start an argument, sit down and just don't join the game: these are the signs of children trying to protect their self concept. As educators, we must realize that children genetically mature at such varying rates. In any third-grade class some children seem as physically advanced as fifth graders. Others have matured more slowly and are like first graders. It's not something the children can control. No one should be penalized for having a different genetic time-clock than another person. Parents do not come to you and say, "This year Susie is really toughening up. She only cries for fifteen minutes this year when she's picked last at school. Last year she cried for 20 minutes. Keep up the good work."

It's time to retire the archaic "Captain" system permanently at school. From now on students will end up on a team without losing any self esteem. They end up on a team just because they showed up to attend school today. Every student does every subject and playing is just another subject that is supposed to be FUN.

The Healthy Play curriculum solution for making teams is the called the double divide. This technique has already been introduced earlier in the book but we feel it bears another look.

Here's how picking equal teams utilizing the double divide works:

Step one: Have everyone in class pick a partner. Children without partners put a hand in the air and look for others who aren't partnered. (Do not become a partner with a student on days when you have an even number of students. On the days when the total is an odd number, you will get a partner.)

Step two: Let the partners choose between two objects. For example, you might pick the Nile River or the Amazon River since you happen to be studying large rivers of the world. Every partnership now must have one person choose to be either the Nile or the Amazon. Now, you ask for all those students who picked the Nile to raise their hands. Quickly check to see that each partnership has one hand up. Have all the Nile partners go to one side of the play area. Have all the remaining Amazon partners go to the other side. Like magic, you will have two equal teams chosen without captains. No one's self esteem is harmed.

Be ready for the obvious learning situation to happen. Two students will be left and one of them refuses to be the other one's partner. Too often it is the child who has become the class scapegoat. Maybe it's a boy not wanting to be with a girl. It could be Skippy and the reasons for not wanting to be his partner are pretty understandable. Whatever the circumstances are, if someone does not wish to be partnered, they can watch the game. You immediately partner with the child no one else wanted. Of course, when they change their mind and talk it over with the person, they can get back into the game immediately. Do not set yourself up to always be saving the unwanted classmate by being their partner. Your students need to learn the compassion you already have mastered. Saving this child only promotes the class belief that they do not have to interact with this person. The teacher will. Let this learning situation occur. Play will be the place where the students have to practice accepting everyone. By doing this you begin the healing process because "scape-goating" will not be tolerated. If you don't deal with this behavior it will continue for the remainder of the year. More than likely, this problem will follow this child into the future unless you intervene. Equally unfortunate will be lesson of acceptance which the other students will not be learning.

Will some students try to manipulate the double divide process? Of course they will. If they don't divide fairly and quickly, send the partners to the side of the game to use Rule # 2 to settle their disagreement. Let the game begin without them. Always keep empowering the healthy peer culture in your class by starting the game up for them. Once your class has played a month or more they will understand that being on a certain team really doesn't matter. The rest of the year will be wonderful.

Obviously, this process can work for whatever number of groups you need. If you want four groups for a science project, have your class get into partnerships of four. Pick four options: winter, spring, summer and fall. Then have the groups complete the quadruple divide.

There are many different ways to create even teams. Another manner is to have everyone get a partner. Have one pair of partners stand in front of you standing side by side. Instruct the other groups of partners to form two columns behind the first pair standing side to side but about one foot from their partner. At this point have each column take an additional step to the side away from their partner. Viola! Like Moses parting the Red Sea you have again created two equal teams.

Other random methods can divide students by odd or even birth dates; odd or even months when they were born; randomly picking either a black or red checker out of a bag; people with siblings and those without; people with dogs as pets, those with cats and so on. For the most part, teams don't have to be even. You are just playing at school. This will be a lesson on doing things a different way for the students. Your focus is to make sure that games are played safely, fairly and that they build trust and compassion.

DOUBLE SIMON SAYS

(Kindergarten and up, generally played indoors, but if the day is nice why not go outside, eight players or more are needed for the game)

As GIANTS, ELVES AND WIZARDS helps older students understand aspects of being on a team, DOUBLE SIMON SAYS is the age appropriate activity for younger students. More importantly this game has been modified so that it really is fun for everyone.

How It's Played

You begin by selecting two DOUBLE SIMON SAYS leaders and place them across the room from each other with an open space for children to walk between them. Pick half of the class to stand by leader X and the rest of the class to go to leader Y. This might be an excellent place to try the double divide method of team creation. Each group will play their own separate game of SIMON SAYS.

As with traditional SIMON SAYS, players must follow the commands which are preceded by the specific words "Simon Says." Players should not follow any commands from the leader if the leader does not use that phrase. **Example:** Leader X states, "Simon Says touch your knees." This means all players must touch their knees. The next command might be "Simon Says meow like kittens." Now everyone should make meowing sounds. If the next command is "Clap your hands three times," none of the players should clap their hands if they were listening carefully.

Here's the big difference in DOUBLE SIMON SAYS. In the regular version of this game when a student made an error they were eliminated from the game. In the old version of this game, when a student playing the game with Leader X clapped her hands without Simon's permission, she was kicked out of the game. Not any more. In DOUBLE SIMON SAYS if you make an error you just say "Oops" and go join the game with Leader Y. Players with Leader Y who make an error say "Oops" and go and continue to play with Leader X. Players can go back and forth an unlimited number of times. In DOUBLE SIMON SAYS you are never eliminated from the game. You just switch groups. This kinder version of the game is so much more appropriate at school.

Be creative with your "Simon says" directions. Here are a few examples:

"Simon says touch another person's arm in slow motion."

"Simon says slowly walk and touch something that is blue and then come back to the group."

"Simon says raise your hand if you know what letter of the alphabet _____ starts with."

"Simon says show everyone your best smile."

"Simon says act like a monkey, elephant, eagle etc."

"Simon says give a soft gentle back rub to the person next to you."

"Simon says touch your chin if your first name has an 'E' in it."

"Simon says slowly walk and touch four different chairs and then come back."

"Simon says count out loud to ten."

GIFT OF THE GAME

The most important dynamic in DOUBLE SIMON SAYS is the trust issue of being included in the game led by the teacher. In the regular version of "Simon Says" students are eliminated. You goof and you're out. It doesn't make sense to banish your students from a school activity. An inadvertent consequence of being eliminated is that it often forces players to learn how to cheat or lie. Would you really intentionally develop a lesson plan to encourage student dishonesty? Of course not. But many students quickly figure out if they are not caught making an error they get to stay in the game. It shouldn't be a surprise to any adult that the kids just want to keep playing. DOUBLE SIMON SAYS fixes this problem. Everyone gets to play the whole time. Goof ups just become an area for the students to practice honesty. Say "Oops" and then try again to do your best with the other group.

The concept of following directions is one of the most useful aspects of the game for younger children. This ability forms an essential foundation for all classroom instruction. However, it has been our experience that too many teachers have limited the learning potential that "Simon Says" can offer. Mostly teachers play a body parts version of the game. Good for learning hips, shoulders, ears and knees, but then the learning stops. The ongoing gift of this game is an opportunity to practice soft touching of each other. Taking a few moments to use your imagination and pretend to be some animal or object. It offers you a chance to review numbers, colors, letters, spelling and everything else you have been teaching. The fact that DOUBLE SIMON SAYS involves walking around and moving from group to group is just another bonus the children need.

SAFETY HAVEN

(Kindergarten and up, 8- 50 players, indoors, outdoors or on grass, play space should be about a basketball court in size 40' by 90', bandannas or markers to identify the players that are "It")

How It's Played

This is a special tag game where the participants are only safe when they seek haven with each other. Choose a playing area and call everyone's attention to the boundary lines. Have several players selected as "It" (one for every 5-6 players) and give them the identifying markers. Players disperse throughout the playing area and the game begins. If a player who is "It" tags another player, "Itness" is then transferred from the original "It" to the person who was tagged. They also transfer the identifying marker to the new person who is now "It," so everyone can easily see the change in roles. Players may choose to run around to avoid being tagged, or they can seek a SAFETY HAVEN (a safe moment of freedom from being tagged "It") with another player. This is done by having two players connect with a side-by-side hug and humming together. Model a sideways hug and humming and then have the group do this. Their safe period only lasts as long as it takes to hum together on one breath of air. After their humming breath is out, they must find a new person to hum and hug with or risk being tagged. In this initial version, a hugging group can be just two people or be made up of any size group. (Allow your students to make hugs that put an arm over the shoulder, touch each others arms or simply hold hands. Let them feel comfortable. Over time the hugs will become more secure.)

Variations during this game keep it feeling fresh. Feel free to change the SAFETY HAVEN rules. Try having students being safe only when hugging people wearing "green," in groups of "four" or people who like "broccoli, etc."

THE GIFT OF THE GAME

Students of all ages have few opportunities to socialize and play together in a positive manner. It seams as if touching has been reduced to only two types in our society: eroticized or violent. This is truly unfortunate, for we, as human beings and especially children, need to experience all the types of appropriate touching to develop physical and emotional intimacy. The beauty of SAFETY

HAVEN is that this activity facilitates appropriate touching within a safe public area. Since everyone is a potential safe "base," the game also makes everybody of equal worth as a "safe port in a storm" of fun.

With simple modifications to the rules, a teacher can gift the class scapegoat or a withdrawn child an opportunity to be actively involved in the game. We can give them a chance to feel needed, accepted or popular. For example, the first time I worked in Ms. Demsey's third-grade class it was immediately obvious which child was the scapegoat. The taunting was merciless and mean-spirited. Once outside, I noted that the class would avoid seeking a "safe haven" with this student. Other students would not hum or hug with him. All the other students kept this child as an "under-dog," so they could feel like "over-dogs." Wanting to break through this trust-defeating dynamic, I happened to notice that this child was one of three children out of 30 who had a cartoon

Safety haven

printed on his tee-shirt. Using the freedom of Creative Play, I changed a rule. I told the children they would be safe only if they were to seek haven by hugging and humming with another child who had a cartoon drawing on their shirt. As if by magic, the child who was the least popular immediately became one of the three most popular children in the game. The "cootie" factor shattered, and from that point on, this child was included as an equal player, even when the rules were changed to share the hugs, hums and "safety havens" with other children. Developing trust does not always need years of intensive psychotherapy. Often, it can be easily accomplished through play.

This same Creative Play dynamic works equally well with shy and withdrawn children. I learned from another teacher that five-year-old Lori avoided all activities, day after day, by sitting on the sidelines because she was afraid of being rejected by the other children. True to form, on the day that I came to her class, she refused to enter any game I initiated even though she was often invited. She was the only child wearing glasses that day, so for 20 seconds the rule was changed to have the children seek haven with those wearing glasses. Well, the mountain came to Mohammed that moment as all the children embraced Lori, showering her with their laughter, hugs and melodically silly humming. Her smile and laughter were evidence enough that her fear of others had melted away. It was this delightful invitation from her peers that mobilized her to participate. After experiencing those 20 seconds of success, she joined in the rest of the games.

REMOTE CONTROL
(Fourth grade and up, two or more players, cones, either inside or outside)

How It's Played
This is a wonderful trust building activity that allows everyone to be in power and under the power of the "remote controller." First,

establish a playing space (A basketball court is good for 20-30 students) and find some obstacles like a row of cones, several chairs, etc. and place them like barricades randomly in the playing field. If you're outside, the primary children's playground area where slides, swings, teeter boards and monkey bars exist will work perfectly. Second, place three destination markers (A, B, C) at strategic locations inside the playing area. Now divide students into small teams of two to four people and have them establish a playing order. Space the teams around the outside parameter of the playing field. The goal of REMOTE CONTROL is to verbally guide your friends safely around the obstacles and to touch all three destination markers while they have their eyes closed. Players can go in any order to the various destinations.

Let's say you have 24 students and made six teams of four. Place the teams around the sides of the playing space and have a 1, 2, 3, 4 order to establish who will be the remote controller. Player 1 from all teams step inside the playing field and will be directed by Player 2 (the remote controller) from outside the field boundary. The remote controller is allowed to walk around the parameter of the field, close enough to be heard by the person with their eyes closed (player 1). Another option is to allow the remote controller to follow directly behind the person they are giving instructions to. Player 1 will search for and touch the markers in the order of A-B-C and then be guided back to the original starting position. During this turn players 3 and 4 will sit quietly and observe the action. As soon as Player 1 finishes, Player 2 will step inside, close his/her eyes and be directed by Player 3 who becomes the remote controller. Players 1 and 4 will sit and watch. Player 2 will be directed in a different order such as B-C-A before returning to the original starting position. Afterwards, Player 3 will be directed through the course by Player 4 and follow the order C-A-B. Lastly, Player 4 will be controlled by Player 1 in the order of A-C-B. When the team finishes they are instructed to quietly sit and watch other teams complete their remote controlling.

THE GIFT OF THE GAME

I remember when we made up this game. We were working with a group of fifth grade peer mentors who assisted us with each of the younger grades when we went out to play. It was the end of our project and we asked them if they would like to do something special by being the first group to test a brand new game. Excitement overflowed. The game was quickly organized and chaos instantaneously developed. Our original concepts, not the ones outlined above, were way too complicated and confusing. The game was terrible. But, just like everything we do, we let the group fix the problems. Voila! A wonderful, sensitive, caring and risk taking adventure was soon created. Everyone liked being guided. Shy students had to practice yelling out commands so they could be heard. The group imposed the rule of quietly watching so "blind" players could easily hear. As expected, peers corrected each other and/or ceased inappropriate behaviors like walking someone directly into a barrier. Many practiced math skills as the remote controller shouting out turns in directions in fractions and/or degrees to aid their "blind" friends. All the students congratulated each other on mastering the difficulty of giving clear instructions. Additionally, they talked, shared, and some even hugged. Now that's the way people can play in a trusting manner!

EMPATHY

(Third grade and older, at least twelve players, inside, no equipment)

How It's Played

We like to tell the story that the game of empathy comes from the wisdom of Native Americans who said, "The best way to know another human being is to walk a mile in his moccasins." Begin this activity by having all players remove their shoes and throw them into a pile in the middle of the floor. The leader begins circling the pile and comments on the unique wonders that the owner of each shoe has to offer. We suggest modeling by having you, the leader, first pick a shoe that would not be a comfortable choice to wear on your foot. (There is always some moderate anxiety in this game, and humorously picking a shoe that is too big or too little helps break the ice.) Now, find another shoe from a very different pair for your other foot and march around as you begin to experience what the original owners feel when they walk in these moccasins. Imagine what it must feel like to be the people whose shoes you are now wearing. Who are these people? Are they happy? Do you share common interests? What do you admire about them? Instruct everyone to find mismatched shoes for their feet, always being sure that a right shoe is on their right foot and a left shoe is on their left. Everyone now parades around and notices the fine choices all the players have made.

Now the tricky part. The goal, at this point, is to rematch the shoes while continuing to wear them. The leader finds someone wearing the mate of a shoe she is wearing and interlocks legs with this other person so that the shoes fit together as a pair, with the right shoe on the right and the left shoe on the left. All players follow the leader's example. Each player now has a shoe that is unmatched and must hold each other together as they precariously move around trying to connect with the other players to match both left and right shoes. The game ends when everyone has paired up both their shoes.

THE GIFT OF THE GAME

This is not the first activity you want to play with your class, because students may feel it is high-risk or an uncomfortable invasion of their personal space. At the right time, however, this is one of the silliest bonding experiences that we know. Every group we have played this with has laughed and laughed while they hold on to each other and scuffle around to attach themselves to another person. The game of empathy breaks down barriers between people. We find out our similarities, such as everyone has warm and sometimes sweaty shoes. We also see that other people have different identities or tastes. They may like shoes that are fashionable, practical, or economical. The important thing about real empathy is that through genuine intimacy with others everyone gets to experience so much more in life, even fun.

COPY MACHINE
(All ages, groups of three players, indoors, no equipment)

How It's Played
Have players get into groups of three. In each group one person becomes the "original," the second is the "copy machine," and the third is the "blank page." We like to begin this activity by having students focus on using their hands. Instruct all the students to close their eyes. The originals form their hands and fingers into some peculiar shape. The copy machines must figure out the position of the originals' hands by feeling them. Finally, the copy machines find the hands of the blank pages and try to reform them to be just like the originals. The copy machines may talk to the players and are allowed to go back and forth between the originals and blank pages as often as necessary. When the final copy is finished, all players open their eyes to see how accurate a job the copy machine did. Everyone trades places until each player has been in all three roles.

As your students demonstrate the appropriate level of trust with each other, they can try more difficult copies using upper body parts, such as head and arms. For truly trustworthy groups of students, you may use whole bodies. You must make an appropriate assessment of your group's readiness. In making a complete body copy, the copy machines do their touching on the back side of the people being copied. In all trust activities it is important to set firm limits and cease any activity at the first sign of inappropriate words or behavior.

THE GIFT OF THE GAME
In 1978 I was playing copy machine at a training for teachers, and

our group included a woman who was blind. I assumed this was probably going to be a rather boring activity for her. I thought that the only fun and challenge in this game occurred after the copy machine had formed the blank page to look like the original and all the players *opened their eyes* to admire the success of the copy machine. How could this woman fully enjoy the game? She could never see the results. Oh, well, we went and played anyway. Almost all the other groups were finished, and the group with the blind woman still needed to let her have a turn as the copy machine. Everyone in the other groups was now watching these three people. I thought, "This could be very awkward."

Insight often occurs when you least expect it. What I thought might be an uncomfortable moment turned into probably the most successful activity of the day. This woman's hands danced with speed, agility, and comfort over the original's body. There were loud gasps of amazement from the onlookers as this woman rapidly and accurately transformed the blank page into an exact duplicate. She received an ovation from the group when she was done, and with a big smile she took a bow. At this moment I clearly saw that everyone really did have an equal capacity for enjoyment. In hundreds of occasions since then I have ignored my preconceptions and allowed the players to just have fun their way.

Cautionary note: Always use good judgment with this exercise and assess your participants before playing. Many groups never get around to playing copy machine because the group dynamics and/or issues of physical touch are so loaded that it is not advisable to play this game. If that is the case with your group, ignore this activity and enjoy the many others that are presented in this book. Always meet the needs of the individuals in your group to experience safety and trust. You have not failed if your group, or individuals within it, cannot tolerate copy machine.

LOST IDENTITY

(Fourth grade and older, the more players the better, inside, paper, tape, pen)

How It's Played

This is a great game for reviewing famous people students have studied in class. One person is selected to have the lost identity. Another player secretly writes the name of a famous person on the sheet of paper and tapes the paper to the back of the person with the identity crisis. Everyone in the group is now shown the lost identity as this player walks around the group.

The player with the lost identity must discover who she is only by asking yes-or-no questions of the whole group. (This can reinforce a great deal of learning about the famous person.) Let's pretend George Washington was chosen as the lost identity. Here are some possible questions and answers:

"Am I a man?"

"Yes."

"Am I a rock star?"

"No."

"Am I living?"

"No."

"Am I a scientist?"

"No."

"Am I an American?"

"Yes."

"Am I a president?"

"Yes."

"Am I Lincoln?"

"No."

"George Washington?"

"Yes!"

Pick another student and start the game again.

If at any point the person in the middle is feeling frustrated, she is allowed to protect her dignity and self-esteem by asking for a hint from the whole group. Hints should be designed so they don't totally give away the answer. The person who has the lost identity may ask for as many clues or hints she needs.

THE GIFT OF THE GAME

One teacher we know shared an innovative way that she improved her children's test scores. On the day before her weekly quiz, she and her class played lost identity. Using historical and current-events figures learned that week, she reviewed their attributes, physical descriptions, accomplishments, and qualities with her class through this game. She saw improved scores the next quiz days because of this activity. Because the children wanted to be more successful at the weekly game, they spent more time doing homework and were generally more attentive in class.

SCISSORS

(Fifth grade and up, the more people the better, inside, a pair of plastic scissors)

How It's Played

This is another game that uses problem-solving skills with a game rule that the players must solve. The objective is to figure out how to pass and receive the scissors in a "crossed" or "uncrossed" manner. All players sit in a circle of chairs. The leader holds a pair of scissors, which she manipulates into one of many possible positions. For example: The leader says, "I have started with the scissors uncrossed, and I am passing them crossed." At this point she may turn the scissors upside down and open or close them with a look of intense concentration. The second person must say, "I have received the scissors crossed [or uncrossed], and, I am passing them crossed [or uncrossed]." The leader and all those who know the solution to this riddle will correct the player if he has made a mistake in how he says he has received or passed the scissors. Play continues to the next (probably bewildered) player, who tries to guess how he or she is receiving and then passing the scissors to the following person.

The scissors have nothing to do with solving this game. They are merely a diversion to what is really going on in the circle. The key to whether they are passing "crossed" or "uncrossed" is whether the player's *legs* are crossed or uncrossed. If players receive the scissors while their *legs* are crossed, this is what they must state. If while holding and manipulating the scissors in their hand, they subtly uncross their *legs,* then this is what they state about passing the scissors to the next person. Hint: Logic-puzzle games can be frustrating to some people. We suggest developing mini-teams of players based on the first three people sitting next to each other, then the next three, and so on. This way no single individual will be upset if he or she can't solve the puzzle alone.

THE GIFT OF THE GAME

You know you are making an impact when your children take what they have learned and share it with others. After Thanksgiving, a fifth-grade girl related that she had played scissors with her family and all eighteen of their relatives. She let her seven-year-old brother in on the secret, and the two of them stumped the adults for over thirty minutes of fun and laughter. They felt empowered, respected, and enjoyed the positive attention from the relatives during this curious activity. This is the true positive social impact of play.

VORTEX

(Large outdoor grassy area, Kindergarten on up)

How It's Played

Everyone holds hands in a large circle facing the center. The leader drops the hand of the person on her left. She then leads the chain of people clockwise around the inside of the circle. Before the circle can no longer tolerate the spiral that is created, the leader switches direction to lead the chain counter-clockwise out of the center. As the line slowly unwinds ask the students to slow down their pace, round out their circle and so that at the end of each round the teacher can once again grasp the hand of the person, originally on her left, who will now be on her right. Be patient if the Vortex doesn't go smoothly at first. This is a great game, especially for primary students, to learn how to work/play cooperatively, problem solve and learn how to hold hands without tugging in a mean manner.

GIFT OF THE GAME

Sometimes more is better. If one class is fun for playing Vortex, two classes makes it more fun. What about four classes? This game has quite the "wow!" factor. A first grade teacher organized a multiple class version after playing this game with just her class. At the end of the lunch period, the four first grade classes were all lined up by their room numbers on the pavement. The teacher coordinated with her colleagues that she wanted to play a brief game before they went inside. Holding hands she began leading her class, starting the spiral movement and attached each of the other classes as the end of the line passed the front of another class. Quickly, all classes were connected and the spiral became really complex. All the kids and other teachers loved this slow walking game which was both exciting and yet very controlled. It gave all the students a common focus before returning to their room. They played the vortex several more times because everyone was having such a good time. What was even more important was the fact that this activity encouraged all the grade level teachers to share more ideas with each other. If one teacher planned something, the others could easily follow along. This dynamic advanced to two classes doing different games together and allowing students to choose which game they wanted to play. It became another method to meet both the needs of the students and the teachers.

THE LEARNING POT

(Second grade on up, small slips of paper, pencil, played indoors)

How It's Played

On slips of paper, the teacher or students write the names of famous people (real or fictitious) and place it in the "learning bowl." We recommend utilizing names of people that your students are currently studying. Each round, a player pulls a slip of paper out of the bowl. The object is for that person to give clues to his/her class or teammates so they can correctly identify the name on the piece of paper. However, the person giving clues can not say or use any part of the name listed on the piece of paper.

Example: name: George Washington. Clue: First president of the United States

If the person giving the clues has no idea who the name on the paper refers to, they are allowed to give verbal and/or charade-like clues. But, they must follow the rules of Learning Bowl and never say any part of the name listed. The teacher should always remind the class of the academic importance of the identified person.

Example: Mother Teresa. Possible Hints: The parent who is not your father is your ___? Mother. A girl's name that starts with the letter after S is? Tammy? No. Tina? No. Teresa? Yes. Teacher: Mother Teresa won a Nobel Peace prize in 1979 for her worldwide work in service for the poor. Beyond current or historical figures, you can utilize the concepts of Creative Play to alter this game to study science and social studies facts as well.

GIFT OF THE GAME

At many of our trainings there is often someone who comes up to us and says, "I do a game that's like The Learning Pot." We always find it an honor to know we have included a good old favorite as part of our program. This is a game teachers have used in one version or another to break the monotony of reviewing test information for years. It's nice when people come up and share their similar experiences with us. I also remember a time this teacher said, "I still use this game, but maybe only twice a year. In the back of my mind when I do occasionally play with my students I'm thinking, 'I'm taking time away from the curriculum.' I use to play a lot more games 23 years ago when I first started teaching. We had a lot of fun in my class and never compromised academics. Being a participant of your HP training has been a reminder to me of how children really do learn. I will once again play more with my students. I'm thankful you have helped me refocus on how I want to teach."

This is a real gift of the game because it's not about the specifics of the game. It's about the bigger picture of education. The gift is the discovery or renewal of a healthy balance in attitude teachers can bring to the learning process. Spencer and I hope many of you will find this gift as you read this book and play with your students.

AMBER'S WORLD

(Third grade on up, dry erase markers, whiteboard at the front of the class)

How it's Played

On your front classroom whiteboard, create a T-graph. Over the T-graph, write out the title of this game, Amber's World. On one side of the middle dividing line, write the word, "inside" and on the other side write the words, "not of." This is a logic puzzle where students try to figure out the riddle to what things or words are "inside" and which are "not of" Amber's World. Pick two children to write down the clues/guesses of their classmates. You will start off the game by giving the first few clues. (We will not give you the rule behind this puzzle right away so you can have fun trying to figure it out as you read the explanation). You might tell your students that even though Amber is a vegetarian and really likes tofu, tofu is not of Amber's World. One of the students will then write Tofu on the "not of" side of the T-graph for Amber's World. And, even though Amber likes to sit on furniture, furniture is not of Amber's World. The word furniture is placed on the not of side of the T-graph. Remember when I said Amber is a vegetarian? Well interestingly enough, Hamburgers are inside Amber's World.

Now the kids might look puzzled with that contradicting information. However, maybe some of the students might think that words and/or things which contradict her actual likes and dislikes might be the solution. Good guess, but that is not the solution to this riddle. I will give a list of some things which are inside and not of Amber's World and see if you can find the solution.

Inside Amber's World	Not of Amber's World
Hamburgers	Tofu
Highway	Furniture
Gridlock	Diamonds
Cupcakes	Pie
Goalkeeper	Soccer
Outdoors	Mountains
Bubblegum	Arizona

I can just imagine the collective readers going, "Aha!" at this point as you quickly discover that compound words are "inside" Amber's World. All other words are "not of" Amber's World.

GIFT OF THE GAME

I have a lot of special feeling for this activity as this game was created by our youngest kiddo, Amber, who was just eight years old at the time. Trying to make the time go by quicker along the long boring ride between Tucson and Phoenix for my wife, Joni and my stepchildren, Amber, Jesse and Malia, I played many of the logic puzzles that are in this book with them. It really made the time go by faster and it was a playful way to interact with our family. As the games progressed we could all see Amber's mind percolating something. She absolutely liked the idea that behind every one of these logic puzzles was a rule created by somebody. It seemed to appeal to her sense of control and quest for power that many eight year olds can desire. During a lull between games she very quickly stated, "I have a game and it is called, Guess What Amber Likes!" (We have since renamed the game to have it be a bit more academic friendly and to incorporate all the compound words listed in the T-graph under the compound-word heading; "inside.") Anyhow, when we played it there in the car, we actually were stumped for the rule behind this game. And frankly, knowing Amber at age eight, it was possible that there might have been some very obscure and creative rule only understood by Amber herself. Initially, we were actually thrown off by thinking the solution was about opposite listings to her actual likes and dislikes. But, a pattern soon emerged and Joni was the first to realize that Amber liked compound words. I asked Amber how she came up with this game and she proudly told us that she had just learned about compound words on Friday at school. I was proud that she was so bright and she was validated for her creativity. This game is another reminder that academics can be reinforced though play, the most natural way children learn.

WHERE AM I?
(First grade and older)

How It's Played
This is another logical puzzle activity which has been designed to reinforce geographic academics. The leader of the game comes up with a secret place (either natural or man-made) that everyone has to guess at via a "twenty questions" style format. All questions asked by students have to be worded so that the leader can answer with either a "yes" or "no" answer. Let us imagine that the leader was thinking of the Grand Canyon. The first student making a guess might ask, "Is this place a land mass?" The leader would answer, "Yes." The next student asks, "Is it in Europe?" "No," responds the leader. "In the USA?" "Yes." "East of the Mississippi?" "No." "Is this place in Texas?" "No." "Arizona?" "Yes" "Is this a man-made structure?" "No." "Is it the Grand Canyon?" "Yes it is." A new leader is now picked and the game continues.

You can use your concepts of Creative Play to adapt this game to reinforce other academic areas such as science by playing, "What am I?" Let's say you are teaching about the different categories of animals in the world and you start the game by thinking of a salamander. Students could narrow down their clues by reinforcing their knowledge whether this particular animal is a mammal, reptile amphibian, etc., what type of food it eats, geographical locations and other identifying traits and so on played in the aforementioned manner.

GIFT OF THE GAME

Using play to support academic curriculum creates some of our favorite gifts of the game. A teacher from California told us how she used this game to bond the love of athletic sports one of her sixth grade boys had with the need to help him in academic areas. She instructed him to think of a sport he really liked (he picked basketball) and that each day he would be in charge of thinking of a different city where a team played. The class would have to guess which city he was thinking of on that day. She allowed him to use the large U.S. map as a reference while everyone played the game. He loved the game and at the end of each session would tell the class about the team's mascot, various great players or other facts. By the second week, he chose the Winter Olympics. It was now a world-wide geography game. By the middle of the second week, other students started taking turns at leading the game and the whole class's interest in geography soared. The playful gift is that the game allowed him to use his competitive abilities to challenge the class while the controlled setting of the game made it so he couldn't have his self esteem hurt in an academic subject. Win/Win is always best.

ON THE WAY TO CLASS TODAY
(Kindergarten up)

How It's Played

Children sit "criss-cross, apple sauce" on the floor. While lightly tapping their thighs they chant along with the leader... "On the way to class today, I (the leader states their name here) saw a _____." At this point, the leader mimes out what they saw. It could have been a gorilla, a ballerina, a guitar player, someone eating ice cream, etc. The children raise their hand to make guesses as to what the leader mimed out. Model about three examples for the children and then start to let them come up to the front of the class and share turns leading the game. Now, when you ask kinder students, "Who would like to lead the next round of On the Way to Class Today?" most children will quickly raise their hands. And, when you additionally ask, "Who knows what they will act out if they are picked to be the leader?" once again they will continue to enthusiastically raise their hands. But, you know once they have been picked and are up in front of the class many children will most likely clam up. They wanted to be the leader, but they never had any idea at all what they would do once they got to be. It is a good idea to have the child picked to be leader first whisper what they will do to the teacher so you know that they do have something that they will demonstrate in front of their class. If they do still freeze up you can gently prod them to show the class what sound and moment their secret creature or person makes. You might even join in with them. However, if they still have stage fright, invite them to have a seat and pick another leader. You may initially have to role play a bunch of ideas for them to choose from. Don't be surprised if one student acts like a monkey that others may also mimic a monkey upon their turn. Once children "get" this activity they often play it very creatively, humorously and for hours. Teachers should appoint someone to be the On the Way to Class Today leader for recess time. This way, children can share turns and have something creative and socially bonding to do at a time in their day when many are bored or isolated from their peers.

GIFT OF THE GAME
This is definitely one of our all time favorites. We were doing our

tenth follow-up at St. Michael's School where I was joined by the seventh and eighth grade kindergarten mentor/buddies. They always bring a wonderful energy to the games and it's kind of special that we have known most of them for the full time that they have been at St. Michael's school.

I had prepared the eighth grade boy who was leading the game to ask a kindergartner what specific animal or object she wanted to demonstrate for the class. Usually we expect a tiger, kangaroo, driving a car, basketball player but after some discussion with the kindergartner the buddy came over to me and said, "She wants to do the tide." I looked as puzzled as the buddy was and asked him, "Does she think she knows how to act it out?" He told me that she says she can so we decided to give it a try. Sitting in the leader's chair the little girl got everyone to be fully attentive and led the chant. She laid down on the floor and with her arms made big curling motions as she rolled toward the group. As she rolled away she made little curling motion. She repeated the process and then asked for guesses. The very first person she called on guessed the tide. I'm still in awe of this talented performance. Like hundreds of similar events, playing again taught us never to underestimate what children are capable of doing.

Trust and Compassionate Play Summary and Overview

Creating compassion in our students and school communities offers children the chance to become their most fully actualized self. Compassion connects us mindfully to ourselves and others and fosters the growth of behaviors which create the highest moral and social possibilities. Academic skills and knowledge, which are often the focus of governmental and bureaucratic policy makers, will never be enough to make children succeed. You can measure skills and knowledge, but the stuff you can measure on tests will not be sufficient to generate greater academic success. Students will need to feel secure in their environment, safe from feelings of isolation, shame, doubt and physical harm. They need to be able to trust their peers and their elders for their well being. Without addressing the underlying issues of what makes students open to skills and knowledge you are asking children to perform a much more difficult function without providing a foundation for that function to grow upon. Even if a child were to develop significant brain power what good would that be if they were unable to learn how to get along with others and make friends? If they never learned how to solve a problem peacefully how will having a high IQ ultimately serve them? When they can't hold a job because they can't get along with others, could we say that their schools provided them with the education that they deserved? If they live alienated and alone because they didn't develop the skills to form bonds and relationships, will being in the top two percent of their class academically keep their hearts comforted? Trust and compassion are the foundations of everything else that follows.

Like all skills, trust and compassion need to be practiced often. Talking about being compassionate is never enough. You can fill your multipurpose room with all sorts of colorful posters that tout being honest, respectful, polite and compassionate, but children will not take on those behaviors unless they have a chance to experience and live those behaviors. Living trustworthy behaviors is critical; it can change the climate of your class and the whole school into an optimum learning environment.

When you continually demonstrate compassion and show your students that trust is a school-wide value, they can count on feeling safe and cared for by their school community. Once that happens, your students can then take that trust, felt within and around them, and balance it with their need to feel safe, take risks, and make necessary changes in their lives to grow into their fullest potential.

Suggested Assignment # 1

Pick two age-appropriate games presented in this lesson and share them with your group of students. Monitor the level of compassion and trust while your students are playing the activities. What limits did you have to set to make the games more trustworthy and the students more compassionate? Did the processing after the games reflect compassionate behaviors and statements?

Suggested Assignment # 2.

Pick two different game activities from this lesson to play for 15-20 minutes. When doing your compliment processing at the end of the game have students say something nice to someone they have not complimented before. As a group, ask the students how they feel about using the Healthy Play games. Ask them what they have liked so far and things they would like to do to make the activities even better.

Lesson Eight:
SOFT AGGRESSION

Introduction

The third game component in the Healthy Play curriculum is "Soft Aggression." In this lesson we will explore the concepts of more aggressive types of play and the appropriateness of such play in the school setting. It is our strong belief that it is NOT necessary to play any aggressive games in elementary school. "Soft Aggression" is at the farthest end of the Healthy Play game continuum. PEOPLE must master both "Creative" and "Compassion" concepts before engaging in any aggressive activities. As we explore aggressive games you will find that we do not encourage their use in any K-3 grades. There are just too many other useful game learning experiences available for these children. For those grades ready to try Soft Aggression activities, this style of play must be carefully supervised for successful applications at school.

Whether you play any aggressive games at school or not, it is still very important to understand these types of activities. Children know of these games. They will often try to model the actions and behaviors they have seen much older students and adults do. Having a healthy perspective about various aspects of aggressive play will enable you to know at what level your students are ready to learn. As much as we will caution you about the use of aggressive games, when the appropriate conditions are present, we believe that "Soft Aggressive" play can offer students positive educational/social skill experiences.

Aggressive Play Dynamics

Let's begin by looking at what does not work. Playing aggressive games because that's what kids have always played is not good reason to use such games at school. Just because your grandfather played Dodge Ball and your father played Dodge Ball doesn't mean you have to teach Dodge Ball to the next generation. It's an aggressive game. You throw things at PEOPLE.

Dodge Ball and many aggressive games are always popular with children who genetically mature faster than their peers. For them, these are the greatest games on the planet. These kids have the strength, coordination and reflexes to protect their safety. Unfortunately, they prey upon others who are not their competitive equals. Those children, who are not as swift or fast, often have painful and intimidating game experiences. Students don't want to be hit so hard with the ball that it leaves a red mark or an impression of the ball manufacturer's name across their forehead. Aggression does not have to be synonymous with violence. School curriculum cannot be designed just for the strongest and the swiftest.

If we were to draw a similar parallel to academics, third grade math would be dominated by the brightest child who could do algebra. All math tests would cover problems trying to find out what "X" equals. Everyone, but Amber, the math whiz, would fail. That's not the mission of elementary school education. In most academics, we wisely try to include all students and not just focus on the smartest children. We must be just as wise when it comes to sports and other game activities that we play in school.

Another example of missing the point concerning aggression happened at a school district that was having problems after their high-school football games. After the game, players were expected to show their good sportsmanship by forming hand-shake lines to congratulate the other team. Unfortunately, the players began to use the hand-shake lines to violently vent their aggression toward the other team by punching them as they passed by. This quickly escalated as players brought brass knuckles and small pieces of pipe to punch the other players with. These conflicts spilled over into parking lots and other parts of the community as the players sought vengeance by fighting.

This example is horrible as it stands. But, to make matters worse, the people, including the administrative staff, who should have been acting as wise elders, chose to solve this problem by eliminating what they believed to be the source of the conflict; the evil and problematic hand-shake line.

They missed the point. In every school sponsored game, players should be able to be good sports. If high school students can't play without fighting at the end of their game, the solution should have been to eliminate football and not the hand-shake line. After suspending one or more games, the coaches, players and parents would have quickly figured out what was truly important about their football games: the PEOPLE playing. This appropriate intervention would have focused on the actual problem and the educational process of finding a solution would have developed important, life-serving skills.

Sports media coverage often presents us with even worse examples of aggression that's not working in professional games. A future Hall of Fame pitcher threw a "six hitter" one day, which for baseball is typically only a fair to good game. Yet, he received four days of media coverage after he hit a batter with a 90 mile-per-hour fastball and the batter came up to the mound to fight him. The pitcher swiftly placed the batter in a head hold and then performed his celebrated "six hitter" as he proceeded to hit him with his fist, six times. That's not baseball, that's assault. Or, what about an ice skater who hires someone to cripple her opponent by hitting her knee with a steel bar? That's not competitive edge, that's battery. A pro hockey player received eight penalties totaling 51 minutes for fighting, slashing and other violent acts. The game is only 60 minutes long. This person wasn't playing hockey. He's wasn't even on the ice for 85% of the game. This player wasn't playing, he was just brawling. The most heinous event happened after a World Cup soccer player accidentally scored a goal for the other team. When he returned to his home country, he was shot. That's not frustrated fan response, that's murder.

All sports and games have not evolved from boxing. We've read the rules. Fighting just isn't there in the rules for baseball, football, hockey or basketball. Even in boxing they won't let you put an opponent in a head hold to hit him. In boxing, they outlawed bare knuckle fighting and have attempted to reduce the physical damage by making the fighters wear padded gloves. Aggression that is out of control is absolutely not part of healthy play.

HEALTHY SOLUTIONS FOR AGGRESSIVE PLAY

To channel aggressive energies in a positive way we must learn to control and soften their overall impact. The Healthy Play philosophy and rules set the tone for how to accomplish this. When children regularly have practiced and internalized compassion and caring for every child in their class, then we begin to soften aggression. When they have practiced using non-abusive words to resolve hundreds of minor squabbles, we soften aggression. When students have taken the next growth step and learned how to prevent injuries and arguments, then the potential problems with aggression have been reduced significantly. These behaviors must be in place before we teach more specifically aggressive games like Dodge Ball.

Additionally, we soften aggression in all our Healthy Play activities by building PEOPLE oriented rules into the games. Hard tags, feet tags, intentionally or accidentally hitting someone in the head with a ball no longer will count as a tag or an out. Hopefully, while in younger grades and before playing aggressive games, children have practiced TOTALLY IT TAG, SAFETY HAVEN, DETECTIVE and RATTLESNAKE TAG where they've learned how to touch each other in compassionate and cooperative ways. We promote fairness with our kids by saying they can't tag, eliminate or score on the players who are engaged in caring for someone. Teachers using Healthy Play concepts empower all the students to be accountable for their behaviors. The positive compliment sessions at the end of the games alter the actions for which children are praised in their play activities. The aforementioned learned and reinforced social skills soften aggression.

Game equipment is also essential to consider in softening aggression. We have chosen to use RuffSKIN™, Nerf™ or similar soft balls when we play Kickball, Soccer or Dodge Ball because they are so kid-friendly. Playing on the correct surface that is free of harmful debris also softens the game.

GUIDELINES FOR LEADING "SOFT AGGRESSION" GAMES

Be vigilant and maintain 100% control. Pay careful attention, observing all the students' actions and behaviors before, during and after the game. Set limits or stop the game immediately when anything seems amiss. When you do this, all of the students in your class can trust that the teacher supervising their activity will keep the games safe and FUN.

Do not condone horseplay. Horseplay often starts out playful and may look insignificant, but such teasing is often filled with aggressive cruelty. Behaviors like punching someone's arm often triggers biological responses beyond the superficial retort, "Nah-nah, didn't hurt at all." The adrenaline released may make the retaliatory punch harder than it was meant to be. Each successive event releases more and more internal bio-chemicals that have a progressively increased effect on the child's body. Often horseplay becomes an actual fight. Even if it doesn't, this is not the time to give such adrenaline pumped up kids an object to throw at their classmates. If kids are horse-playing, announce, "I don't think we're ready for Dodge Ball today. We'll try again tomorrow when everyone shows that they are ready." Not playing a game is an effective way to teach healthy social skills. Don't stop playing completely. Just pick a different game that day so the students can achieve success. It's both their responsibility and yours to intervene when a game becomes potentially threatening or unsafe. Processing disappointments will create quality learning.

Spencer and I are so firm on our stance about horseplay that we do not tolerate any fake fighting. Often while you are explaining a game, two students (usually boys) start pretending to do karate kicks and punches. There are usually smiles on their faces, but sometimes, they even start practicing their best mock tough looks and stares. Without hesitation we send these two students over to the side to use Rule # 2 to discuss how they can play with the class without these violent looking poses or actions. By publicly dealing with these actions we continue to model the effective limits for the whole class to see. If you want to play, you must always act appropriately

Always keep your focus on the people and not on winning. There's no score without PEOPLE, so keep the focus on what's important. If some players are driven to score regardless of the consequences to their peers, use individual time outs or stop the game completely. Competition is wonderful, but it is only one of the 20 things the students said were important about play. At school, keep competition in balance. It is meant to be a spice, which can make things better. No one ever eats a whole plate of oregano by itself.

When Charlie and I are conducting our trainings I often bring up the following when it comes to the importance of people vs. scoring. I remember back in 1960 when I was a third grader in Mrs. Whitesell's class. We often played kickball. But, I couldn't tell you a single score of any of those games even if my life depended upon it. Here is what I could tell you. I could tell you if I played often in the games and whether I enjoyed them. I could tell you if I was liked by the other students or not and if I learned anything. I could even tell you the names of some of the bullies in our class. However, I couldn't tell you the score to any of those games. When all is said and done we don't remember numbers. Instead, we always remember our experiences and feelings and whether they were positive or negative. If we don't make a big deal out of the score then the children won't either. Always keep the primary focus on the people planning and not the score or winning.

Anticipate problems. One way you can use a "Soft Aggression" game is to anticipate problems or failure. You may know that your class isn't ready, but it may be useful to choose a particular game some kids want to play, just to let it fail. We learn from our failures. Thomas Edison failed at creating hundreds of filaments before he found the right one to illuminate the light bulb. Play is a safe arena where we can fail or struggle with our problems without momentous repercussions. When arguing, or other expected incidents occur in a game, stop the play. When you do, you can give concrete feedback to students on what they need to practice for a certain amount of time before you'll let them try the game again.

Successful games deserve lots of praise. When your game is played and it turns out to be FUN, be sure to celebrate and reinforce particular behaviors you saw in specific students. Praising what goes well is one of the strongest teaching tools you have.

Add humor. To soften aggressive and other acting out, add humor to foster buy-in and cooperation for all activities. When you attend one of our trainings, it is side-splittingly apparent that we use a lot of shtick. And, that's more than okay. After a HP training, we encourage participants to borrow our shtick or feel free to make up their own. Not only does humor and story telling facilitate buy-in and cooperation, it really softens and sets the tone for the kind of energies that children put out. Humor and story telling can gently put scoring and competition in their proper place.

Keep competition in a healthy perspective. Competition really is okay. The Healthy Play curriculum endorses a positive belief in competition. It just needs to be placed in a healthy perspective. The only person you truly compete against is yourself. The benefits of competition must not be gleaned at the damaging expense of another. Remember, all the people are the most important part of the game.

To begin softening aggression in our play activities we must address the definition of competition. Our current definition originated during the Roman era and it reflected conflicts between gladiators. Clearly, the perspective of, "Winning isn't every thing, it's the only thing!" had great deal of significance when competition was truly a matter who would be alive for the next game. But, this original idea regarding competition is now obsolete like so many other beliefs which have changed radically over 2000 years. We no longer play any sports or games to the death. It is therefore essential that we update and make relevant the meaning and focus of competition. Competition should now reflect a set of values far greater than an archaic and violent combat between gladiators.

Our new definition needs a foundation in the elements of life that all human beings compete and struggle with; time, space and gravity. These are the universal factors we all face as challenges when we play.

Regarding the concept of time we wonder, how fast can I swim 100 meters or run a marathon? How many points can a team score in four quarters, nine innings or three periods? How quick are my reflexes or how long is my stamina? Am I a better chess player when I play by e-mail because the games may take weeks or months to complete? This is what our games actually reflect when we conceptualize ourselves as competing with or against time.

Space is our challenge with the infinite. Play is one way humans attempt to achieve brief mastery over the environment in which we live. How big should we make a basketball court or soccer field? How long or far should a foot race, horse race or auto race be? How many squares on a checker board? Should we substitute a six sided star for Chinese checkers? Should parallel bars be at the same height or should they be uneven? Will our play space be ice, grass, water, inside or outdoors? In order to compete with space we establish specific limits and parameters so we can measure and give meaning to what we have accomplished.

It is natural for us to strive against the ever present force of gravity. Through our play we attempt to gain control of its confining bounds. How far can a football be kicked, golf ball be hit or a discus be thrown? Can I jump high enough to dunk a basket or do a triple toe loop? How much energy has the moon given the wave that I surf or the collision of tectonic plates given the mountain slope under my skis? Gravity is a fair, impartial, and equal competitor for everyone.

When we compete against time, space and gravity there's no need for violence and hostile aggression. People are simply demonstrating what they can accomplish. It allows each individual to see that, in reality, their competition is always against themselves and the natural elements. The question becomes, "Have I done the best that I can do?" If you want, you can compare the results of your play successes with others. However, this comparison is ultimately not necessary or relevant. For as you mix the dynamics of time, space and gravity it becomes difficult to determine who or what is the best. Is the fastest runner the one who finishes first in the 100 meter, 1,500 meter or 10,000 meter race? Do swimmers, hockey players, skiers and surfers compete equally with each other because they all do a sport that requires water? Is the best jumper a four foot, ten inch, 90 pound gymnast who can do summersaults, flips and turns and land without moving or the six foot, eight inch, 220 pound basketball player who can thunderously dunk a ball by leaping from the free throw line?

Regardless of these comparisons, the focus of a new definition of competition is about what each living individual person can achieve. It's not about aggression, violence and death. With our new understanding we can go back to the original Latin definition of competition and re-interpret its meaning. We no longer need to struggle against another. Our new definition can embrace struggling together with somebody against common forces of nature. When we do this, we receive a wonderful opportunity to have a new definition of competition where instead of struggling against each other to polarize ourselves into winners and losers we now learn to struggle together to improve our skills

This better exemplifies how we can play our games at school. We can learn that these struggles allow us an opportunity to improve our skills. When we accept this perspective of competition we are learning when we play.

Regarding sports played as teams, we, as responsible elders and educators, have another wonderful opportunity to help children get beyond our Western cultural concept that the other team, or that the other players, are our enemies. If we think of them as our enemies, we can feel more comfortable hurting them. Pay attention to the language your students may use when you divide your class into teams. Often, there will be a few kids who might say the following, "You're dead. You are going down. We're gonna trample you! You're losers." Do not tolerate this kind of threatening and cruel taunts. Help the children understand that the other team is just the "opposition."

Enable them to see that the other team is not their enemy. They are not at war with their classmates they are just playing a game with them. At school, at work and in our neighborhoods, we must teach the idea that the other team is just our opposition and is made up of people like us. We encourage you to have the teams celebrate their worthy opponents with special cheers. When you think about it, a team truly needs their opposition. We should honor and respect our opposition and be glad that our opposition showed up because without them we would have a boring game.

Be concrete with your students. Ask them, "Who would chase after the kickball if you didn't have the other team? Who would pitch to you?" Focus must be placed on FUN AND PEOPLE and much less importance placed on competition and scoring. This revolutionary thought will bring great benefits to your students.

An insightful and creative woman named Ann Herbert has written a wonderful piece of satire. We were delighted and amused when we read it. She puts the concepts of scoring, competition and playfulness into humorous perspective. We'd like to share it with you. It's called "The Art of Play":

> In the beginning, God didn't make just two people; he (she) made a bunch of us because he wanted us to have a lot of fun. And, he said you really can't have fun unless there's a whole gang of you. So, he put us in Eden, which was a combination garden, playground and park and told us to have fun. At first, we did have fun, just like he expected. We rolled down the hills. We waded in the streams, we climbed on the trees, we swung on the vines, ran in the meadows. We frolicked in the woods; we hid in the forest and acted silly. We laughed a lot.
>
> Then, one day, this snake told us we weren't having real fun because we weren't keeping score. Back then, we didn't know what score was. When he explained it, we still couldn't see the fun. But, he said we should give an apple to the person who was best of all the games and that we would never know who was best without keeping score. Well, we could all see the fun of that because we were all sure that we all were the best.
>
> Oh, it was different after that. We yelled a lot. We had to make up new scoring rules for most of the games. Others, like frolicking we stopped playing because they were just too hard to score.
>
> By the time God had found out what had happened, we were spending about forty-five minutes a day actually play-

ing, and the rest of the time, working out scoring. God was wroth about that, very, very wroth. He said we couldn't use his garden anymore because we weren't having fun. We told him we were having lots of fun. He was just being narrow-minded because it wasn't exactly the kind of fun he originally thought of. But God wouldn't listen. He kicked us out and said we couldn't come back to the garden until we stopped keeping score. To rub it in, to get our attention, he told us we were all going to die and that our scores wouldn't mean anything anyhow.

But he was wrong. My cumulative, all game score is 16,548 and that means a lot to me. And, if I can raise it to 20,000 before I die, I'll know that I've accomplished something. And, even if I can't, my life has a great deal of meaning because I've taught my children to score high, and they'll be able to reach 20,000 or even 30,000.

Really, it was life in the garden that didn't mean anything. Fun is great in its place, but without scoring there's no reason for it. God actually has a very superficial view of life and I am certainly glad my children are being raised away from his influence. We were all lucky. We were all very grateful to the snake. (Herbert, 1984)

We believe the snake has given us a really bum deal. Like I mentioned earlier in this lesson, I personally don't know what my score was at the end of the Kickball game in my third-grade class on October 19, 1960. I do know whether I was able to make friends. I do remember if I was liked or not. No one remembers scores years after the event. In fact, as Charlie often points out, just ask anyone what the score was in the Super Bowl game five years ago. Most people can't remember who even played, much less what the score was. At the time it seemed so very important, but what remains are our feelings and experiences, not the numbers. So it is with children when they play. It is more meaningful to remember feeling good, accepted and respected than remembering a meaningless, "7 to 15."

Good sportsmanship is presented by our media, but positive examples are reported far less often than examples of poor sportsmanship, aggression and violence. We need more examples like the following to share with our students, one of which was reported by National Public Radio and the others on network news channels:

The National Cuban Baseball League, winners of the Gold Medal in Barcelona, demonstrated that though they play to win, all players are important and celebrated even when they are on the other team. When a member of the opposing team made a good play, they publicly applauded their opponent's skills. Additionally, when the Cuban pitcher accidentally hit the batter with a curve ball, he and the managers of both teams immediately went to the batter to see if he was okay. They enacted Rule # 1!

We like to tell the following story of Lance Armstrong. He is the well known winner of the Tour de France cycling event many years in a row. There he was one year, once again, in the lead when his nearest competitor had a mishap and when off the road and down the mountain. Lance slowed down and waited until his opponent could get back up from the slope, back unto his bike, and rejoin the race. Now the race continued and Lance, as per usual, won the race. But, after the race many people came up to Lance and asked him why he waited until his opponent was able to get back in the race. Clearly, millions of dollars in endorsements were riding on his winning and people couldn't understand why he would stop and jeopardize his advantage. Lance said, he "could not win any other way." Now that is quite competitive and yet also quite mindful.

Another touching story was when two Japanese Olympic athletes scored the same points in an Olympic event. At that time, the Olympic committee did not yet have a process for two athletes ending up with a tie score, so they randomly gave one the Silver medal and the other the Bronze. However, on their return to Japan, each athlete had their medals cut down the middle and presented the other with a half. They then had the halves fused together so each one could have an equal Silver/Bronze "Medal of Eternal

Friendship." Can you imagine what a story like that teaches the children who heard it? If one can be compassionate and mindful, one could also possibly be competitive in the healthiest of manners. This is what truly being a good sport is all about. Only when the focus of game stays firmly on the PEOPLE can aggressive games be fun, exciting and useful.

Soft Aggression Activities

We would like to share with you games that involve more physical interaction between students when they play. No, we're not going to teach tackle football, wrestling or judo. The following are games we think model a potential for learning how to control and safely vent aggressive energy and feelings. For the most part, your students should demonstrate the 100% effective use of the philosophy and the two rules for at least a month before moving on to the more aggressive games. You do not have to play them now just because we have included them in our course. Save them until you know the time is right.

DRAGONS DODGEBALL

(Fourth grade and older, 10-40 players, large playing area free of breakables, three or more RuffSKIN™ or soft sponge balls)

How It's Played

Start by having the players form a very large circle, about half a basketball court in size. Select four players if you have 20 or fewer students and six players for a larger group. These selected players will pair off into groups of two people each and become the dragons at the start of the game. Each group of two must decide who will be the head and who will be the tail of the dragon. The student who is the tail holds the shoulders or the waist of the front person of the dragon with both hands (do not hold on to belt loops when holding at the waist). The dragons are free to roam and run around inside the circle.

The object of the game is for the players of the circle to throw the sponge or RuffSKIN™ balls and hit the tail of the dragon directly on the bottom (butt). Only the dragon's butt counts. The player who hits a dragon's butt moves into the circle to become the new tail of the dragon. The previous tail now becomes the head of the dragon. The former head of the dragon returns to the circle and the game continues. It is not easy to hit the tail of a dragon because the head person is always trying to move so that no one can get a clean throw at the tail person. Teamwork is essential! We also have a three-second rule to encourage players of the circle to pass their ball to someone else quickly if they don't have a clear shot. This three second rule will foster sharing. During the game you will have to frequently call out to remind the students to pass after three seconds. It is useful to have three or more balls in action.

Remember, throwing things at people is aggressive. Quickly stop playing if players are throwing too hard or violently. All the players have to do is hit the dragon's butt. They are not trying to knock anyone out. To enhance safety and soften the aggression we also have a rule that too hard a throw just won't count. As always, if someone is hurt, Rule # 1 is used immediately. However, even though the other member of the dragon is the closest, the person who threw the ball must do the caring. This will help players learn that PEOPLE are the most important part of the game. Use creative play to adjust the size of the circle, the number of dragons, and the numbers of balls to discover which factors make the best game for your group.

THE GIFT OF THE GAME

Overall, we're not too keen on Dodge Ball. It's an aggressive game easily misused. You're throwing something at others in a very hard manner. If you've got a cannon arm and lightning reflexes, then Dodge Ball is fun for you. If you are like the rest of us, most likely you're not enjoying being pummeled by a hard rubberized playground balls traveling at the speed of sound. We were surprised and grateful to discover Terry Olick's DRAGONS DODGEBALL. With this discovery, we finally can teach our children a Dodge Ball game where they can learn and practice compassion, empathy and teamwork. Can you imagine a Dodge Ball game teaching all that? You can pick your jaws off the floor now. A child learns not to throw the balls as hard because they quickly discover that if they are successful with their throwing tag, their butt will become the next target. That golden rule, do on to others as you would have them do on to you, is concretely evident in this game. Compassion and empathy emerge victorious. Teamwork comes into action because the head of the dragon will protect its rear by foiling clear shots. That factor, plus the three-second holding rule encourages players to share the ball with someone on the other side of the circle who has a clearer shot.

Finally, we always suggest using soft sponge or RuffSKIN™ balls. If throwing still becomes rough, assist children to problem solve this issue by ultimately having students making hard throws play with their non-dominant hand or throw underhand rather than take time outs. These students who get to continue to play, but now have to throw underhanded or with their non-dominant hand will not find the game as much FUN. This will then be a motivating factor for them to learn how to throw normally without violence. Once this lesson is learned it might be appropriate to give them another chance to see if they can now successfully throw overhand compassionately. If they do, make sure you praise then genuinely for their improved behavior.

TRIAD

(Third grade and up, four or more players, an open play area, no equipment)

How It's Played

We don't know of a game that has as much flexible teamwork or can tire you out as fast as TRIAD. Have players divide into groups of four. (If teams don't divide evenly, just allow some of the groups to have five players.) Three of the players join hands and form a TRIAD (or in the larger groups of five have four people join hands to make a QUADDRAD). The remaining player becomes the challenger.

The object of this game is for the challenger to tag one of the players of the TRIAD. This is easier said than done. The game starts by having the challenger announce to the TRIAD who they will try to tag. The TRIAD will adjust to move that person farthest away from the challenger. Now play begins. The challenger moves left, moves right, tries to crawl underneath, gets back up and goes around and around, but each time the TRIAD moves to protect the player that the challenger is after. Any tag counts. When the challenger finally catches the person, they trade places and the new challenger announces who they are after. Play continues until everyone has a turn being chased and being the challenger. One special rule is that the members of the TRIAD should not let go of each others hands. If this happens, it counts as a tag for the challenger. Obviously, the challenger cannot pull the hands of the TRIAD players apart.

Modifying the TRIADs makes for extra fun and protects everyone's self-esteem. If the challenger has been unable to tag the person they are after, try having members of the TRIAD hop on one leg. Another idea is to have the players doing the protecting close their eyes and be directed by the person that the challenger is after who keeps their eyes open as well. Let your group have multiple TRIADS and multiple challengers. Use marker handkerchiefs to identify who are the target players in each TRIAD and let any challenger catch any target person. Always keep the games safe, and use this activity to support team work between all the different players.

THE GIFT OF THE GAME

After years of playing TRIAD, an old New Games Foundation favorite, I thought that this game was primarily useful to ventilate pent-up physical energies. I had discovered that kids spent so

Triad

much energy playing the game, even if for only five minutes, that TRIAD was the perfect activity for older students who were acting restless. But as I've learned over and over again, don't count the PEOPLE out on what they might gain from the game.

We were playing with a group of third graders on the fourth day of the school year. There was a new student from China who had only been in the United States for three weeks and didn't speak English. She colored as the class discussed the values of play, and she barely followed along as we went to the playground to play some games.

First we tried LIKE, TOTALLY IT TAG. She stood there, never moved an inch and looked kind of scared. Wanting to get her involved, I then tried SAFETY HAVEN. Surely, I thought the concept of hugging and humming would get her involved. She didn't understand a word I said. Failing to convince her by a simple hum-hug demonstration, I had the whole class hum and hug while facing her. Again, she showed no response of understanding and continued to look afraid, but we went ahead and played the game. In this instance, SAFETY HAVEN, which had always worked at bringing children together, did not succeed.

A little flustered, I suggested we play TRIAD. What was I thinking? This activity is too physical. It might only scare her more. Oh well, I'll just have her watch, I thought to myself. Everyone broke up into groups of four, except three girls who seemed to be very close friends and this little girl from China. I gently moved them together to make a TRIAD of girls holding hands with the remaining girl the challenger. I announced to the class to begin, and to my surprise there was all this giggling and laughing streaming out of our Asian friend's mouth. In fact, her whole group was running this way and that way, laughing and giggling. Just like that, she had shown the others a language they all knew. With each passing moment, the bond between that group grew stronger.

After the game, the class expressed their positive feelings with each other. Once again, she didn't know what we were saying and no one gave her any compliments. But, the game had worked its magic. As we started to walk back to the class, the other three students put her between them and held hands again. They immediately resumed laughing and giggling. I felt overjoyed watching them swing their arms back and forth as they crossed the playground. They were no longer strangers.

For the rest of the day the four of them spent time teaching languages to each other. The girls would race up to the teacher and relate each breakthrough. "She said, 'Pizza.' "She said my name!" Later in the day, her older brother, who spoke English, translated for her. He said this was the first day she had enjoyed being at school. She liked having friends. The whole class won that day because of how those four students played together.

STRATEGY TAG

(Fourth grade and older, ten or more players, outside or in a gym, no equipment)

How It's Played

Ever feel like everyone was trying to get you? Well, this game playfully lives up to that feeling. Players begin by making a straight line of students standing shoulder to shoulder. Place cones or identify lines to use as a boundary about twelve feet both in front and behind the line of students. At this point, have every other person turn and face the opposite direction so that the line has a person facing forward, backward, forward, backward and so on. The people of the line are called "Chasers." A "Quarry" and one "Chaser" are chosen from the group to start the game. The "Quarry" is the person who is being chased after.

The object of the game is for the two active players to run around the line as the Chaser attempts to catch the Quarry. The problem for the Quarry is that the Chaser can choose a replacement from the line at anytime to continue the chase. In order to pick a replacement, the Chaser comes up from behind and taps another player on their back. The player who was tapped steps forward and becomes the new Chaser while the previous Chaser steps into the vacant spot the other player just left. Eventually the Chaser catches the Quarry. Once tagged, the roles immediately reverse. The Chaser becomes the new Quarry. The Quarry becomes the Chaser and can now use the line of players as replacements.

Only the Chaser can tap someone as a replacement. The Quarry is stuck running away from the Chaser until he is caught and the roles reverse. Players must stay within 12 feet of the line at all times. Players running around the line can change directions at any time. Be prepared for this game to be confusing at first. Be patient and correct the errors that occur. What will frequently happen is that the Quarry will try to use the line to get a replacement. Sorry, only the Chaser can do that. Other times, the Chaser will pick a replacement but forget to take their position in line. Another

Strategy tag

frequent confusing factor occurs because students sometimes get too excited watching the people running around. In their excitement and to get a better view, students in the line end up turning sideways. This is problematic because it will make it harder for the Chaser to figure out who they can tag on the back. Have fun and remember this game takes STRATEGY.

THE GIFT OF THE GAME

Teamwork: it's on every poster that we make in the classrooms. This is a perfect game to allow children to practice the teamwork they think they believe in. Initially, your class will have long drawn out races between two students who refuse to give up chasing each other. You might as well plan for this to happen. When it does, you'll have an opportunity for the class to make up a rule like, "You can't circle the line more than two/three times without picking a replacement." Players actually make the game more difficult when they don't use the line. Eventually, children will learn that the excitement and pace of the game improves when they use each other very quickly. At this point, the insight about the simplest form of teamwork will have been accomplished. Additionally, some kids will get picked over and over while others do not get a chance to run at all. Take a brief time out to identify this problem and then have people who have not been chosen raise one arm. Now the Chaser can only pick students with their arm raised who have not had a turn. You can even suggest that the game cannot end until Susie Cue tags Skippy. This will require the class to figure out how to get the right players out there to end the game. With a lot of practice, your class will actually transfer this learning to other sports like Kickball, Soccer and Basketball. This awareness should help stop that one player who will race all over the field trying to make every play alone. Remember to return to and use your posters to help the children focus and perform the values they identified about play.

BE MY FRIEND, ONE, TWO, THREE

(Third grade and up, ten or more players, a large safe playing space, no equipment)

How It's Played

This is a soft-aggression game that can be played with lots of enthusiasm and energy. Mark off a large space (approximately 100 by 40 feet if you have twenty-five players). Have everyone stand on one of the long sides of the field, and pick two boys and two girls to be the first set of friends. These four players go to the inside of the playing area and begin the chant, "Lonely people standing there, won't you be my friend?" At the end of the chant, the people on the side race across the playing field, trying to reach the other side without being caught. The friends in the middle attempt to "catch" the running players and must touch them long enough to say the phrase, "Be my friend, one, two, three." If contact is maintained, the person touched becomes one of the friends and helps catch other people. Eventually, everyone becomes part of the group of friends. At the end of the round, the two original boys pick two new girls and the original girls pick two new boys, and the game starts over.

THE GIFT OF THE GAME

The gift of this game came from its metamorphosis over the years that we have played it in its various incarnations. Initially, we observed a game called British bulldog. British bulldog happens to be a brutal activity with questionable usefulness. Mostly, children just got hurt trying to break through the arms of the players in the middle. We eliminated the action of breaking through people's arms. Instead, we had players try to pick other players up off the ground. The game was renamed American eagle to disassociate the play from British bulldog. The game still proved unsatisfactory for many players, so we then changed from picking people up to having prolonged tags. This improved the game significantly, yet there was still an aspect of uncontrolled aggression as people raced by, thinking they were unstoppable American eagles. The last piece we needed to shape this soft-aggressive game into one that reminded us that all the players were really our friends was a change in title. Be my friend, one, two, three conveys the right message while providing plenty of physical action.

BALLOON SOCCER

(Third grade and up, twelve or more people, an inside open space, a bunch of balloons at least twelve inches in diameter)

How It's Played

This is a moderate soft-aggressive activity. First, blow up your balloons and store them (in a balloon corral) away from the game. Define a clear space of approximately 20 by 20 feet. Set two sturdy chairs (the goals) at opposite sides and encircle the chairs with cones or some other boundary marker, like tape on the floor. Randomly divide into two teams and have players *sit* on the floor. Be sure to scatter the members of each team all over the playing area, and have one player from each team sit in each goalie chair.

The object of the game is to tap the balloons to your own goalie, who must pop the balloon using his fingers. Instruct goalies to pop balloons far away from their own and others' faces. Do *not* allow sharp objects, such as pens or needles, to be used to pop the balloons, for obvious safety reasons. All players must keep their *bottoms* on the floor at all times, and they cannot rise on their knees to get an extra height advantage. Players may scoot around to get to different positions, but they cannot crawl, stand, or roll around to get there. The balloons can only be tapped by the hand. For safety reasons, kicking, carrying, or holding a balloon is not permitted. The goalie must stay seated in the chair while trying to catch a balloon that is being tapped toward them. The boundary area around the goalie is a safe zone. Players may reach into the safe zone with their arms to deflect the balloons from the goalie. However, they may not scoot their bodies into the safe zone. Adjust the size of the safe zone to meet your students' needs.

Many variations are possible in this game. First of all, players don't have to pop the balloons to make a score. This makes the game last longer and cost less. Also, kids who are uncomfortable around loud noises may not like popping balloons. Some balloons will pop during play, so be prepared and have some extras. Try having two or more balloons in play at a time. This becomes especially funny when the goalie is holding several balloons yet still tries to catch another. Many a goalie has lost several caught balloons while trying to get another. Have the goalies wear blindfolds or close their eyes to make scoring even harder. Having fixed positions where the players are not allowed to move may be a necessary step to take if you want to slow the action down or if some players become too rowdy. Always explain why you are making such changes, so that the children can learn from the experience.

We've tried this game standing up, and it's just not as safe. Players got too excited jumping around and accidentally hurt each other. We found the only safe, soft-aggressive way to play this game was to start and stay on the floor. Once again, sharp objects to pop the balloons are not allowed.

THE GIFT OF THE GAME

We like this soft-aggressive activity because it's perfect to blow off energy on a day when you can't get outside. It helps kids practice setting boundaries around their bodies. They also learn how to stay in control while still playing hard with other people and with objects in a room. Be sure to allow time for the teams to plan some offensive and defensive strategies. We are amazed at the inventive ideas that groups create, especially if they have played this game five or six times.

There is so much action going on in balloon soccer that it is almost impossible to know what the score is after the first few pops. We love using this method to deemphasize scoring: At the beginning of the game, we tell each team that they will receive a point for every balloon that their goalie pops. When all but one remaining balloon has been popped, we explain to the whole group that the other balloons were really just practice and that the final balloon we are holding is the only one that really counts. We then set up an impossible task, saying, "Both teams only have five seconds to pop this last balloon or the game ends in a tie." Nine out of ten times the balloon remains unpopped, and the children are satisfied with the tie score. This game generates so much laughter.

OH, FIDO
(Any grade, ten to forty students, inside, sturdy chairs)

How It's Played
Arrange all the players in a circle, sitting in chairs. Ask someone in your class to give you the name of their pet. Let's say the child has a dog they call Fido. Then that becomes the title of your game: oh, Fido. Select one player to be it. Remove her chair from the game and have her stand in the middle of the circle. The object of this game is for the person in the middle to get a chair.

Movement in oh, Fido occurs when two players who are sitting down make eye contact with each other and make a nonverbal agreement to exchange chairs. When they think the person in the middle isn't looking, they get up and try to switch places. If the person in the middle sees them move, he can try to beat the players to one of the empty chairs. Often there are several people making chair switches at the same time, which causes confusion and usually allows the person in the middle to find a seat. More action happens because other players can get up and sit in an empty seat while the players are trying to make a switch.

To protect the self-esteem of the player in the middle in case she can't get a chair, we give her special power. At any time, she can yell the name of the game, "Oh, Fido!" and everyone sitting down has to get up and move at least two chairs away from where he or she started.

Practice safety! We always make a rule that if someone touches a chair first, it becomes that person's chair. This reduces the number of people colliding and crashing into chairs. If students are knocking each other down while running around, you may want to slow the game down by making everyone walk heel-to-toe. Or you can stop the game and have the kids offer suggestions.

THE GIFT OF THE GAME

The naming aspect of this activity can give gifts to a child even before the game has started. Being chosen to name this activity empowers and acknowledges the child. This can help to gently quiet attention-seeking children who become relaxed and less anxious when they are recognized. Or maybe you want to boost the self-esteem of the isolated or ostracized child. Giving her a chance to name the game validates her. This often tears down another group barrier and "de-cootiefies" this child as the group learns more about her. You also might reserve the naming of this activity for the child who has been the most nurturing to her peers. This action always reinforces the positive peer culture.

The rule that the person in the middle can yell out, "Oh, Fido," when unable to get a seat goes a long way. Some children don't possess the skills, cunning, or power to get themselves out of impossible situations. Using creative-play dynamics to make up rules

Oh, Fido

like this one enables *all* children to play this aggressive game. Kids who are fast won't need to yell, "Oh, Fido," because they will probably always get a seat quickly. For children who are a bit slower, this is a safety valve to protect their self-image when they think they need to use it. When children can trust that their humanity and skills will be honored and taken into account, they will feel better able to take risks. We also like how this game gently assists in developing eye contact and other nonverbal communication skills.

OFF BALANCE

(Fifth grade and older, groups of two players, space to stand, no equipment)

How It's Played

This is an aggressive activity, but it can help players learn to control their physical energy. Begin by having everyone find a partner. Partners stand about two feet apart with their feet directly under their shoulders. Players raise their hands in front of their bodies with their arms slightly flexed. The object of off balance is for students to rapidly push at their opponents' hands, making them lose balance and move their feet. It might seem like strength will always prevail in such a contest, but it's not so. A highly effective strategy is to avoid hand contact with the opponent, so he topples forward and moves his feet. Only the hands can be used as a target area. A player may not push an opponent in the chest, shoulders, or head.

THE GIFT OF THE GAME

I find this game useful because it so carefully controls the act of aggression. Players clearly have to face and look at their opponent. It becomes obvious that they need their opponents, or they would look silly standing there alone thrusting their hands into the air. Opponents are good! Without them there are few games. To control aggression only one target area can be attacked. When they play, kids hear the slapping together of the hands. This has the sound of aggression, yet the actual physical impact causes less discomfort than enthusiastic clapping. I especially like the lesson of the game, which teaches that excessive aggression is not successful. Students learn that when they passively

Off balance

stand there with their knees bent slightly and give their arms no tension at all. Using this dynamic, opponents will never push them off balance.

ACCUMULATOR

(Fourth grade and older, eight or more players, large outside or inside area free of breakables, three RuffSKIN™ balls)

How It's Played

The object of accumulator is to accumulate all the lost friends, thus making them all winners. Begin by setting up your boundaries, which should be the size of a basketball court. Select two to four players to start as the accumulators. The accumulators take possession of the RuffSKIN™ balls in the center of the playing area. The lost friends scatter to the outskirts, as far away as they can get from the people with the balls. The game starts when the accumulators. say, "*Hasta la vista*, baby!" Accumulators may throw the balls to hit any lost friend, turning her into another accumulator.

Accumulator

The newly captured accumulators now assist in gathering everyone else.

Accumulators do have one major challenge. When they are *holding* a ball, they cannot run or move their feet. However, accumulators without the ball can move freely on the playing field. The best strategy is for the accumulators without a ball to get close to or surround a lost friend and then have the ball-holding, feet-frozen accumulator(s) pass a ball to them for a successful short throw. Long throws usually miss, and the accumulators can spend a lot of time chasing after the erratic balls. Teamwork is the essence of this game.

Instruct the accumulators that they should keep one arm waving in the air so all accumulators are easily identified for ball passing and teamwork. Fair-play rule: Only the accumulators may raise their hands and shout that they are accumulators.

There is a lot of action in this one, but lost friends can only be turned into accumulators if they are hit between the knees and the shoulders. Head and feet hits don't count for obvious safety reasons. If someone is hit too hard, the tag won't count, and the thrower will need to stay with the injured person until he or she feels ready to play again.

THE GIFT OF THE GAME

No one likes getting kicked out of a game, and here people are accumulated, not eliminated. Sometimes children learn the value of teamwork when it's missing. We recall many classes who became frustrated that the same three dominant or skilled kids were hogging the ball. Often these greedy ballplayers were the ones who sent the balls flying outside boundary lines without accumulating more lost friends. The frustrated children who were tired of chasing wayward balls could ask that the game stop. During the processing time, they identified solutions so that everyone could be included and every lost friend would be turned into an accumulator.

Remember that your group has not failed if it needs to stop a game that is not working out well. Often this is the point where most of the learning occurs, where most behavior changes begin. Try to see discomfort and frustration as tools. Never lose sight of the fact that most positive behavioral changes occur after children become comfortable with their uncomfortable feelings. Using these simple games, you can help schoolchildren overcome their difficulties with teamwork. You can appreciate why Jean Piaget and Erik Erickson advocate team sports for seventh graders and older children.

BLOB

(Third grade and older, eight to forty players, very large playing area, no equipment)

How It's Played

This is an accumulation tag game of blobs and amoebas. Blobs know life is better when there are lots of friends hanging together. Amoebas think life is fine alone and celebrate the freedom of individuality. The object of the game is for the blobs to catch all the free amoebas. Select a large rectangular playing area about 60 by 100 feet, and start the game by picking one person to become a blob for every seven people playing the game. The blobs start a three-two-one countdown, and each blob, acting independently from the other blobs, begins chasing the amoebas all over the playing field. If a blob touches an amoeba, that amoeba becomes part of that blob by holding hands with the person who tagged her. The blobs grow and grow every time another amoeba is caught.

Teamwork and cooperation are essential. If the blob comes apart while they are chasing someone, the tag does not count. Moving slowly, stretching out, and chasing one specific amoeba at a time are all good strategies. Amoebas may not break through or run between the members of the blob. At some point near the end of the game, several blobs may wish to connect, making one huge blob that stretches across the entire playing field. This makes rounding up the last few amoebas simple work if the blob walks

Blob

down the field, not letting anyone get past its ends.

THE GIFT OF THE GAME

To discover what it is like to be really, really excited without losing self-control and awareness is a fantastic gift for children and teenagers. To discover that effective strategies and teamwork can get the job accomplished more efficiently is another valuable lesson to be gleaned from this game. As the game facilitator, be aware that this game is difficult for most young children the first time they try it. Don't give up. Help your children explore solutions of cooperation and teamwork. The successes they gain with repeated play cultivate their abilities to work collectively with others. Can you see how we have further redefined the role of the players in all our games by regularly calling them "friends"? This is a social-skills education that is lived and not just read in a conflict-resolution program.

Also, if you want to teach some practical applications of geometry, play blob. My favorite tactic is to have my blob chain choose the fastest kid in the class to catch. I tell my blob, "We will walk while our amoeba quarry will have to jog or run." My blob members all like this idea. "In fact," I tell my blob, "we will chase this amoeba until it is so tired that it will ask to be tagged, on purpose, just so it can walk with us." And that's what usually happens.

Here's how this strategy works. Our blob will move to the center of the field and begin chanting the name of our amoeba quarry. The person closest to the center remains almost stationary while the other blob members move like a door on a hinge, forcing our quarry to stay outside our reach. To avoid us, the amoeba must jog or run in a circle about ten feet away from us. This extra ten feet really changes the distance the amoeba must travel to stay out of reach. When the amoeba reverses direction, the blob simply yells, "Switch," as we all let go of one another's hands, turn around, reconnect hands, and then walk in the opposite direction. For advanced-math connections to your class's game of blob, try having your class measure different circle circumferences with a string or calculate the distances.

SWITCHER SOCCER
(4th grade and up, outside soccer field, soccer balls, bandannas)

How It's Played
Teams are divided equally at first. Three to four balls are placed mid-court. Goalies are picked. "Switchers" (one to two per team) are picked and given bandannas to identify them. Switchers have the power, once play begins, to tag opposite team players and make them now members of the Switcher's team. The game leader (teacher or identified student) has the option to yell out, "Change Switchers." If this occurs, switchers must give the bandanna to a member of their own team who now becomes the new Switcher. Every time a ball is scored it is taken out of play. When one ball remains each team only gets 30 seconds to score or the game ends as

a draw. Whatever team players were on at the end of the last round becomes the team they must start out on for the next round. At this point the teams will most likely not be even. New goalies and Switchers are picked.

GIFT OF THE GAME

It is a really special treat when you make up a new game. Spencer and I were back at one of our favorite schools for the sixth or seventh time. We couldn't think of an exciting outdoor game for their fifth graders that we hadn't already played. To solve this problem we offered them a chance to play Switcher Soccer, a game I was just beginning to formulate. A quick vote confirmed their enthusiasm to participate as the experimental group for our brand new game.

Since they were familiar with Three Ball Soccer the new adaptations seemed easily explained and it looked like there would be no problems. Well, it was easier said than done. The first round of the game was fairly confusing. We had not yet established that the "switchers" needed to identify the team that players had to now play for. Thus, recently tagged players ran around tagging other people but didn't know the name of which team they belonged too. Our first huddle with the kids solved that problem.

The next round had one "switcher" wanting to play more soccer than doing the switching. When the game was over there were only three people left on his team. Again the students quickly processed what the focus of the "switcher" need to be.

The third round had two of the three balls score quickly and then it took forever to score the last ball. More importantly, Spencer noticed that the level of competition to score the last ball started to demonstrate more than the desired level of aggression among the players. In a wonderfully serious manner, the students acknowledge their behaviors in the last game and re-affirmed how they wanted to play. Additionally, some students found the game got kind of boring when there was only one ball and they felt left out of the play. As always, the kids came up with the idea of a time limit after the second ball got scored and the game was made better.

The fourth round was a really successful game. Everyone was totally exhausted from all the running. The compliments after the game were equally divided between reflections on how people played the game and to those who offered ideas to make it better. Seeing the excitement of the students discussing the new strategies and making plans for the next time was a wonderful reward. They all felt very special to be the first group to play this game. It's fun to experiment. We can't encourage you enough to try new ways of playing a game.

DRAGON TAILS

(Third grade up, best played outdoors or in a large indoor space without obstacles, bandannas)

How It's Played

Divide class into Dragons. Each Dragon is a line of students, between three to eight maximum, each holding on to the waist of the person in front of them. The last person in line tucks a bandanna or paper towel in the back of their belt or in their back pocket. The object is for the people at the head of the dragons, who have their arms free, to try and snatch a bandanna from another dragon's tail. If a line happens to fall apart, the "catch" will not count. This is a good safety rule to help students act cooperatively while maintaining a better sense of safety. Once a tail has been taken from your dragon those students head off behind the side boundary lines and cheer on the remaining dragons.

GIFT OF THE GAME

Most Healthy Play activities have all the students playing at the same time. We have eliminated the elimination factor of most games to increase the self-esteem and activity of all students. However, there is also value in giving children opportunities to learn how and when to tolerate not always having their "turn." But, to do this you really need to make sure that any down time is structured or else children will become bored or fidgety. The down time for not being actively involved in Dragon Tails is short. If your dragon has lost its tail you will only be out of the game for a few moments until the next round. Additionally, once any dragon becomes eliminated you will find those children are now very active spectators invested in all the action remaining on the playing field. Safety factor: We have learned that adding all the dragons together who have lost their tails into one long dragon is not safe. The line becomes too whip-like and almost impossible for children to maintain integrity of a full and unbroken line.

ULTIMATE BALL

(Grade four and up, full basketball court or large outdoor grassy play area, one RuffSKIN™ ball)

How It's Played

Divide your class into two teams. Using a basket ball court or a larger field on the grass, define each team's back end-zone line. The object of the game is for a player to toss the ball to another member of their own team behind the other team's end-zone. That person has to catch the ball for it to count as a score.

To start the game, players line up along their end-zone. Team A tosses the ball to Team B. Now there are very specific rules in the game of Ultimate Ball that make this game both fun and challenging. Whenever a player is in possession of the ball they may not run from their position. They are allowed to pivot on one foot but can no longer run. To keep the game safe, no other player can cross the "pivot reach" of a player who has the ball. When they do toss the ball to another teammate they are, once again, permitted to run. However, the person who caught the throw may now no longer run with the ball. If at any time the ball is dropped or intercepted by the opposing team, the opposing team gains possession of the ball and play continues towards the opposite end-zone using the same rules. To keep the game from being dominated by your best throw-ers or dominant children we suggest that you inform the class that any team cannot have a score count unless their ball has been passed to at least two boys and two girls on their team prior to the final throw behind the opposing team's end-zone. If a team scores, everyone lines up again along their end-zones and the scoring team tosses off the ball to the opposing team to start the next round. Game ends when a team reaches 18,000 points. Just kidding. But, do use your Creative Play dynamics to soften the competition and move the focus from the score back to the people!

GIFT OF THE GAME

This game has the most wonderful opportunities to help students come to grips with what the proper levels of increased competitiveness mean during a school game. In every game of Ultimate Ball be ready to discuss the crowding in on the person who has the ball. One discussion by the whole group usually solves the problem, but just in case, a reminder to use Rule # 2 really fixes things quick. We really can teach kids to play fair.

The second predictable gift occurs after two or more rounds when you ask "Who hasn't caught the ball yet?" Many times some rather hurt feelings are shared by the non-included team players. The great thing is that the team fixes the problem immediately.

My favorite solution to include everyone on the team is called the "decoy." By the third round, both teams were earnestly trying to get their last people involved in catching the ball. Unfortunately, the other team could see who you were trying to get the ball to and swarmed over by the person making it impossible to pass the ball to them. During the huddle after the next point was scored, a sixth grade boy developed this strategy. He asked a student, who had already caught the ball, to cause a great commotion about needing to pass the ball to him. The majority of the rest of the team was to run over there and keep shouting for the ball. Anyone who hadn't caught the ball was to go to the other side of the field. The opposition fell for that strategy hook, line and sinker. They swarmed the decoy. Seconds later the ball was successfully passed to the opposite side of the playing field where no one was guarding the people who needed to catch the ball. Now everybody on the team felt good. Healthy Play endorses competition. The real gift is when you and your students can see that it was a higher level of competition to figure out how to include everyone vs. only having the four or six best players do the playing.

SPONGE WARS

(Third grade and up, best played with a lot of players, outdoors, two sponges or more per player and two water buckets)

How It's Played

Set up a playing space about the size of a basketball court outdoors, and place a boundary line across the middle. Place the safety bases (buckets of wet sponges) in the middle of the opposite end lines of the playing area. Divide players, using a double divide, into two teams and place the teams in their half of the playing area. Be firm on the rule that players from opposite teams *cannot* cross the middle line or they'll become frozen solid at the point where they crossed.

Players will try to tag opposing team members with laser blasts. Laser blasts are represented by thrown wet sponges. If a player is hit by a laser blast, he becomes stunned or frozen. Once hit, frozen players cannot move (that is, pick up or throw sponges) and are at the mercy of players on the other team, who can continue to *softly* bombard them with wet sponges. Frozen players are permitted to turn and face away from the opposing team, so they will only be hit with sponges from behind. Fortunately, each team will choose a "healer," who becomes the *only* person on their team with the amazing ability to unfreeze frozen teammates. When a healer touches a frozen player, the player is free to move again. Players can be frozen and unfrozen any number of times. Prior to the start of the game, teams must announce (using lots of fanfare) to the opposition just who their healer is.

Sponge wars

Because of his or her great thawing abilities, the healer is the most important player on a team. If the healers are hit by a sponge, they are removed from the game because no one has the power to unfreeze the healers. If a team's healer is tagged with a sponge, it loses a great strategic advantage. From that point, none of their frozen players can be thawed out. So it is a very important team strategy to choose one or two players to act as shields to protect their healer. Explain that a player who becomes frozen should turn around and call out for his healer. The healer, protected by her human shield, goes to the frozen player, tags him, and lets him reenter the game as an active players. As long as the healer is touching her shield(s), the shield(s) can't be frozen because his healer's touch is constantly unfreezing him. If a healer accidentally becomes separated from her bodyguard, the healer should immediately run back to her safety base (the bucket of wet sponges). Healers are only safe from the laser blasts of wet sponges if they are touching their water-bucket safety base.

If a healer is tagged with a wet sponge while not on the safety bucket, we recommend taking a brief time-out. All action must cease. Remove the healer and all currently frozen players on the frozen healer's team from the court. They will now root and cheer their remaining teammates from the sidelines. From this point on, any player on that team when hit by a sponge must leave the playing area. Remember, they have no healer left to unfreeze them. When there are only five players left on a team, the other team has only thirty seconds to "sponge" the remaining players or the game ends as a tie.

Most games end in a draw, but don't worry if a single team wins. By the time you are ready to play sponge wars with your group of children they should have had a great deal of practice in healthy social skills. So they should be able to tolerate this dynamic without teasing and taunting. Plus, there will be an advantage given to the "losing" team when you start the game over. At the end of a game, the losing team usually has a lot of extra sponges on their side of the playing field. They get to keep them. Yahoo! The other team cannot cross the middle line to get these sponges. You can reassure the team with few sponges that they'll have plenty of sponges in their territory real soon after the game begins again.

Reminder: Be sure that all the players understand completely that people are the most important part of the game and that vicious, aggressive acts and rule breaking will not be tolerated *before, during,* or *after* the game. Be sure all rules, concepts, and boundaries are established and explained before letting teams pick up their wet laser blasts. Before and after each game, no throwing of sponges is allowed. Be especially firm with the rule that even players on the same team cannot attack each other with water or sponges. Always start the game with everyone counting down, "Five, four, three, two, one, go." Now go have fun!

THE GIFT OF THE GAME

We have often described this game as the carrot in front of the pony. When we do trainings at schools, there are always children around who watch their teachers play our games. No other game we play excites the students as much as watching their principal, teachers, and parents throw wet sponges at each other. The students' response is always, "When do *we* get to play sponge wars?" The excitement about playing this game often becomes a catalyst for teaching the social skills, values, and responsibilities that must be mastered before engaging in a soft-aggression activity. Sponge wars is intentionally placed at the end of our trainings and at the end of this book. It will not succeed without a strong framework and understanding of creativity, compassion, and soft aggression by all the participants. When your children have earned the opportunity to play this game, they will truly possess the skills to have fun with all the people in a safe and enthusiastic manner.

Soft Aggression Summary

It is not necessary to play aggressive games in an elementary school setting. It is much more important to offer a program and activities which promote social skills growth and bonding while creating a safe learning environment. However, if your students can master being compassionate and empathetic with each other then the benefits of playing more aggressive games become another effective school-worthy tool for venting competitive and aggressive energies safely.

When conditions are right, the Healthy Play curriculum includes games that involve more physical energy and contact. In order to play these games effectively at school you must develop rules and strategies which "Soften the Aggression." We recommend that you do not move on to soft aggression activities until your students have mastered the usage of both HP rules and the HP philosophy is ensconced in your students' behaviors.

While playing soft aggression games make sure you are vigilant and maintain firm control of your group before, during and after all activities. Limits will need to be set on "horseplay," fake fighting and bullying behaviors. Intimidation in even its subtlest forms can have a trust defeating impact on the integrity of your group of students.

Competition is something that Charlie and I do endorse but it can never come at the expense of another child or group of children. Develop a healthy school-oriented definition of competition that children can feel comfortable with. We do want them to succeed and be their best. We want them to be able to face disappointments and failures with a sense of renew vigor to do better the next time. And, we want them to know they are free to take needed risks without threats, both, physical or emotional, from their classmates. With a classroom and school-wide focus on the PEOPLE and not just the winners, all children are free to compete and become winners.

Your attitude alone will have a major impact on softening aggression at school. When you add humor, laughter and story-telling to games, automatically students will lighten up and engage in bonding and not polarizing behaviors. Your modeling "team" games where the other team is treated as worthy opposition and not enemies will give helpful clues to students on how to better treat their classmates on the other team. Most powerfully of all, when you frequently praise your students when they behave well, they will take your compliments along with their internalized good feelings and externalize them back as socially acceptable actions. Then, all that high-level excitement that can be gleaned from playing aggressive games is now put into balance with empathy. Former potentially destructive and aggressive energies now have the possibility to be expressed compassionately and cathartically. When this occurs, aggressive games can be both useful and fun.

Suggested Assignment:

It is now time to play again for twenty minutes. Pick one or more of the games we have shared with you over the past lessons to practice learning social skills. By this point, the students should be more actively implementing the rules during the game, but keep reminding them if they forget. If you feel your students are ready, try an activity from the Soft Aggression Lesson. You might want to pick a student to lead your compliment session and fun applause at the end of the game. Whenever you can, turn the responsibilities over to the students.

FINE TUNING THE ROLE OF PLAY IN EDUCATION

Introduction

In this chapter, you will find a summary of some of the more important points of the HP curriculum, two editorials along with ideas on how you can further support yourself and your students by fine tuning the HP program.

The biggest mistake that a teacher can make that will sabotage any character education program is not doing it. Even doing it haphazardly and infrequently may actually do more harm than good. There always seems to be something important that needs to get done in any school setting. In the education arena, there is the constant bombardment of IEPs, parent-teacher meetings, various deadlines or the threat of standardized testing requirements. Don't let the reason of why you got into teaching and your service to children be subjugated by your heavy workload and the well, or not-so well, intentioned whims of politicians or other officials who may not truly know how to meet the needs of students nor know the most efficient way to reach children. Test scores will rarely get better if you don't provide a safe environment of caring for students. There is a natural order that works best for children. Safety and trust needs have to come first. Once their basic needs for safety, support, trust and empathy are met, only then can your students go on to higher levels of successful cognitive and intellectual functioning. Character education programming must be part of your curriculum's foundation. If you diminish its importance, than you will sabotage all the powerful lessons that the children will have gained from the HP program.

Think on this: You have to be consistent and congruent with any effective programming, whether it is ours or another. We are not advocating that you ever continue a program that is ineffective, but we are asking that when you clearly see that a program IS effective you do not abandon it. Abandoning a potential valuable program means you will ultimately abandon your students. Character education is lifelong learning and not something that you can reduce down into a week's worth of lessons for the students and then move on to the teaching of academic requirements, never returning to your character education programming. If, for a week, you set up the HP curriculum with your students, they'll come to accept that you have provided a safer way to be at school. They will blissfully and happily buy into that their school is now going to be a place where emotional and physical injuries are attended to, bullying is reduced and arguments are solved without violence. Yet, if after this week, you no longer play with your students, quickly your playground and school culture will return to the usual "Lord of the Flies" scenario. You will have effectively broken a trust that the children placed in you to do the right thing by them. You had effectively made them vulnerable and trusting only to have abandoned them. You forgot to walk your talk. Don't lose track of being dependable and consistent for your students.

You cannot let the children totally run any character education program by themselves. Some teachers want to leave many adult responsibilities up to the students and have the children "run" programs. "Let's let our fourth graders become peer mediators. Let's let the fifth graders run the HP program." These are ten year olds, eleven year olds. They have not been professionally trained to lead groups or mediate. You don't say, let's let the fifth graders run the cafeteria, teach the third graders language arts and drive the school buses. Yet, there is this desire to place students in charge of projects that many adults have difficulty doing or following through with. Yes, children can practice being peer mediators, if there is an adult supervising them. Yes, your fifth graders can mentor/buddy with students in the younger grades if there is an adult supervising them. However, be realistic about appropriate developmental expectations. Don't ever put students in charge of something because you might feel pressured about your own time restraints or commitments.

Teaching is not just a profession, it is actually a commitment. It is a commitment to do what is right and best for children in a manner that appreciates where they are at developmentally, cognitively and emotionally. The Healthy Play curriculum recognizes, respects and appreciates what motivates children and what they can successfully live up to. By giving your children consistent opportunities to play, under your wise guidance, you will not only being gifting them opportunities to hone their character skills, but provide a foundation for classroom and playground management. All this will bring a joy into learning for them and a joy of teaching for yourself. Enjoy!

Editorials:

Charlie and I have strong opinions regarding the potentially problematic effects which have been created by the high-stakes testing hysteria that has gripped our educators, legislators and students around this country. We are not at all against accountability. Accountability is very good. But, we do seriously wonder about the operationalization of the high-stakes testing movement that has lost sight of how children truly learn, develop and flourish and how teachers should actually try and reach them. We are also concerned about what important basic attributes and skills are lost in the shuffle when focus is only placed on testing for math and language skills.

Perhaps it was writing the following on Martin Luther King Day that inspired the tone of my editorial. I humbly admit it may feel preachy in its passion. The truth is; I feel very passionate about the subject of how to effectively enable children to reach all their potentials. So if you want to visual yourself as a member of the congregation, go right ahead. And, if you care to throw in a few, "Right On's and Amen's!" please do. It would put a smile across my face.

Measuring Tenderness

How does one measure tenderness? What are the standards? Can someone tell me how to assign a number to it? And, if it can't be measured is it therefore not necessary? Does tenderness even have a place in school? Will children learn more if teachers show tenderness or develop it within themselves? What about values like integrity, kindness or even more abstractly, character? We in education always talk about character education. We know through research and experience that it is paramount to learning. Yet, what was once the focus of courageous educational leaders now feels forgotten, overshadowed by the specter of high stakes standardized testing. (Are you with me!?!)

Schools are now mandated into meeting numerical values as standardized testing becomes the new norm; the new focus. Having standards is good. It has the potential to equalize quality education for all. It helps define specific goals to meet. But having standards does not mean that there is a standardized method to achieving those goals. This is where I believe many of our advocates of standardized testing fail. There is a failure to look at the process of achieving genuine long-lasting solutions. A process, or perhaps many processes, cognizant of the big picture, that are proactive and not reactive and not done to win votes. After all, we are educating vibrant, dynamic, non-static children and not building widgets. Try as we might, or are ordered to, there is no by-pass route to learning without developing character.

How much more anxiety will we subject our children (and educators) to? At what expense will teaching out character harm kids? And, who really wants this? Are parents of elementary children really saying, "Forego ethics and values and just make sure my child can read and multiply?" Are we in such a state of collective amnesia that the lessons of Columbine and Santee can be so easily forgotten? Most ironically, why do we ignore our own educational research, which has validated the importance of learning and character?

Values and academics must exist concurrently. Fostering this relationship is the only way to truly realize learning and meet standards. This then brings us back to the process of effecting academic achievement. Who will advocate for how our children really learn and live? Do we just follow political leaders whose federal mandates dictate desired outcomes but do not recognize the importance of local control? Local communities are the authorities to best recognize their own local character. If effective learning is the desired outcome, the local school or community system knows itself better and of what is needed to optimize its unique learning environment. They know what nutrients are needed to plant in their own soil.

It seems to me that we need to trickle UP from a grassroots level, despite our political leaders' good intentions, because history shows us that things often do not trickle far enough down. Additionally, local communities have the larger role in effective learning. Education advocate, Thomas J. Sergiovanni, offers the following:

"Schools develop academic capital by becoming focused communities that cultivate a deep culture of teaching and learning. The rituals, norms, commitments, and traditions of this culture become the capital that motivates and supports student learning and development."

At both local and more expansive levels, let's recognize and celebrate these young creatures we work for. They ARE different than us and cannot have their boundless energy and enthusiasm squashed by an imposed system, focused on only outcomes, not the process, and be expected to achieve. Let us not give in to testing hysteria and fear. As recent national tragic events have shown us, fear ripples quickly through our individual being and connecting systems. But so does optimism. Fear versus optimism, I know which fuel I want to run on.

Spencer Gorin

Keep the Joy in Learning

Ah, spring is here! Time to test the kids...the final act in the stress-filled, year-long educational fear that my school's students will disappoint the adults and not achieve properly. To compensate for this adult fear we have created the district measurement test, state achievement test and a national standards test. This must be based on the concept that sooner or later students are bound to show improvement on one of the tools. "It's for their own good," we tell each other, and at some level of understanding, that is true. However, on another level it strikes me that we adults are demanding to give our children too much of a good thing for their own good. The sum total of attending school for years and years must be something other than a countable number of beans each child accumulates. LIFE for children at school must be more than that. Real learning should be a stimulating, pleasurable and exciting effort. But for this to occur, we must keep the joy in learning.

It's clear to me that we're not asking kids for any input about their overall educational life as we've gotten swept up in the current testing mania. I doubt that they'd agree with the over-reaction of some schools, which are now built without playgrounds at all. How did the parents, teachers, principals and administrators come to such a decision? While many successful businesses are discovering that gyms, sports fields and swimming pools keep employees happy building company loyalty and productivity, schools now only focus on work.

At what district meeting do you think the kids voiced the opinion that summer programs should not have choices for outdoor activities? I must have missed the uprising of children when they pleaded for adults to eliminate or greatly minimize the teaching of music, art and physical education because of the lack of relevance to testing. I can't imagine the kids voted to eliminate morning and afternoon recesses at their school. I'm sure they were not consulted about having to sit quietly at the lunch table for the full 30-minute lunch period and then return straight to the classroom. Neither did children asked school architectural committees to design new classrooms without those distracting views of the outside world. In some schools it's like being in the movie, "Cool Hand Luke." You're gonna spend the day in the box!

Of course, we adults are not going to let the children run the school. But somewhere (constantly) along the way we've got to remember who we're making these decisions for! Even the simplest of obvious observations should tell adults that we're forgetting how children really function. Where else, other than in every school in the country, is there a constant problem with people running? All of these educational changes are impacting students by taking the joy out of going to school and learning.

We cannot approach the education of 5, 8, 11, 16 year olds with the expectation that it's an inconvenience that they aren't 23 with concentration skills of an adult capable of earning a master degree. We've got to remember that kids don't have six-hour attention spans. Intellectual learning is at the top of the hierarchy of human needs. Learning takes time to physiologically bond in our neurons and cannot occur all day long. I'm too often reminded of the Gary Larson cartoon where a student raises his hand and says, "May I be excused? My brain is full."

Yes, adults are going to set expectations for learning. It's essential that we do this. But let's react to these needs with a healthy balance. Advocate and encourage laughter and singing in school. Use play, which involves all of the multiple intelligences, to regularly support learning or to take a frivolous break from the tedium of lectures and work pages. It's got to be okay for seven and ten year olds to be children! Insist that every day must have multiple opportunities for kids to burn off their natural physical energy. We must meet our children's needs to learn how to care for and respect each other. Some of our most important learning is about overcoming shyness, controlling aggression and learning tolerance. These are not testable qualities, but if they are not mastered, they will lessen the abilities of our children to succeed in life. Make coming to school the best place to spend the day for our children and they will learn.

As we've conducted the Healthy Play program throughout the country, I've universally heard educators at every school grieving about the preoccupation of teaching all year to standardized tests. "We haven't got time to do that," is the chorus's response to anything but math and reading.

I don't think a lot of adults really know how the testing pressures negatively effect the hour-by-hour life in the classroom. All of us who care for our children must put reason back into discussions at faculty meetings, curriculum forums, PTO gatherings and every day conversation. Respectfully challenge potentially destructive ideas like no playgrounds and no recess. Speak up for the kids about taking curriculum time away from music, art and PE to meet your testing goals. Advocate that it is not okay to build classrooms without windows. Get real. What adult doesn't want the office with the window?! Regularly share your thoughts about

education by emailing legislators or sending comments to the editor. Take action! Keep the joy in learning.
Charlie Steffens

TIPS and Fine Tuning the HP Curriculum

We have compiled a list of useful items so that you can effectively continue the Healthy Play program with your students. Of special note are tips reflecting information gleaned from the results of surveys which principals, teaching, counseling and ancillary staff completed for the GOALS 2000 study. Probably the most significant factor reported by teachers was that 94.3% of the teachers surveyed who used Healthy Play three, four, or five times each week observed a 50% to 100% reduction in aggressive and problematic behaviors. It's clear that frequent repetition gives students enough practice to learn and implement positive behaviors.

Many of the other ideas included in our "Tips" continue to come from teachers and students who are using these concepts successfully. Also included are some basic reminders on what to do to re-initiate the process of Healthy Play for each school year. Finally, we would also like to address some frequently made comments from youth servicing professionals asking us for assistance in furthering the program with their students. We hope these tips keep children focused on how to practice getting along with each other and that the time invested in using this process will allow them to complete more academics without distractions caused by socialization problems.

1. Always start the year by creating the two posters, which answer the questions, "Why do we play?" and "What is the most important part of every game?" Remember, when discussing the "Why do we play?" question, to also encourage your students to express how they want "To feel" during play. Continue to strongly reinforce the number one answers of FUN and PEOPLE. Use the posters regularly to point out positive times that

the children played. Return to the posters when your students (as a group) may deviate from living up to the values listed on their posters. Don't laminate last year's poster and use with your new group of students.

2. Discuss the two rules.

Rule # 1: If someone is hurt, the person closest to them must stop and check to see if they are okay and stay with them until they feel better.

Rule # 2: People with disagreements or arguments must leave the game and settle their issues peacefully before coming back to play. (It is always vital to remind students that the school conduct codes apply and that fighting, pushing, swearing, yelling etc. will not be permitted.)

3. Have playground monitors meet and plan out the week's noon recess activities. There may be a need to have two activities planned each day so that different age groups will have the right age-appropriate activity to play. During your school's morning messages broadcasted over the PA system, announce what the recess activity will be and where on the playground it will be located. (**Hint:** be flexible with your weekly planning. When a game becomes a favorite with the kids they may want to play it every day for a while). At recess time, have one of the playground monitors lead an activity and the other(s) invite/direct children to go join in. Many schools have picked class leaders who meet with the monitors to successfully suggest and plan the recess games.

4. Set up a student PE planning committee for each week. Allow them (with your supervision) to determine some PE activities. When picking the weekly group, try to have a mix of students that like various types of activities. (As you can see

with both Tips 4 and 5, we encourage you to share the planning responsibility with students. This will hopefully make less work for you and achieve fuller buy-in from the kids. However, please do not expect the children to do all the work.)

5. Turn over the "NOMINATION/COMPLIMENT" sessions to the student leader of the day. This processing of good feelings must be part of the allotted time to play. Feedback from almost every school indicates that this is one of the most important parts of every school day for community building, personal sharing and the cementing of positive behaviors.

6. We'd like to address one of the frequent remarks made by teachers, "Healthy Play is going fine in our room and when we play outside as a class, but at lunch-time recess there is still a problem." We encourage the faculty to walk around the campus for part of their lunchtime, especially for the first four to six weeks of school. The goal is to both briefly acknowledge all good things that teachers see students doing and to quickly call to students' attention when they need to cease an inappropriate interaction. The goal here is two-fold. Firstly, it will set a positive tone that teachers will see lots of good things. Secondly, teachers will feel a natural relaxation which occurs by getting a little exercise. It will make the afternoon much calmer.

7. Use some name recognition games at the beginning of school. Rumpelstiltskin, Cosmic Motions, Are You a Good Learner, are some activities you might want to use.

8. Start your classes off with active games that focus on equality and trust. We recommend Like, Totally It Tag as a warm up game almost every day. Other games, like Safety Haven, Triad, Magic Shoe and Peace Patrol and Gremlins set a good tone for everyone to feel included. These are also terrific games for students to observe how well they are doing with playing by the

rules, being honest and caring for each other. Just like your other academic areas, anticipate some regression over the summer and don't start with the most aggressive or competitive game.

9. Play to have fun! STOP all unsafe, non-productive games. Completion of a tortuous activity for the full period is not useful. Teachers across the country validate that this is one of our most useful concepts. When necessary, calmly process with the class what is not working well and allow them to suggest ways to improve the situation. Many classes have determined that certain games cannot be played for a while. Banning an activity for a short period of time can be an effective incentive for having students practice desired social behaviors successfully in other games and then later returning to the original game which was a problem. Sometimes it works and sometimes the children find out that they still haven't mastered certain social skills to a satisfactory level and the game is put on hold again.

10. Numerous teachers have processed with their classes that score keeping causes too many problems. When this is occurs, try keeping total class scores. Use single digit scores. Reward team cooperation with bonus scores. Some classmates just get too competitive and loose track of the PEOPLE when any scoring is involved. These classes just don't keep score at all for a while and might try a few weeks, or a month later, to see if any improvement has occurred.

11. Utilizing older students in the school to model and lead activities with younger grades is highly recommended. It will take some coordination to identify student groups who will adopt a class and attend HP or PE periods on a regular basis. This action promotes the positive peer pressure model which the Healthy Play program advocates by demonstrating expected social skills one should possess when you get into an older grade.

12. Remember that play is a natural way to learn. In both urban and small town environments our children need to practice the skills of how to get along with each other. Too much of their play at home is solely sold to the children as entertainment. Violence is often portrayed in a pedestrian and promoting manner on video games, other media and in professional sports. At school, keep your focus on teaching social skills and promoting a safe school community.

13. In class, have a monthly curriculum assignment where students write and describe different values that they have demonstrated, i.e. honesty, friendship, caring, cooperation, trust, competition, sportspeopleship, etc. Send these assignments into the editor of the local newspaper. In younger grades, use such values assignments for verbal expression during show and tell, i.e., "Tell of a nice time you had playing at home with _____. Have your parents or coach write you a note to bring in about a time you played well or demonstrated good character skills." Read the note and process with the class.

14. Have one or more art projects each year that focuses on Healthy Play at school, or home, etc. Put it in the hallway for everyone to see. It is important to update your original poster. If you don't occasionally change the scenery in the room and hallway it soon becomes ignored.

15. Plan a parent/student game night and let parents have some fun with their kids. Most likely there will be much familial joy gleaned from playing together. Have a group of students (with teacher support) become the leaders for this event. Teachers and families find this to be quite enjoyable and it bonds parents to HP concepts you want promoted. For safety reasons and greater family connection we highly recommend doing this classroom-by-classroom and NOT multi-classrooms or total schools at the same time. Promote safety and never play in

places that are too confined or filled with too many people.

16. Talk about what is going well with your colleagues. Keep your focus on successes and share them. Make your faculty interactions as enjoyable as possible. This is an option, which you can control. Don't get hooked into competing with each other as to who has the most to complain about.

17. As often as possible spend ten minutes of your staff meeting times being playful with each other. Every school staff identified how wonderful it felt when they got to see each other laugh and feel connected with each other. Even playing one round of Personality, presented in Lesson Seven, can set a positive and warm tone for the rest of the meeting.

18. "My kids want to play the traditional games." There are no wrong games. The traditional games are fine. The philosophy is what is important to implement at school. If the students are having FUN and PEOPLE are the most important part of the game they can probably play anything. Students still must care for each other if hurt, teasing is not allowed, arguing is done outside the game, include others, etc. If a traditional game causes a problem, then help students problem-solve a solution. If problems persist, cancel that activity for a short period of time and try it again later. What we have tried to do with the Healthy Play format is give you some alternatives which allow children to see what they need to do at school while playing. When they have mastered fairness, honesty, caring, and kindness concepts they will transfer this learning to other traditional games and areas of their school environment.

19. "I can't remember the games. We need more different games." The kids will remember many of the games. Have them compile a game list. Let them teach new activities to each other. Create an index card with a list of the games. Keep a copy of our

book, Learning to Play, Playing to Learn (available through our website; www.joyinlearning.com in your classroom and reference it often. There are also dozens of game books in the library which you or the students can explore to find something new to do. We hope you will not be discouraged if you don't do lots of different games. Remember that kids on their own seem to only play about five different games regularly each year. (Also, our training video, which has over twenty games, can be played to refresh your memory.)

20. "We need more consistency among all the teachers, monitors, after-school leaders etc. at the school to do this." This is an issue that you will need to process among the faculty at your school. First discuss your thoughts with your principal to clearly identify what the expectations are for the Healthy Play program. Each school has their own unique approach. In some schools, implementation is optional by the teachers, at recess or as part of after-school. In others, a curriculum frequency has been determined for weekly teacher use and expectations for structure during recess and after-school have also been implemented. There are many priorities and each school needs to set its own agenda.

21. "You need a newsletter to share more information and games." Our Joy in Learning Newsletter is a wonderful way to give and receive inspiration and garner more information about the Healthy Play Program. You can not only read it, but also contribute to it. Once again, you can receive the newsletter by going to our website: www.joyinlearning.com. Please send us good sportspeopleship stories, write-ups about games that you like to play or invented, questions, solutions, editorials etc. and we will possibly include them in a future copy.

22. It would be wonderful to have a school wide HP training and in-classroom consults with the originators of Healthy Play,

Charlie and Spencer. If you interested in a Healthy Play training for your school or district contact us at 1-800-742-0708.

Special Addendum:
Learning to Play at Home

Although the majority of our text has been devoted to using play in an educational setting, our overall belief about play is that it belongs everywhere. In reality, all people are both teachers and students when it comes to play. Focusing on an educational format has enabled us to explain lessons of critical importance within a larger social setting before bringing play back home where it belongs.

The Playful Family

Using play with your family is easy. You will find that the games described in this book are perfect for children's birthday parties, for teen sleep-overs, long car trips, vacations, family picnics, holiday gatherings, and daily use. Think of this section as a crash course on general rules for smaller groups. Use your new knowledge of creative-play concepts, presented earlier in this book, to modify any game to meet your family's requirements. For example, imagine you are having a small birthday party of ten children and want to play sponge wars. Unfortunately, it is raining outside and you don't want to have the neighborhood children tossing wet sponges at each other in the house, demolishing your favorite picture of Uncle Elmo while trashing your living room. Modify the game and play sock wars instead. Ball up about twenty-five old socks. You now have softer and safer objects for you and your children to play with indoors. Think small, and remember the old adage that less is more. Charlie and I always joke that we once had to do one of our trainings in a stairwell because that was the only place available. This was a much smaller space than we had anticipated, but we were still able to do our whole six-hour training. We used creative-play dynamics to modify the activities to fit the limited space. Though at times it felt a bit cramped, joy was still experienced by all present.

Birthday parties don't have to be expensive. We've played just about every one of these games at birthday gatherings and laughed until our sides ached. Your home or the local park are perfect places to play. You can plan either inside or outside activities and not have to worry about the weather. Maybe start with something like the iPod™ of the '50s until everyone arrives, then progress to who's in charge? Younger children will play ghost and safety haven until they burn off some energy, and then you can play cooperative musical chairs and Simon says times two. (Imagine two independent and simultaneous Simon-says games; players who do something without Simon's permission are not kicked out of the game but merely join the other group.) Older kids like giants, elves, and wizards, triad, and strategy tag. If it's hot outside, you'll probably want to play sponge wars, but be sure to set some limits, such as not dumping buckets of water on any of the players. Since balloons are almost always present, you will probably want to play balloon soccer. To cut down on the cost of balloons, or if you are playing with young children who might be frightened by the sound of popping balloons, modify the game so that the goalies are instructed not to pop the balloons. Instead, goalies throw the three balloons that are always in play back into the group immediately after they catch one. At one party, there were six helium balloons, and we invented a game on the spot of racing the balloons across the ceiling by hitting them with rubber bands to make them move. Most important, adults don't have to remain spectators. Invite everyone present at the party to join in the fun. You may need to encourage parents and older guests to join more than once, but they'll always have a better time once they get involved.

The goal of teen sleep-overs does not have to be a contest of who can rent and endure the most video games and DVDs for the night. Probably one of the best games for teens is called I Know Medusa found on page 159.

A group of six or more can play this game for hours. One of our favorite things to do with I KNOW MEDUSA is to start the game and then begin doing other things throughout the evening.

Play in the Neighborhood

Bring play to your neighborhood. Being with your children and their friends is an issue of both quality and *quantity* time. Kids don't have to be in leagues to play sports. We adults have made life far too complicated for us and our children. What works is just to be with them after work and on weekends. It often takes less time commitment and management to join your children's lives this way than to have them on a team. In fact, it's really quite relaxing when you're not trying to win anything, just having fun with people you love.

When my son started third grade and joined his first sports league, I realized that he had joined because everyone else had. If you weren't on the team, you were basically alone in the neighborhood. The teams were fun but a lot of work and commitment from parents for twelve to sixteen weeks.

My solution was to start the Sunday free-play games. My modeling for this came from my father and all the other fathers in my neighborhood as a child. At least five nights of every week during summer vacation, we kids played kick ball in the street. There were always at least two fathers who supervised the games, and sometimes as many as six. The other parents pulled up chairs and chatted with each other on the sidelines. No parents screamed at us to do better or became obnoxious, red-faced, obscenity-yelling monsters because the umpire made a call against their kid. The parents either played with us or happily watched us have a good time being kids. No pressure. Wow! There's an idea for how to learn how to play.

On my very first week at the park with my son and about eight of his friends, I met another father playing with his kids. I asked Steve if he wanted to join and immediately made a good friend. Between the two of us we played at the park on Sundays probably forty weeks a year for the next four years. At times as many as twenty-four kids showed up, but often there were a dozen or so. We mostly played traditional games. However, they were all modified with the *Learning to Play, Playing to Learn* philosophy. Your team's score didn't count in flag football until everyone caught a pass. Everyone had to have a turn as quarterback. In basketball, the fathers could only block three kids' shots in a game. Five-year-olds played with twelve-year-olds, big with small, fast with slow. It was grex!

When older kids tried to bring a mean aggressiveness to the games, the fathers present established that such behavior was not acceptable. Everyone was welcome to play with us, but our games were just for fun without hurting anyone. Many of these once-aggressive kids stayed and only a few chose to leave.

For those two hours every Sunday, the park and the games were ours. The kids were safe; free from neighborhood bullies or undesirable criminal pressures and supervised by playful adults. No one had to pay any enrollment fees, offer birth certificates, buy special uniforms, sell candy bars, or make banners in order to play. When your family had other plans for the day, you could miss a Sunday without any feelings that you were letting the team down. Heck, we picked different teams every thirty minutes. Everyone played with everyone as friends. Trophies were represented by smiles.

As our kids grew up, they joined the adults playing basketball. For years I continued to play twice a week with Forrest, his friends, other fathers, and their kids. Even now, they still play every week. As always, there is a special "gift of the game." In this case, it became the tradition of celebrating one another's birthdays. It is absolutely wonderful to see six semi-macho men and six testosterone-filled teen boys finish their basketball game and sit down to open silly cards, blow out candles, and stuff their face with birthday cake.

Playful Adults

Don't be afraid to have fun! One of our favorite comments at the end of a training is when someone states, "I can't wait to have a party and do this with my friends." The benefits from play occur for all ages. Adult play groups are the best. Over the years, our friends have played all the games in this book and the ones that will be in our next book. It's easier to play sit-down games with adults, but the physical activities often offer the most enjoyment when they are played compassionately.

For years now, I and my adult friends have been playing kick the can. Yep, the very same game we played as kids but now played by forty-year-olds. It's better as an adult, because now when you run off to hide in the bushes you can make out with your wife before you try to kick the can. This is a truly major improvement that I didn't even think of when I was ten. Our kick-the-can games got so popular that we soon had to keep them a secret because we only wanted ten players. One night, more than twenty people showed up all dressed in their darkest camouflage clothes. Of course, we modified the rules so that no one could be it for more than fifteen minutes and you could only be it once a night. Adults are very creative with their strategies in play. One player got a woman walking her baby in a big baby buggy to stroll toward the can while she crouched behind the buggy. She snuck right up on the can and kicked it before she was ever seen by the person who was it. One of the funniest scenes I can remember occurred when one of our friends who was very eight months' pregnant tried to outsprint a young teen who was trying to kick the can. It truly put in perspective the concept of competing against time, space, and gravity. FYI, she got to the can first!

We encourage you to play as adults. It's worth taking the healthy risk to lead these activities with your friends. If you aren't ready to be the leader, we encourage you to be an active follower of the natural playmaster in your group. Be supportive and compassionate with your friends, for many adults, just like children, need to learn how to play.

Playing with Scouts and Other Children's Groups

Learning to Play activities, rules, and philosophies are perfect for Girl Scouts, Boy Scouts, Campfire Girls, 4-H clubs, and other youth groups. The games will help teach and reinforce the values that your organization represents. Besides, after sitting all day in school, the kids are ready for some good, clean, wholesome action.

At a recent training one of the parents was so excited with triple tag and endangered species that she couldn't wait to try them with her scout troop that evening. She got the kids together and immediately started playing. To her absolute disappointment, the outcome of their games were horrible. The kids played just as poorly as they always had. They were mean and rough, and they argued constantly for twenty minutes until she stopped the games. At that point, she smartly went back to the beginning of our program. She had the kids sit down and make the posters to answer the two key questions and explained the two essential rules. Afterward, they went back and played the same games but now had fun. The children ran, laughed, and cared for each other.

As a scout leader, try figuring out which merit badges can be earned by playing in a healthy manner. Maybe a new merit badge will need to be created. If your scout group is located at a school or a church, be sure to do the eco-walk activity to clean up the play area, and praise the kids for this good-citizenship act. Delegate responsibility to your scouts by having two of them plan the game period for next week. This is great for promoting leadership skills. Make sure they know what equipment they will need to have, and let them read this book for ideas. If they forget to plan something, you may want to allow this situation, when appropriate, to be a lesson learned by not having the game period. They won't forget more than once. Being the scout leader doesn't mean you have to do all the work. In fact, it's more effective when you share these suitable tasks with your kids.

Play with Church and Synagogue Groups

Church is fun.

We did a training four years ago at a church for their middle-school-age children. Ever since, their Tuesday-night group has made play a part of their activity agenda. Some of the kids who first started with us now go back to carry on the tradition by teaching the games and playing with the new kids. What a perfect way to have the young people in your church live out the values your church group represents.

Teen retreats are a regular part of many synagogues and churches. The objective of most church retreats is to teach younger members of the congregation the beliefs of their faith. Without a doubt, you will find dozens of the games in this book perfect for your teen or children's retreat. Often retreats will have a specific theme for the weekend. Use your creative-play dynamics to change the names of the games in this book so that the play activity reflects the goals you are trying to achieve. A trip to Washington could easily become a trip to Jerusalem. Safety haven might be called love thy neighbor. Generally, when games are played with compassion for all people, every activity in this book will lend itself to achieving your positive goals. Healthy teamwork and cooperation are achieved by playing three-ball soccer or over, under, and around kick ball. Endangered species and vennis are perfect fun breaks for teens and can easily be added to a day-long agenda. In the evening, when you are trying to set a quieter tone, your group will attain maximum benefit from such trust activities as action/reaction, copy machine, and personality. Your teens will probably want to play personality all night long if they're anything like the teens we've played with. Always remember to save time at the end of your game period to discuss the positive. These discussions will reinforce everything that you are hoping to achieve on your retreat.

Another wonderful thing that your church or synagogue teen group can do is to plan the activities for the annual family picnic. This is the perfect place for teens to make responsible contributions to their church community. When planning several hours of play, be sure to have a balance of active and quiet activities.

Begin by having teens practice out loud, explaining the rules and the expectations of how the games are to be played. Have the teens practice playing the games themselves so they know what to expect. (A gentle reminder: Often teenagers are very self-conscious and reluctant to do silly things like playing games. Teens have their sense of cool to maintain. Additionally, they've already watched too many adults sit and become spectators in life and naturally have begun to emulate them. By giving your teen group the responsibility of leading the games, you are adding a new factor to the equation for breaking down their self-conscious barriers. Now, not only is there a specific reason to do the games, but they quickly discover that they are also having a grex time. Once this barrier is broken, it becomes a safe, acceptable norm of your teen group to play. They will become more open to other healthy risks and have greater fun with each other.)

Games are also perfect for your church singles groups. Nothing mixes people up faster than games that allow everyone to relax and meet each other without any unnecessary expectations. Start off with light, breezy games like oh, Fido or change are you a PeaceBuilder? to do you like fun dates? ("Yes, and I like fun dates that ———.") After a while, a game of empathy would be funny and enjoyable. If you start to play kick the can, we'll know you've read the other parts of our book.

Playing at Work

"Our company makes widgets. I don't pay people to play games and have fun. I pay them to do their job!" This is the way many employers feel about work. This statement is most often made by the highly valued, extremely productive executive who conducts some of the company's most important business on the golf course or at the racket club. It's time to stop the double standard of who can have fun while doing work. If you want a big boost in company morale, let play be a positively sanctioned part of your employees' workday.

Of course, we're not advocating that you close down the office and let everyone play golf for four hours every Thursday. That's not where the majority of employees can work or play to get their job done. What we are advocating is that the same dynamics that help the executive land big deals at the golf course (being playful, relaxed, open, happy, and creative and having enjoyable camaraderie with others) are the same essential needs of every worker, every day, in every company.

In order to bring play into the workplace, management must wholeheartedly endorse it. Employees cannot sense any doubt that appropriate playfulness will be viewed as poor work performance. It's best when the boss models playful activities or is present for them. At one company we worked at, our boss encouraged us to play every Friday afternoon. The last four work hours of the week were always the most stressful and the busiest, yet we were always encouraged to take our 2:45 P.M. break together and do something fun. We did such things as seeing who could slide in their socks the farthest on the gleaming solid oak floor in the board room. (Women wearing nylons really slid well.) We held a staple-removing contest to see who could collect the most staples out of ten on the upper side of their staple remover. (The secretarial staff was by far the best at this, but everyone, including the boss, tried.) Sometimes we even had prizes. The most popular prize at our organization was first-in-line privileges at the copy machine anytime on Monday. These fun breaks essentially renewed our energy, made us relaxed, and kept us in contact with different people from different departments. Then we went back to our office feeling renewed and worked real hard.

At your business, some afternoon, clear out a space and put some chairs in a circle and play oh, Fido with your employees. If a customer walks in, add a chair for him. We know of one boss who had so much fun with this game that he periodically yells, "Oh, Fido!" during meetings when people are getting that blank, glazed-over look. This is a signal for everyone to get up and move to another chair. Sometimes he does it two or three times in a row. It doesn't take much time, but it gets people attentive while having some fun.

One manager in a technology department picked up half a dozen noise-making ray guns and gave them to everyone in the office. That afternoon, and on other spontaneous occasions, the employees spent odd moments sneaking up and blasting each other. Simple, quick, ongoing, and revitalizing.

As the boss, you can easily bring fifty balloons to work and play balloon soccer. We know this activity works well even in very large groups. One time we played it with 220 members of U.S. West Communications' Presidents Club, and they all loved it.

Your goal is not to turn employees into overboard pranksters but to revitalize morale and increase productivity. Have a short staff meeting to outline some goals for fun in the workplace. Obviously, squirt guns in an expensive technology department could cause a lot of expensive damage. Noise-making rays guns do no harm. Discuss among your staff the idea of people being the most important part of the company, and explain that games that honor everyone will be encouraged.

Encourage your employees to play games during their lunch break or give fifteen to twenty minutes of extra time on Monday, Wednesday, and Friday for them to join in company games. Delegate a "spirit-master" to create no-cost special events each month, and be sure the boss shows up and joins in when possible. Inexpensive equipment can allow you to play vennis-style volleyball. It's a great company game because it is so inclusive. Forget score keeping, or keep only the accumulated total of successful volleys without an error. Post the accumulated score and try to beat it the next time you play.

Remember, you are not trying to determine whether accounting has a better team than sales. What you want is for sales, janitorial, production, secretarial, accounting, data processing, and management to all mix together and get to know each other as full human beings. The benefits of playing at the office are identical to those of doing business at the golf club. Employees benefit by having a shared goal of making their company and their lives successful. Play is productive and meaningful, and it will enhance cooperation and loyalty among coworkers.

Company picnics are the perfect place to play totally it; giants, elves, and wizards; who's in charge; rattlesnake tag; and maybe even sponge wars. There are dozens of activities in this book that are perfect for these events. What could be better than having the family and friends of your employees share the positive joy of having fun together. Feeling good about where you work and how the company treats your family is not derived from the dollars-and-cents columns on a pay check, but those feelings can make a difference in how many dollars your company ultimately generates.

It is desirable to have employees go home to spouses and friends and tell them, "You won't guess what crazy, fun thing we did at work today. Our boss got us all together with three paper wads, a buzzing pager, and an empty coffee cup [using creative-play dynamics to spontaneously adapt cosmic motions to the workplace], and we had to pass them around in different ways. It was so wild, and we laughed so hard. I'm not sure I can explain it, but it was fun. It made my time at work more enjoyable and fruit-ful." The alternative is, "Finally, the weekend. I'm so tired of this job. I've got a stack of work I'll never finish. It just goes on and on." Which kind of thoughts do you think will create the happier and more productive worker?

Company teams can be wonderful, but they are not what we advocate as a means to bring play to the workplace. Sometimes company teams cause as many internal morale difficulties as they were intended to help.

What we're encouraging managers and employees to do is to choose the second strongest motivator in forging cooperation: fun. Fun forges cooperation quicker than any other human dynamic other than a catastrophe. Gosh, let's see here. Our organization can choose to attempt productivity through managing frequent crises or by having fun at work. Well, duh, which one would you like your company to choose?

Some wise men once said, "If you can't play together, how can you possibly work together?" Oh, that was us. In his book *This Job Should Be Fun*, Bob Basso, Ph.D., states that the values found in healthy play—fun, open communication, teamwork, and innova-tion—are the same ones found in the most productive companies on our planet. We hope you are ready to bring play into the work-place. If you are ready but feel you'd like some expert help getting started, give us a call. After all, our whole business is about play-ing while you work.

Play Belongs Everywhere

If you've read everything in this book to this point, we can tell we're probably preaching to the choir. You clearly understand how play can make you feel. You know how it can teach valuable lessons, bring people closer together, make us laugh, compete, cooperate, allow us to care, be silly and free. We at Creative Spirit hope you will share what you've learned about how to play with the other people who are important in your lives.

Tips and Fine Tuning Summary

Safer Schools- Smarter Students

Everyday we seem to hear about another event of violence perpetrated towards children by other children. Our media is ripe with the most horrendous stories, which too often, end in murder. The common thread through all these stories are children living lives in fear of each other and perpetrators having histories filled with isolation, not fitting in, diminished empathy and poor socialization.

Blame for this increasing problem is placed everywhere, "It's the movies and television our children watch, the influence of gangs, lyrics of the music they listen to, the rising rate of divorce and single parent homes." Solutions suggested by our leaders focus on symptoms and never seem to get at the heart of the problem. We have forgotten about our responsibilities to our children. We've forgotten to teach them how to nurture and show compassion to each other; how to notice when another needs our support and how to address that situation. We have lost track of how to resolve problems realistically without finding that one formula which could never reach everyone anyhow. We live in fast times and we want fast answers to our problems.

But, this will not work with our children. Children grow over time. They learn, over time, and from practice and repetition. Children learn in a manner that is both linear and more primitive than how we adults learn. They cannot learn by adults spoon-feeding them answers, especially when we do not give them chances to practice solutions. They can rarely learn unless they feel safe. And many of our children don't feel safe.

We have to get back to the right way of being adults again in our communities and start acting as responsible communities. We all, every one of us, raise all our children. Every one of us must become a responsible and wise elder to all our children. And, as elders, our responsibility is to mentor. This way, we create a protected place where children become apprentices, beginners at their craft of becoming loving, socialized, and compassionate people.

As elders/mentors we must be open enough to our past and current failures. To see that some of what we've created has damaged our children and sent them forward, acting out their righteous rage. We must acknowledge how we have let them down. How we have stood by for so many years turning a blind eye to the growing signs that our children were in trouble, putting out attention and energies into the most empty of solutions. All the metal detectors in every high school in the world will not address the reasons why we need metal detectors in the first place. All the conflict resolution programs will not address how conflicts get started in the first place. All the special needs programming and psychiatric facilities will not change the factors that cause children to need these isolating programs. All the workbooks touting words like responsibility, respect and safety fall short when delivered in a manner that is not how many, if not most children learn. And, if children are not taught in the manner by which they truly discover and dance through their experiences, then they will not learn. Children learn through play. Their learning is reinforced with repetition and honed only in pockets of safety and support.

As elders and educators, we must be wise enough to create the most optimal interventions for our children. And, where we start is by creating safe environments of compassion, excitement, innovation and wonder...an environment, which respects the birthrights of all children placed in our care. We no longer pretend that we teach just language, math, physical education, etc. We instead, teach children. And we teach children to reach their highest potential, which addresses what is good within and around us all.

When this happens we accept that teachers, youth-servicing professionals and paraprofessionals, parents and grandparents don't work for the schools or organizations. We humbly accept that we work for our children and our children are no longer invisible. It is then that we see them, their needs, their developmental status, and their seemingly endless openness to praise, joy and curiosity. And, we fill that openness with a bounty of gifts, which motivates their evolution.

Our places of learning become places of being. Places of mindfulness that nurture; attuned to how children learn. We delight in being consistent and congruent in our actions. In turn, our children learn to trust themselves and us within surroundings of safety. And it is then that our children flourish.

Safer schools create smarter students filled with hope and compassion. May the lessons that you've learned through the Healthy Play curriculum serve you in the most noblest of professions and in the most joyous and playful manner. Have Fun!

Suggested Assignment:

Identify two things that you could do to make the Healthy Play curriculum even more effective for you and your students. What did you come up? Implement those interventions and report on their effectiveness.

Addendum

Healthy Play Bullet Points

Introduction:

- Play is the most natural way that children learn
- Purposeful and therapeutic play can provide a solution to classroom and playground socialization and management problems
- Research supports the importance of play on healthy childhood development, socialization and learning

Lesson One: Philosophy, Why Do We Play?

- Play is active, joyous, inclusive and experiential
- Creating the WHY DO WE PLAY poster for your setting is

essential. Remember to also ask your children how they want to feel when they play

- We play to have FUN is the only number one answer for this poster
- Leave the poster up all year. Return to the poster for validation of successful play and to assist in problem solving

Lesson Two: Philosophy, What IS the Most Important Part of Every Game?

- The creation of a classroom poster to identify the most important part of the game is essential for promoting character skills and managing student behavior
- People are the most important part of every game
- People are the most important part of your setting
- Utilize positive peer pressure and voting to influence appropriate behaviors. Give voice/influence to students who are doing well to act as role models for those who need interventions

Lesson Three: Rule # 1, the Empathy Rule:

- Children most often perpetrate violence between each other because they lack empathy
- Rule # 1: If anyone is hurt, either physically or emotionally, the closest person must stop playing, take care of and stay with that person
- Rule # 1 helps delegate compassion and caretaking among students. It is encouraged that the children personally implement Rule # 1. However, the teacher should also exercise good judgment. Actively and immediately intervene when you witness a situation of a higher level of physical or emotional injury that a student could not age-appropriately address

Lesson Four: Rule # 2, the Disagreement Rule:

- It's normal to have disagreements
- The teacher does not always have to resolve these disputes
- By utilizing play experiences, students can practice peaceful resolutions
- Rule # 2: If two individuals have an argument or disagreement during a game, they must leave the game until their argument is peacefully settled
- Rule # 2 allows for the game to go on while students arguing go to the side
- Arguments are only done by two students at a time
- There is a difference between a problem and trouble. Problems can be solved by the individuals having the problem. Trouble often requires the intervention of others like the teacher, principal or parents
- The teacher will always use good discretion on when to get involved
- Flexibility is necessary because students come with a wide variety of skills
- The skills gained while playing will carryover into the whole day

Time to Play:

- Have your kids chant the answers to: "Why do we play? What is the most important part of the game? If someone is hurt do you stay with them or run away? Do you have your disagreement in the game or out of it?" before leaving the classroom
- Plan to be in the middle of the activity
- Practice the 5, 4, 3, 2, 1 countdown before starting your first game
- Be ready (eager) to find opportunities to delegate the responsibilities of the rules to the students

- Plan to give frequent positive verbal feedback to students during the games
- When students have questions and ideas about the rules, bring these ideas up for a class vote
- Gather your kids together at the end of the game to say only positive things to each other

Creative Play:

- All games are made up (This means they are not sacred, so they can be altered)
- There are really only six types of games: Follow the Leader, Tag, Keep Away, Capture, Logic Puzzles, and Accumulation
- Keep safety a # 1 priority
- Reward teamwork with bonuses
- Have multiple "Its"
- Change game speed
- Add more bases
- Have more balls in a game
- Experiment with the size and shape of the boundaries
- Create rules that deal with difficulties surrounding score
- Allow everyone a chance to offer ideas
- Processing at the end of activities cements positive behaviors

Trust and Compassionate Play:

- Trust is experienced both physically and emotionally
- Trust is a basic human need and must be present before higher intellectual learning goals can be achieved
- The 5 Cs: A trustworthy activity is contained, cushioned, controlled and played with a sense of caring and community
- Choosing "Captains" is often a trust defeating mechanism for picking teams
- Trust and Compassionate Play can facilitate positive physical contact among students which creates a greater sense of be

longing and community
- Changing different aspects of a traditional game like "Simon Says" can promote honesty vs. dishonesty
- When trust is present, a game can fail miserably, but the group can effectively cope with this situation to try to make things better.

Soft Aggression Play:

- There should be a solid foundation and consistent use of the philosophy and two rules before trying aggressive games
- The teacher must maintain firm control of the activity before, during and after the game
- Set limits on "horseplay" or fake fighting behaviors
- Keep the class focus on PEOPLE vs. winning
- Add humor to lighten up games played at school
- Develop a healthy school oriented understanding of competition
- Make sure students understand that the other team is the opposition and not the enemy
- Be sure to give praise when students follow rules and play games in the appropriate manner

References and Readings

Acton, Heather M., and Lynne Zarbatany. "Interaction and performance within cooperative groups: Effects on nonhandicapped students' attitudes toward their mildly mentally retarded peers." American Journal on Mental Retardation, 93, 16–23 (1988).

Bay-Hinitz, April K., Robert F. Peterson, and H. Robert Quilitch. "Cooperative games: A way to modify aggressive and cooperative behaviors in young children." Journal of Applied Behavior Analysis, 27, 435–446 (1994).

Blank, M., and B.R. McCandless. "A methodology for fostering abstract thinking in deprived children." Ontario Institute for Studies in Education, Monograph, 9, 1–25 (1970).

Fauth, B., (1990) Linking the visual arts with drama, movement, and dance for young children. In Moving and Learning for the Young Child. Ed. W. J. Stinson, 159-87. Reston, VA: American Alliance for health, Physical Education, Recreation and Dance.

Fluegelman, Andrew. (1976) New Games. New York: Bantam Doubleday Dell Publishing Group, Inc.

————, More New Games. (1981) New York: Bantam Doubleday Dell Publishing Group, Inc.

Herbert, A., (1984). Structured exercises in stress management. (Vol. 2). Duluth, MN: Whole Person Associates Inc. Reprinted with permission

Howard, Pierce. Ph.D., (2006) Learning That Sticks: Insights for Enhancing Memory. In   OWNER'S MANUAL for the BRAIN, Everyday Applications from Mind-Brain   Research. (pp.531-561, third edition), Austin, TX: A Bard Productions.

Klugman, E., (1990), Children's Play and Learning, Teachers College Press, Columbia   University, New York

Loomans, Diane, and Karen Kolberg. (1993) The Laughing Classroom, Tiburon, Calif: H. J.   Kramer, Inc.

Murphy, H.A., J.M. Hutchinson, and J.S. Bailey. "Behavioral school psychology goes outdoors: The effects of organized games on playground aggression." Journal of Applied Behavior Analysis, 16, 29–35 (1983).

Orlick, Terry. (1978 & 1982) The 1st & 2nd Cooperative Sports and Games Book. New   York: Random House Inc. (excellent for younger children)

Pellegrini, A.D. "Elementary-school children's rough-and-tumble play and social competence." Developmental Psychology, 24, 802–806 (1988).

Pellegrini, Kato, Blatchford, & Baines. (2002) A short-term longitudinal study of   children's playground games across the first year of school: Implications for   social competence and adjustment to school. American Educational Research   Journal, Vol.39. No 4, Winter 2002, pp.991-1015.

Rogers, M. "Cooperative games as an intervention to promote cross-racial acceptance." American Educational Research Journal, 18, 513–16 (1981).

Sapp, M. "Irrational beliefs that can lead to academic failure for African American middle school students who are academically at-risk." Journal of Rational-Emotive & Cognitive Behavior Therapy, 14, 123–134 (1996).

Sponseller, D., (1974) Play as a Learning Medium, National Association of the Education of Young Children, Washington D.C.

Thomas, Jerry R., and Amelia M. Lee, Lea McGee, and Stephen Silverman. "Effects of individual and group contingencies on disruptive playground behavior." Journal of Research & Development in Education, 20, 66–76 (1987).

Walker, H.M., G. Colvin, and E. Ramsey. Anti-social behavior in schools: Strategies and best practices. Pacific Grove, Calif: Brooks/Cole, 1995.

Weinstein, M. & Goodman, J (1980) Playfair. San Luis Obispo, Calif: Impact Publishers

White, A.G., and J.S. Bailey. "Reducing disruptive behaviors of elementary special education students with sit and watch." Journal of Applied Behavior Analysis, 23, 353–60 (1990).

Index

1. Games listed alphabetically

2. Games; by behaviors you want to manage or promote.

Remember, that every game opens itself to a variety of behaviors and skills that it can address. The following games are suggestions based on years of experiencing repetitive benefits from their use. However, we encourage you to use an open mind and look towards other games to achieve results that you desire.

COMMUNICATION

CONFLICT RESOLUTION

COOPERATION

DECREASING FIGITY BEHAVIORS

EMPATHY

HELPING OTHERS

3. Games; by age groups of (P) Primary (Kindergarten through 2nd grade), (I) Intermediate (Third through sixth grade), (T) Teens and (A) Adults.

Remember, that every game opens itself to a variety of age groups by utilizing Creative Play dynamics. For instance, we know of a kindergarten teacher who routinely plays Cosmic Motions, as one would play with a teen group, with his four and five year olds. And, even though the game of Personality requires abstract thought, we know of a second grade teacher whose children adore playing this game. In a reverse manner, if you don't tell your fifth graders that Broken Wheel is really just advanced Duck, Duck, Goose they will play this activity with as much youthful abandon as do first graders. Charlie and I fondly remember having a psychiatric unit full of adolescent boys, many diagnosed as having conduct disorders, willingly playing Broken Wheel. We smartly never told them they were just playing advanced Duck, Duck, Goose. The lesson here is to remain open and you will find that a great majority of these games transcend age barriers.

? = assess your group